GLENCOE LANGUAGE ARTS

P9-CCK-160

Grammar and Language Workbook

GRADE 12

Glencoe
McGraw-Hill

New York, New York   Columbus, Ohio   Woodland Hills, California   Peoria, Illinois

Glencoe/McGraw-Hill

A Division of The **McGraw·Hill** *Companies*

Send all inquiries to:
Glencoe/McGraw-Hill
8787 Orion Place
Columbus, Ohio 43240-4027

ISBN 0-02-818312-6

Printed in the United States of America

6 7 8 9   024   04 03 02 01

Contents

*H*andbook of Definitions and Rules

PARTS OF SPEECH

Nouns

1. A **singular noun** is a word that names one person, place, thing, or idea: brother, classroom, piglet, and joy. A **plural noun** names more than one person, place, thing, or idea: brothers, classrooms, piglets, and joys.

2. To help you determine whether a word in a sentence is a noun, try adding it to the following sentences. Nouns will fit in at least one of these sentences:
   I know something about _____.   I know something about a(n) _____.
   I know something about **brothers**.   I know something about a **classroom**.

3. A **collective noun** names a group. When the collective noun refers to the group as a whole, it is singular. When it refers to the individual group members, the collective noun is plural.
   The class meets two days a week. (singular)
   The board of trustees come from all walks of life. (plural)

4. A **common noun** names a general class of people, places, things, or ideas: soldier, country, month, or theory. A **proper noun** specifies a particular person, place, thing, event, or idea. Proper nouns are always capitalized: **G**eneral **S**chwartzkopf, **A**merica, **J**uly, or **B**ig Bang.

5. A **concrete noun** names an object that occupies space or that can be recognized by any of the senses: tuba, music, potato, and aroma. An **abstract noun** names an idea, a quality, or a characteristic: courage, sanity, power, and memory.

6. A **possessive noun** shows possession, ownership, or the relationship between two nouns: Raul's house, the cat's fur, and the girls' soccer ball.

Pronouns

1. A **pronoun** takes the place of a noun, a group of words acting as a noun, or another pronoun.

2. A **personal pronoun** refers to a specific person or thing. **First person** personal pronouns refer to the speaker, **second person** pronouns refer to the one spoken to, and **third person** pronouns refer to the one spoken about.

	Nominative Case	Possessive Case	Objective Case
First Person, Singular	I	my, mine	me
First Person, Plural	we	our, ours	us
Second Person, Singular	you	your, yours	you
Second Person, Plural	you	your, yours	you
Third Person, Singular	he, she, it	his, her, hers, its	him, her, it
Third Person, Plural	they	their, theirs	them

3. A **reflexive pronoun** refers to the subject of the sentence. An **intensive pronoun** adds emphasis to a noun or another pronoun. A **demonstrative pronoun** points out specific persons, places, things, or ideas.
   Reflexive: **They** psyched **themselves** up for the football game.
   Intensive: **Freddie himself** asked Julie out.
   Demonstrative: **That** is a good idea!   **Those** are my friends.

4. An **interrogative pronoun** is used to form questions. A **relative pronoun** is used to introduce a subordinate clause. An **indefinite pronoun** refers to persons, places, or things in a more general way than a noun does.
   Interrogative: **Which** is your choice?   With **whom** were you playing video games?

Relative: The cake **that** we baked was delicious.
Indefinite: **Everyone** has already voted.   **No one** should enter without knocking.

5. The antecedent of a pronoun is the word or group of words referred to by the pronoun.
Ben rode **his** bike to school. (*Ben* is the antecedent of *his.*)

Verbs

1. A verb is a word that expresses action or a state of being and is necessary to make a statement. Most verbs will fit one or more of these sentences:
We _____.   We _____ loyal.   We _____ it.   It _____.
We **sleep**.   We **remain** loyal.   We **love** it!   It **snowed**.

2. An action verb tells what someone or something does. The two types of action verbs are transitive and intransitive. A transitive verb is followed by a word or words that answer the question *what?* or *whom?* An intransitive verb is not followed by a word that answers *what?* or *whom?*
Transitive: Children **trust** their parents.   The puppy **carried** the bone away.
Intransitive: The team **played** poorly.   The light **burned** brightly.

3. A linking verb links, or joins, the subject of a sentence with an adjective, a noun, or a pronoun.
The concert **was** loud. (adjective)   I **am** a good card player. (noun)

4. A verb phrase consists of a main verb and all its auxiliary, or helping, verbs.
My stomach **has been growling** all morning.   I **am waiting** for a letter.

5. Verbs have four principal parts or forms: base, past, present participle, and past participle.
Base: I **eat**.   Present Participle: I am **eating**.
Past: I **ate**.   Past Participle: I have **eaten**.

6. The principal parts are used to form six verb tenses. The tense of a verb expresses time.

Simple Tenses

Present Tense: She **eats**. (present or habitual action)
Past Tense: She **ate**. (action completed in the past)
Future Tense: She **will eat**. (action to be done in the future)

Perfect Tenses

Present Perfect Tense: She **has eaten**. (action done at some indefinite time or still in effect)
Past Perfect Tense: She **had eaten**. (action completed before some other past action)
Future Perfect Tense: She **will have eaten**. (action to be completed before some future time)

7. Irregular verbs form their past and past participle without adding *-ed* to the base form.

PRINCIPAL PARTS OF IRREGULAR VERBS

Base	Past	Past Participle	Base	Past	Past Participle
be	was, were	been	catch	caught	caught
beat	beat	beaten	choose	chose	chosen
become	became	become	come	came	come
begin	began	begun	do	did	done
bite	bit	bitten *or* bit	draw	drew	drawn
blow	blew	blown	drink	drank	drunk
break	broke	broken	drive	drove	driven
bring	brought	brought	eat	ate	eaten

Base Form	Past Form	Past Participle	Base Form	Past Form	Past Participle
fall	fell	fallen	run	ran	run
feel	felt	felt	say	said	said
find	found	found	see	saw	seen
fly	flew	flown	set	set	set
freeze	froze	frozen	shrink	shrank *or* shrunk	shrunk *or* shrunken
get	got	got *or* gotten			
give	gave	given	sing	sang	sung
go	went	gone	sit	sat	sat
grow	grew	grown	speak	spoke	spoken
hang	hung *or* hanged	hung *or* hanged	spring	sprang *or* sprung	sprung
have	had	had	steal	stole	stolen
know	knew	known	swim	swam	swum
lay	laid	laid	take	took	taken
lead	led	led	tear	tore	torn
lend	lent	lent	tell	told	told
lie	lay	lain	think	thought	thought
lose	lost	lost	throw	threw	thrown
put	put	put	wear	wore	worn
ride	rode	ridden	win	won	won
ring	rang	rung	write	wrote	written
rise	rose	risen			

8. **Progressive forms** of verbs, combined with a form of *be,* express a continuing action. **Emphatic forms**, combined with a form of *do,* add emphasis or form questions.
   Kari **is scratching** the cat.   Loni **has been washing** the walls.
   We **do support** our hometown heroes. (present)   He **did want** that dinner. (past)

9. The **voice** of a verb shows whether the subject performs the action or receives the action of the verb. The **active voice** occurs when the subject performs the action. The **passive voice** occurs when the action of the verb is performed on the subject.
   The owl **swooped** upon its prey. (active)   The ice cream **was scooped** by the cashier. (passive)

10. A verb can express one of three moods. The **indicative mood** makes a statement or asks a question. The **imperative mood** expresses a command or request. The **subjunctive mood** indirectly expresses a demand, recommendation, suggestion, statement of necessity, or a condition contrary to fact.
    I **am** overjoyed. (indicative)   **Stop** the car. (imperative)
    If I **were** angry, I would not have let you in. (subjunctive)

Adjectives

1. An **adjective** modifies a noun or pronoun by giving a descriptive or specific detail. Adjectives can usually show comparisons. (See Using Modifiers Correctly on pages 9 and 10.)
   cold winter   **colder** winter   **coldest** winter

2. Most adjectives will fit this sentence:
   The _____ one looks very _____.
   The **dusty** one looks very **old**.

3. Articles are the adjectives *a, an,* and *the.* Articles do not meet the above test for adjectives.

4. A proper adjective is formed from a proper noun and begins with a capital letter.
Marijka wore a **Ukrainian** costume.   He was a **Danish** prince.

5. An adjective used as an object complement follows and describes a direct object.
My aunt considers me **funny.**

Adverbs

1. An adverb modifies a verb, an adjective, or another adverb. Most adverbs can show comparisons. (See Using Modifiers Correctly on pages 9 and 10.)

   a. Adverbs that tell how, where, when, or to what degree modify verbs or verbals.
   The band stepped **lively.** (how)   Maria writes **frequently.** (when)
   Put the piano **here.** (where)   We were **thoroughly** entertained. (to what degree)

   b. Adverbs of degree strengthen or weaken the adjectives or other adverbs that they modify.
   A **very** happy fan cheered. (modifies adjective)   She spoke **too** fast. (modifies adverb)

2. Many adverbs fit these sentences:
She thinks _____.   She thinks _____ fast.   She _____ thinks fast.
She thinks **quickly.**   She thinks **unusually** fast.   She **seldom** thinks fast.

Prepositions, Conjunctions, and Interjections

1. A preposition shows the relationship of a noun or a pronoun to some other word. A compound preposition is made up of more than one word.
The first group **of** students arrived.   They skated **in spite of** the cold weather.

2. Some common prepositions include these: *about, above, across, after, against, along, among, around, at, before, behind, below, beneath, beside, besides, between, beyond, but, by, concerning, down, during, except, for, from, into, like, near, of, off, on, out, outside, over, past, round, since, through, till, to, toward, under, underneath, until, up, upon, with, within, without.*

3. A conjunction is a word that joins single words or groups of words. A coordinating conjunction joins words or groups of words that have equal grammatical weight. Correlative conjunctions work in pairs to join words and groups of words of equal weight. A subordinating conjunction joins two clauses in such a way as to make one grammatically dependent on the other.
Coordinating conjunction: He **and** I talked for hours.
Correlative conjunctions: Russ wants **either** a cat **or** a dog.
Subordinating conjunction: We ate lunch **when** it was ready.

4. A conjunctive adverb clarifies a relationship.
He did not like cold weather; **nevertheless,** he shoveled the snow.

5. An interjection is an unrelated word or phrase that expresses emotion or exclamation.
Wow, that was cool!   **Aha!** You fell right into my trap!

PARTS OF THE SENTENCE

Subjects and Predicates

1. The simple subject is the key noun or pronoun that tells what the sentence is about. A compound subject is made up of two or more simple subjects that are joined by a conjunction and have the same verb.
My **father** snores.   My **mother** and **I** can't sleep.

2. The simple predicate is the verb or verb phrase that expresses the essential thought about the subject of the sentence. A compound predicate is made up of two or more verbs or verb phrases that are joined by a conjunction and have the same subject.

The night **was** cold.   The elves **sang** and **danced** in the flower garden.

3. The complete subject consists of the simple subject and all the words that modify it.

The bright lights of the city burned intensely.   **The warm, soothing fire** kept us warm.

4. The complete predicate consists of the simple predicate and all the words that modify it or complete its meaning.

Dinosaurs **died out 65 million years ago.**   The sun **provides heat for the earth.**

5. Usually the subject comes before the predicate in a sentence. In inverted sentences, all or part of the predicate precedes the subject.

There **are** two **muffins** on the plate.   Over the field **soared** the **glider.**

Complements

1. A complement is a word or group of words that complete the meaning of the verb. There are four kinds of complements: direct objects, indirect objects, object complements, and subject complements.

2. A direct object answers *what?* or *whom?* after an action verb.
Sammi ate the **turkey.** (Sammi ate what?)
Carlos watched his **sister** in the school play. (Carlos watched whom?)

3. An indirect object receives what the direct object names.
Marie wrote **June** a letter.   George Washington gave his **troops** orders.

4. A subject complement follows a subject and a linking verb and identifies or describes the subject. A predicate nominative is a noun or pronoun that follows a linking verb and further identifies the subject. A predicate adjective follows a linking verb and further describes the subject.
Predicate Nominative: The best football player is **Jacob.**
Predicate Adjective: The people have been very **patient.**

5. An object complement describes or renames a direct object.
Object Complement: Ami found the man **handsome.**
Object Complement: Carlo thought the woman a **genius.**

PHRASES

1. A phrase is a group of words that acts in a sentence as a single part of speech.

2. A prepositional phrase is a group of words that begins with a preposition and usually ends with a noun or pronoun called the object of the preposition. A prepositional phrase can modify a noun or a pronoun, a verb, an adjective, or an adverb.
One of my favorite meals is pigs **in a blanket.** (modifies the noun *pigs*)
The supersonic jet soared **into the sky.** (modifies the verb *soared*)
The love of a household pet can be valuable **for a family.** (modifies the adjective *valuable*)
The child reads well **for a six year old.** (modifies the adverb *well*)

3. An appositive is a noun or a pronoun that is placed next to another noun or pronoun to identify it or give more information about it. An appositive phrase is an appositive plus its modifiers.
My grandfather **Géza** takes me fishing.   C.S. Lewis, **my favorite author,** lived in England.

4. A verbal is a verb form that functions in a sentence as a noun, an adjective, or an adverb. A verbal phrase is a verbal plus any complements and modifiers.

   a. A participle is a verbal that functions as an adjective: Gary comforted the **crying** baby.

   b. A participial phrase contains a participle plus any complements or modifiers: **Thanking everyone,** my uncle began to carve the turkey.

   c. A gerund is a verbal that ends with -ing. It is used in the same way a noun is used: **Skiing** is a popular sport.

   d. A gerund phrase is a gerund plus any complements or modifiers: **Singing the national anthem** is traditional at many sports events.

   e. An infinitive is a verbal that is usually preceded by the word to. It is used as a noun, an adjective, or an adverb: I never learned **to dance.** (noun) She has an errand **to run.** (adjective) I will be happy **to help.** (adverb)

   f. An infinitive phrase contains an infinitive plus any complements or modifiers: My father woke up **to watch the news on television.**

5. An absolute phrase consists of a noun or a pronoun that is modified by a participle or a participial phrase but has no grammatical relation to the sentence.
   His legs terribly tired, Honori sat down.

CLAUSES AND SENTENCE STRUCTURE

1. A clause is a group of words that has a subject and a predicate and is used as a sentence or part of a sentence. There are two types of clauses: main and subordinate. A main clause has a subject and a predicate and can stand alone as a sentence. A subordinate clause has a subject and a predicate, but it cannot stand alone as a sentence.

          main   sub.
   The book bored me, until I read Chapter 5.

2. There are three types of subordinate clauses: adjective, adverb, and noun.

   a. An adjective clause is a subordinate clause that modifies a noun or a pronoun.
      The students **who stayed after school for help** did well on the test.

   b. An adverb clause is a subordinate clause that modifies a verb, an adjective, or an adverb. It tells *when, where, how, why, to what extent,* or *under what conditions.*
      When the sun set, everyone watched from the window. (modifies a verb)
      Today is warmer **than yesterday was.** (modifies an adjective)

   c. A noun clause is a subordinate clause used as a noun.
      Who will become president has been declared.   I now remember **what I need to buy.**

3. Main and subordinate clauses can form four types of sentences. A simple sentence has only one main clause and no subordinate clauses. A compound sentence has two or more main clauses. A complex sentence has one main clause and one or more subordinate clauses. A compound-complex sentence has more than one main clause and at least one subordinate clause.

		main	
Simple:		The stars fill the sky.	

	main	main	
Compound:	The plane landed,	and the passengers left.	

	sub.	main	
Complex:	Although the children found the letter,	they couldn't read it.	

	main	main	sub.
Compound-Complex:	The earth is bountiful;	we may destroy it	if we abuse it.

4. A sentence that makes a statement is classified as a declarative sentence: The Cleveland Browns are my favorite team. An imperative sentence gives a command or makes a request: Please go to the dance with me. An interrogative sentence asks a question: Who would abandon a family pet? An exclamatory sentence expresses strong emotion: Look out!

SUBJECT-VERB AGREEMENT

1. A verb must agree with its subject in person and number.
   Doli **runs**. (singular)   Doli and Abay **run**. (plural)
   He **is** singing. (singular) They **are** singing. (plural)

2. In inverted sentences the subject follows the verb. The sentence may begin with a prepositional phrase, the words *there* or *here,* or the verb form of *do.*
   Out of the bushes **sprang** the *leopard.*   There **is** never enough *time.*
   Do those *pigs* **eat** leftover food?

3. Do not mistake a word in a prepositional phrase for the subject.
   The **boss** of the employees **works** very hard. (The verb *works* tells the action of the boss.)

4. Make the verb in a sentence agree with the subject, not with the predicate nominative.
   Her problem **was** the twins.   The twins **were** her problem.

5. A title is always singular, even if nouns in the title are plural.
   The War of the Worlds **was** a radio broadcast that caused widespread panic.

6. Subjects combined with *and* or *both* use plural verbs unless the parts are of a whole unit. When compound subjects are joined with *or* or *nor*, the verb agrees with the subject listed last.
   Chocolate, strawberry, and vanilla are common ice cream flavors.
   Peanut butter and jelly is a good snack.   Neither **books nor a briefcase is** needed.

7. Use a singular verb if the compound subject is preceded by the words *many a, every,* or *each.*
   Every **dog and cat** needs to be cared for.   Many a **young man** has stood here.

8. A subject remains singular or plural regardless of any intervening expressions.
   Gloria, as well as the rest of her family, **was** late.
   The **players,** accompanied by the coach, **enter** the field.

9. A verb must agree in number with an indefinite pronoun subject.
   Always singular: *each, either, neither, one, everyone, everybody, everything, no one, nobody, nothing, anyone, anybody, anything, someone, somebody,* and *something.*
   Always plural: *several, few, both,* and *many.*
   Either singular or plural: *some, all, any, most,* and *none.*
   Is any of the **lemonade** left?   **Are** any of the **biscuits** burnt?

10. When the subject of an adjective clause is a relative pronoun, the verb in the clause must agree with the antecedent of the relative pronoun.
    He is one of the singers who dance. (The antecedent of *who* is *singers,* plural: singers dance.)

USING PRONOUNS CORRECTLY

1. Use the nominative case when the pronoun is a subject or a predicate nominative.
   She eats cake.   Is **he** here?   That is **I**. (predicate nominative)

2. Use the objective case when the pronoun is an object.
   Clarence invited **us**. (direct object)   Chapa gave **me** a gift. (indirect object)
   Spot! Don't run around **me**! (object of preposition)

3. Use the possessive case to replace possessive nouns and precede gerunds. Never use an apostrophe in a possessive pronoun.
   That new car is **hers**.   They were thrilled at **his** playing the violin.

4. Use the nominative case when the pronoun is a subject or a predicate nominative.
   We three—Marijian, his sister, and I—went to camp.

5. Use the objective case to rename an object.
   The teacher acknowledged **us**, Burny and **me**.

6. When a pronoun is followed by an appositive, choose the case of the pronoun that would be correct if the appositive were omitted.
   We the jury find the defendant guilty.   That building was erected by **us** workers.

7. In elliptical adverb clauses using *than* and *as*, choose the case of the pronoun that you would use if the missing words were fully expressed.
   Kareem is a better sprinter than **I**. (I am)   It helped you more than **me**. (it helped me)

8. Use a reflexive pronoun when it refers to the person who is the subject of the sentence. Avoid using *hisself* or *theirselves*.
   Jerry found **himself** in a mess.   The candidates questioned **themselves** about their tactics.

9. In questions, use *who* for subjects and *whom* for objects. Use *who* and *whoever* for subjects and predicate nominatives in subordinate clauses. Use the objective pronouns *whom* and *whomever* for objects of subordinate clauses.
   Who roasted these marshmallows?   **Whom** will you hire next?
   This medal is for **whoever** finishes first.
   The newspaper will interview **whomever** the editor chooses.

10. An antecedent is the word or group of words to which a pronoun refers or that a pronoun replaces. All pronouns must agree with their antecedents in number, gender, and person.
    Colleen's **friends** gave up **their** free time to help.   The **Senate** passed **its** first bill of the year.

11. Make sure that the antecedent of a pronoun is clearly stated.
    VAGUE: The people who lost their dogs stayed in their yards, hoping **they** would return.
    CLEAR: The people who lost their dogs stayed in their yards, hoping **the dogs** would return.

    INDEFINITE: If you park the car under the sign **it** will be towed away.
    CLEAR: If you park the car under the sign **the car** will be towed away.

USING MODIFIERS CORRECTLY

1. Most adjectives and adverbs have three degrees of form. The positive form of a modifier cannot be used to make a comparison. The comparative form of a modifier shows two things being compared. The superlative form of a modifier shows three or more things being compared.
   The year went by **fast**.   This year went by **faster** than last year.
   I expect next year to go by the **fastest** of all.

2. One- and two-syllable adjectives add -er to form comparative and -est to form superlative.

POSITIVE: bold   happy   strong
COMPARATIVE: bolder   happier   stronger
SUPERLATIVE: boldest   happiest   strongest

3. For adverbs ending in -ly and modifiers with three or more syllables, use more and most or less and least to form the comparative and superlative degrees.

He was the **least** exhausted of the group.   She spoke **more** caringly than some others.

4. Some modifiers have irregular forms.

POSITIVE:	good, well	badly, ill	far	many, much	little
COMPARATIVE:	better	worse	farther	more	less
SUPERLATIVE:	best	worst	farthest	most	least

5. Do not make a double comparison using both -er or -est and more or most.

INCORRECT: That musical was the **most funniest** I have ever seen.
CORRECT: That musical was the **funniest** I have ever seen.

6. Do not make an incomplete or unclear comparison by omitting other or else when you compare one member of a group with another.

UNCLEAR: Joey has missed more school than any kid in the ninth grade.
CLEAR: Joey has missed more school than any **other** kid in the ninth grade.

7. Avoid double negatives, which are two negative words in the same clause.

INCORRECT: I have **not** seen **no** stray cats.
CORRECT: I have **not** seen **any** stray cats.

8. For clarity, place modifiers as close as possible to the words they modify.

MISPLACED: The fire was snuffed out by the storm **that we accidentally started**.

CLEAR: The fire **that we accidentally started** was snuffed out by the storm.

DANGLING: **To avoid the long walk,** a friend drove us.

CLEAR: **To avoid the long walk,** we were driven by a friend.

9. Place the adverb only immediately before the word or group of words it modifies.

Only Afi wants choir rehearsal next week. (No one but Afi wants rehearsal.)
Afi wants **only** choir rehearsal next week. (She wants no other rehearsal.)
Afi wants choir rehearsal **only** next week. (She does not want rehearsal any other week.)

USAGE GLOSSARY

a, an   Use the article a when the following word begins with a consonant sound. Use an when the following word begins with a vowel sound.

a house   **an** understudy   **an** hour   **a** united front

a lot, alot   Always write this expression, meaning "a large amount," as two words.

With his help, we will learn **a lot** about photography.

a while, awhile   In or for often precedes a while, forming a prepositional phrase. Awhile is used only as an adverb.

Let us listen to the forest for **a while**.   The students listened **awhile**.

accept, except *Accept,* a verb, means "to receive" or "to agree to." *Except* may be a preposition or a verb. As a preposition it means "but." As a verb it means "to leave out."
I will **accept** all of your terms **except** the last one.

adapt, adopt *Adapt* means "to adjust." *Adopt* means "to take something for one's own."
Species survive because they **adapt** to new situations. My church will **adopt** a needy family.

advice, advise *Advice,* a noun, means "helpful opinion." *Advise,* a verb, means "to give advice."
I must **advise** you to never take Jakel's **advice.**

affect, effect *Affect,* a verb, means "to cause a change in, to influence." *Effect* may be a noun or a verb. As a noun it means "result." As a verb it means "to bring about."
Is it true that the observer can **affect** the results? (verb)
I have no idea what **effect** that may have. (noun)
How can the president **effect** a good approval rating? (verb)

ain't *Ain't* is unacceptable in speaking and writing. Use only in exact quotations.

all ready, already *All ready* means "completely ready." *Already* means "before or by this time."
We had **already** purchased our plane tickets, and we were **all ready** to board.

all right, alright Always write this expression as two words. *Alright* is unacceptable.
Because she is your friend, she is **all right** with me.

all together, altogether The two words *all together* mean "in a group." The single word *altogether* is an adverb meaning "completely" or "on the whole."
The hikers gathered **all together** for lunch, and they were **altogether** exhausted.

allusion, illusion *Allusion* means "an indirect reference." *Illusion* refers to something false.
Mr. Lee made an **allusion** to *The Grapes of Wrath.*   The magician performed **illusions.**

anyways, anywheres, everywheres, somewheres Write these words and others like them without a final *-s: anyway, anywhere, everywhere, somewhere.*

bad, badly Use *bad* as an adjective and *badly* as an adverb.
We watched a **bad** movie.   He sang the national anthem quite **badly.**

being as, being that Use these only informally. In formal writing and speech, use *because* or *since.*

beside, besides *Beside* means "next to." *Besides* means "moreover" or "in addition to."
Who, **besides** Antonio, will offer to sit **beside** the window?

between, among Use *between* to refer to or to compare two separate nouns. Use *among* to show a relationship in a group.
I could not choose **between** Harvard and Princeton.   Who **among** the class knows me?

borrow, lend, loan *Borrow* is a verb meaning "to take something that must be returned." *Lend* is a verb meaning "to give something that must be returned." *Loan* is a noun.
People **borrow** money from banks.   Banks will **lend** money to approved customers.
People always must apply for a **loan.**

bring, take Use *bring* to show movement from a distant place to a closer one. Use *take* to show movement from a nearby place to a more distant one.
Bring in the paper, and **take** out the trash.

can, may *Can* indicates the ability to do something. *May* indicates permission to do something.
Anyone **can** use a credit card, but only the cardholder **may** authorize it.

can't hardly, can't scarcely These terms are considered double negatives. Do not use them. Use *can hardly* and *can scarcely.*

continual, continuous *Continual* describes repetitive action with pauses between occurrences. *Continuous* describes an action that continues with no interruption in space or time.
We make **continual** trips to the grocery.   **Continuous** energy from our sun lights the sky.

could of, might of, must of, should of, would of Do not use *of* after *could, might, must, should,* or *would.* Instead, use the helping verb *have.*
That **must have been** the longest play ever!

different from, different than The expression *different from* is preferred to *different than.*
Baseball is **different from** the English sport of cricket.

doesn't, don't *Doesn't* is the contraction of *does not* and should be used with all singular nouns. *Don't* is the contraction of *do not* and should be used with *I, you,* and all plural nouns.
My dog **doesn't** like the mail carrier.   Bobsled riders **don't** take their job lightly.

emigrate, immigrate Use *emigrate* to mean "to move from one country to another." Use *immigrate* to mean "to enter a country to settle there." Use *from* with *emigrate* and *to* with *immigrate.*
Refugees **emigrate** from war-torn countries.   My great-grandfather **immigrated** to America.

farther, further *Farther* refers to physical distance. *Further* refers to time or degree.
Traveling **farther** from your home may **further** your understanding of different places.

fewer, less Use *fewer* to refer to nouns that can be counted. Use *less* to refer to nouns that cannot be counted. Also use *less* to refer to figures used as a single amount or quantity.
If **fewer** crimes were committed, there would be **less** misery in the world.
The box measured **less** than 100 cm².

good, well *Good* is an adjective, and *well* is an adverb.
That spot is a **good** place for a picnic.   We dined **well** that day.

had of Do not use *of* between *had* and a past participle.
I wish I **had eaten** my sundae when I had the chance.

hanged, hung Use *hanged* to mean "put to death by hanging." Use *hung* in all other cases.
In the Old West, many were convicted and **hanged**.   I **hung** my coat on the hook.

in, into, in to Use *in* to mean "inside" or "within" and *into* to indicate movement or direction from outside to a point within. *In to* is made up of an adverb *(in)* followed by a preposition *(to).*
The fish swim **in** the sea.   We moved **into** a new house last year.
The student walked **in to** see the principal for a meeting.

irregardless, regardless Always use *regardless. Irregardless* is a double negative.
Root beer tastes great **regardless** of the brand.

this kind, these kinds Because *kind* is singular, it is modified by the singular form *this* or *that.* Because *kinds* is plural, it is modified by the plural form *these* or *those.*
I love **these kinds** of desserts!   I do not feel comfortable with **this kind** of situation.

lay, lie *Lay* means "to put" or "to place," and it takes a direct object. *Lie* means "to recline" or "to be positioned," and it never takes an object.
I taught my dog to **lay** the paper at my feet and then **lie** on the ground.

learn, teach *Learn* means "to receive knowledge." *Teach* means "to impart knowledge."
I want to **learn** a new language and later **teach** it to others.

leave, let *Leave* means "to go away." *Let* means "to allow" or "to permit."
My guest had to **leave** because his parents do not **let** him stay up too late.

like, as *Like* is a preposition and introduces a prepositional phrase. *As* and *as if* are subordinating conjunctions and introduce subordinate clauses. Never use *like* before a clause.

I felt **like** a stuffed crab after the feast.   The pigeons flew away, **as** they always do when scared.

loose, lose Use *loose* to mean "not firmly attached" and *lose* to mean "to misplace," or "to fail to win."

You don't want to **lose** your nice pair of **loose** jeans.

passed, past *Passed* is the past tense and the past participle of the verb *to pass*. *Past* can be an adjective, a preposition, an adverb, or a noun.

He **passed** the exit ramp because he could not see the sign **past** the bushes.

precede, proceed *Precede* means "to go or come before." *Proceed* means "to continue."

We can **proceed** with the plans.   From a distance, lightning appears to **precede** thunder.

raise, rise *Raise* means "to cause to move upward," and it always takes an object. *Rise* means "to get up"; it is intransitive and never takes an object.

Raise the drawbridge!   For some, it is difficult to **rise** in the morning.

reason is because Use either *reason is that* or *because.*

The **reason** why he left **is that** he was bored.   He left **because** he was bored.

respectfully, respectively *Respectfully* means "with respect." *Respectively* means "in the order named."

We **respectfully** bowed to the audience.

Abla, Héctor, and Shelly, **respectively,** play first, second, and third base.

says, said *Says* is the third-person singular of *say*. *Said* is the past tense of *say*.

Listen carefully to what she **says.**   I love what the keynote speaker **said.**

sit, set *Sit* means "to place oneself in a sitting position." It rarely takes an object. *Set* means "to place" or "to put" and usually takes an object. *Set* can also refer to the sun's going down.

Sit anywhere you would like.   **Set** the nozzle back in its slot before paying for the gas.

Today the sun will **set** at seven o'clock

than, then *Than* is a conjunction that is used to introduce the second element in a comparison; it also shows exception. *Then* is an adverb.

Julio hit more home runs **than** Jacob this year.   Call for help first, and **then** start CPR.

this here, that there Avoid using *here* and *there* after *this* and *that.*

This bunk is yours.

who, whom *Who* is a subject, and *whom* is an object.

Who first sang the song "Memories"?   To **whom** should I throw the ball now?

CAPITALIZATION

1. Capitalize the first word in a sentence, including direct quotes and sentences in parentheses unless they are contained within another sentence.

   Shakespeare asked, "**W**hat's in a name?" (**T**his is from *Romeo and Juliet*.)

2. Always capitalize the pronoun *I* no matter where it appears in a sentence.

   Because **I** woke up late, **I** had to race to school.

3. Capitalize the following proper nouns.

   a. Names of individuals, titles used in direct address or preceding a name, and titles describing a family relationship used with a name or in place of a name

   President Nixon   **George Burns**   **Sis**   **Sir Anthony Hopkins**   **Uncle Jay**

b. Names of ethnic groups, national groups, political parties and their members, and languages

African Americans   Mexicans   Republican party   Hebrew

c. Names of organizations, institutions, firms, monuments, bridges, buildings, and other structures

National Honor Society   Vietnam War Memorial   Brooklyn Bridge   Parliament

d. Trade names and names of documents, awards, and laws

Kleenex tissues   Declaration of Independence   Academy Award   Bill of Rights

e. Geographical terms and regions or localities

North Carolina   Arctic Ocean   Nile River   West Street   the South   Central Park

f. Names of planets and other heavenly bodies

Jupiter   Horsehead Nebula   the Milky Way

g. Names of ships, planes, trains, and spacecraft

Challenger   *Spirit of Saint Louis*   USS *George Washington*

h. Names of most historical events, eras, calendar items, and religious terms

Fourth of July   Jurassic   Gulf War   Friday   Yom Kippur   Protestant

i. Titles of literary works, works of art, and musical compositions

"The Road Less Traveled" (poem)   *The Old Man and the Sea* (book)
Venus de Milo (statue)   *The Magic Flute* (opera)

4. Capitalize proper adjectives (adjectives formed from proper nouns).

Socratic method   Jungian theory   Chinese food   Georgia clay   Colombian coffee

PUNCTUATION, ABBREVIATIONS, AND NUMBERS

1. Use a period at the end of a declarative sentence and at the end of a polite command.
Robin Hood was a medieval hero.   Pass the papers to the front.

2. Use an exclamation point to show strong feeling or to give a forceful command.
What a surprise that is!   Watch out!   That's just what I need!

3. Use a question mark to indicate a direct question. Use a period to indicate an indirect question.
DIRECT: Who ruled France in 1821?
INDIRECT: Gamal wanted to know how much time was left before lunch.

4. Use a colon to introduce a list or to illustrate or restate previous material.
For my team, I choose the following people: Zina, Ming, and Sue.
In light of the data, the conclusion was not hard to obtain: Earth is not flat.

5. Use a colon for precise time measurements, biblical chapter and verse references, and business letter salutations.
10:02 A.M.   John 3:16   Dear Ms. Delgado:

6. Use a semicolon in the following situations:

a. To separate main clauses not joined by a coordinating conjunction
My computer isn't working; perhaps I need to call a technician.

b. To separate main clauses joined by a conjunctive adverb or by *for example* or *that is*
Cancer is a serious disease; however, heart disease kills more people.

c. To separate items in a series when those items contain commas
I have done oral reports on Maya Angelou, a poet; Billy Joel, a singer; and Mario van Peebles, a director and actor.

d. To separate two main clauses joined by a coordinating conjunction when such clauses already contain several commas
   According to Bruce, he spent his vacation in Naples, Florida; but he said it was a business, not a pleasure, trip.

7. Use a comma in the following situations:

   a. To separate the main clauses of compound sentences
      She was a slow eater, but she always finished her meal first.

   b. To separate three or more words, phrases, or clauses in a series
      Apples, oranges, grapefruit, and cherries are delicious.

   c. To separate coordinate modifiers
      The prom was a happy, exciting occasion.

   d. To set off parenthetical expressions
      He will, of course, stay for dinner.   Mary, on the other hand, is very pleasant.

   e. To set off nonessential clauses and phrases; to set off introductory adverbial clauses, participial phrases, and long prepositional phrases
      Adjective clause: The bride, who is a chemist, looked lovely.
      Appositive phrase: The parade, the longest I've ever seen, featured twelve bands.
      Adverbial clause: After we had eaten, I realized my wallet was still in the car.
      Participial phrase: Laughing heartily, Milan quickly left the room.
      Prepositional phrase: At the sound of the final buzzer, the ball slid through the hoop.

   f. To separate parts of an address, a geographical term, or a date
      1640 Chartwell Avenue, Edina, Minnesota   September 11, 1982

   g. To set off parts of a reference
      Read *Slaughterhouse-Five*, pages 15–20.   Perform a scene from *Hamlet*, Act II.

   h. To set off words or phrases of direct address and tag questions
      Sherri, please pass the butter.   How are you, my friend?   We try hard, don't we?

   i. After the salutation and close of a friendly letter and after the close of a business letter
      Dear Richard,   Sincerely,   Yours,   Dear Mother,

8. Use dashes to signal a change in thought or to emphasize parenthetical matter.
   "Remember to turn off the alarm—oh, don't touch that!"

9. Use parentheses to set off supplemental material. Punctuate within the parentheses only if the punctuation is part of the parenthetical expression.
   I saw Bill Cosby (he is my favorite comedian) last night.

10. Use brackets to enclose information inserted by someone besides the original writer.
    The paper continues, "The company knows he [Watson] is impressed."

11. Ellipsis points, a series of three spaced points, indicate an omission of material.
    The film critic said, "The show was great . . . a must see!"

12. Use quotation marks to enclose a direct quotation. When a quotation is interrupted, use two sets of quotation marks. Use single quotation marks for a quotation within a quotation.
    "This day," the general said, "will live on in infamy."
    "Yes," the commander replied. "The headlines today read, 'Allies Retreat.'"

13. Use quotation marks to indicate titles of short works, unusual expressions, and definitions.
    "The Gift of the Magi" (short story)   "Ave Maria" (song)

    Large speakers are called "woofers," and small speakers are called "tweeters."

14. Always place commas and periods *inside* closing quotation marks. Place colons and semicolons *outside* closing quotation marks. Place question marks and exclamation points *inside* closing quotation marks only when those marks are part of the quotation.
    "Rafi told me," John said, "that he could not go."
    Let me tell you about "Piano Man": it is a narrative song.
    He yelled, "Who are you?"
    Did she say "Wait for me"?

15. Italicize (underline) titles of books, lengthy poems, plays, films, television series, paintings and sculptures, long musical compositions, court cases, names of newspapers and magazines, ships, trains, airplanes, and spacecraft.
    The Last Supper (painting)   *Bang the Drum Slowly* (film)   *Roe* v. *Wade* (court case)
    Titanic (ship)   *Time* (magazine)   *Boston Globe* (newspaper)

16. Italicize (underline) foreign words and expressions that are not used frequently in English and words, letters, and numerals used to represent themselves.
    Please discuss the phrase *caveat emptor.*
    Today, *Sesame Street* was sponsored by the letters *t* and *m* and the number *6.*

17. Add an apostrophe and -*s* to all singular indefinite pronouns, singular nouns, plural nouns not ending in -*s*, and compound nouns to make them possessive. Add only an apostrophe to plural nouns ending in -*s* to make them possessive.
    anyone**'s** guess   the dog**'s** leash   the women**'s** club
    student**s'** teacher   singer**s'** microphones   runner**s'** shoes

18. If two or more people possess something jointly, use the possessive form for the last person's name. If they possess things individually, use the possessive form for both names.
    mom and dad**'s** checkbook   Carmen**'s** and Sumil**'s** projects

19. Use a possessive form to express amounts of money or time that modify a noun.
    a day**'s** pay   fifty dollar**s'** worth   a block**'s** walk

20. Use an apostrophe in place of omitted letters or numerals. Use an apostrophe and -*s* to form the plural of letters, numerals, and symbols.
    cannot is *can't*   *do not* is *don't*   1978 is *'78*
    Mind your **p's** and **q's.**

21. Use a hyphen after any prefix joined to a proper noun or a proper adjective. Use a hyphen after the prefixes *all-, ex-,* and *self-* joined to a noun or an adjective, the prefix *anti-* joined to a word beginning with *i-,* the prefix *vice-* (except in *vice president*), and the prefix *re-* to avoid confusion between words that are spelled the same but have different meanings.
    all-inclusive   ex-wife   self-reliance
    anti-immigrant   vice-principal   re-call *instead of* recall

22. Use a hyphen in a compound adjective that precedes a noun. Use a hyphen in compound numbers and in fractions used as adjectives.
    a green-yellow jersey   a red-hot poker   jet-black hair
    ninety-nine   one-fifth cup of sugar

23. Use a hyphen to divide words at the end of a line.
    daz-zle   terri-tory   Mediter-ranean

24. Use one period at the end of an abbreviation. If punctuation other than a period ends the sentence, use both the period and the other punctuation.
    Bring me the books, papers, pencils, etc.   Could you be ready at 2:00 P.M.?

25. Capitalize the abbreviations of proper nouns and some personal titles.

U.K.   C.E.O.   R. F. Kennedy   B.C.   A.D.   Ph.D.

26. Abbreviate numerical measurements in scientific writing but not in ordinary prose.

Measure 89 g into the crucible.   Jim ran ten yards when he heard that dog barking!

27. Spell out cardinal and ordinal numbers that can be written in one or two words and those that appear at the beginning of a sentence.

Five hundred people attended.   I look forward to my **eighteenth** birthday.

28. Use numerals for dates; for decimals; for house, apartment, and room numbers; for street and avenue numbers greater than ten; for sums of money involving both dollars and cents; and to emphasize the exact time of day and with A.M. and P.M.

April **1, 1996**   Room **251**   **$2.51**   **2:51** P.M.

29. Express all related numbers in a sentence as numerals if any one should be a numeral.

The subscriptions gradually rose from **10** to **116**.

30. Spell out numbers that express decades, amounts of money that can be written in one or two words, streets and avenues less than ten, and the approximate time of day.

the **seventies**   **fifty** cents   **Fifth** Avenue   half past **five**

VOCABULARY AND SPELLING

1. Clues to the meaning of an unfamiliar word can be found in its context. Context clues include definition, the meaning stated; example, the meaning explained through one familiar case; comparison, similarity to a familiar word; contrast, opposite of a familiar word; and cause and effect, a cause described by its effects.

2. Clues to the meaning of a word can be obtained from its base word, its prefix, or its suffix

telegram **gram** = writing   psychology **psych** = soul, mind

antibacterial **anti** = against   biology **-logy** = study

3. The *i* comes before the *e*, except when both letters follow a *c* or when both letters are pronounced together as an $\bar{a}$ sound. However, many exceptions exist to this rule.

f**ie**ld (*i* before *e*)   dec**ei**ve (*ei* after *c*)   r**ei**gn ($\bar{a}$ sound)   w**ei**rd (exception)

4. Most word endings pronounced *sēd* are spelled *-cede*. In one word, *supersede*, the ending is spelled *-sede*. In *proceed*, *exceed*, and *succeed*, the ending is spelled *-ceed*.

pre**cede**   re**cede**   con**cede**

5. An unstressed vowel sound is not emphasized when a word is pronounced. Determine the spelling of this sound by comparing it to a known word.

hesitant (Compare to *hesitate.*)   *fantasy* (Compare to *fantastic.*)

6. When adding a suffix that begins with a consonant to a word that ends in silent *e*, generally keep the *e*. If the suffix begins with a vowel or *y*, generally drop the *e*. If the suffix begins with *a* or *o* and the word ends in *ce* or *ge*, keep the *e*. If the suffix begins with a vowel and the word ends in *ee* or *oe*, keep the *e*.

encourag**ement**   scar**y**   chang**eable**   flee**ing**

7. When adding a suffix to a word ending in a consonant +*y*, change the *y* to *i* unless the suffix begins with *i*. If the word ends in a vowel +*y*, keep the *y*.

heart**iness**   read**iness**   sp**ying**   stra**ying**

8. Double the final consonant before adding a suffix that begins with a vowel to a word that ends in a single consonant preceded by a single vowel if the accent is on the root's last syllable.
   plan**ned**   fin**ned**   misfit**ted**

9. When adding *-ly* to a word that ends in a single *l*, keep the *l*. If it ends in a double *l*, drop one *l*. If it ends in a consonant +*le*, drop the *le*.
   real becomes real**ly**   dull becomes dul**ly**   inexplicable becomes inexplicab**ly**

10. When adding *-ness* to a word that ends in *n*, keep the *n*.
    lean**ness**   mean**ness**   green**ness**

11. When joining a word or prefix that ends in a consonant to a suffix or word that begins with a consonant, keep both consonants.
    quiet**ness**   great**ly**   red**ness**

12. Most nouns form their plurals by adding *-s*. However, nouns that end in *-ch*, *-s*, *-sh*, *-x*, or *-z* form plurals by adding *-es*. If the noun ends in a consonant +*y*, change *y* to *i* and add *-es*. If the noun ends in *-lf*, change *f* to *v* and add *-es*. If the noun ends in *-fe*, change *f* to *v* and add *-s*.
    can**s**   chur**ches**   fax**es**   sp**ies**   hal**ves**   loa**ves**

13. To form the plural of proper names and one-word compound nouns, follow the general rules for plurals. To form the plural of hyphenated compound nouns or compound nouns of more than one word, make the most important word plural.
    Shatner**s**   Stockholder**s**   brother**s**-in-law   Master Sergeant**s**

14. Some nouns have the same singular and plural forms.
    sheep   species

COMPOSITION

Writing Themes and Paragraphs

1. Use prewriting to find ideas to write about. One form of prewriting, freewriting, starts with a subject or topic and branches off into related ideas. Another way to find a topic is to ask and answer questions about your starting subject, helping you to gain a deeper understanding of your chosen topic. Also part of the prewriting stage is determining who your readers or audience will be and deciding your purpose for writing. Your purpose—as varied as writing to persuade, to explain, to describe something, or to narrate—is partially shaped by who your audience will be, and vice versa.

2. To complete your first draft, organize your prewriting into an introduction, body, and conclusion. Concentrate on unity and coherence of the overall piece. Experiment with different paragraph orders: chronological order places events in the order in which they happened; spatial order places objects in the order in which they appear; and compare/contrast order shows similarities and differences in objects or events.

3. Revise your composition if necessary. Read through your draft, looking for places to improve content and structure. Remember that varying your sentence patterns and lengths will make your writing easier and more enjoyable to read.

4. In the editing stage, check your grammar, spelling, and punctuation. Focus on expressing your ideas clearly and concisely.

5. Finally, prepare your writing for presentation. Sharing your composition, or ideas, with others may take many forms: printed, oral, or graphic.

Outlining

1. The two common forms of outlines are sentence outlines and topic outlines Choose one type of outline and keep it uniform throughout.

2. A period follows the number or letter of each division. Each point in a sentence outline ends with a period; the points in a topic outline do not.

3. Each point begins with a capital letter.

4. A point may have no fewer than two subpoints.

SENTENCE OUTLINE	TOPIC OUTLINE
I. This is the main point.	I. Main point
A. This is a subpoint of *I*.	A. Subpoint of *I*
1. This is a detail of *A*.	1. Detail of *A*
a. This is a detail of *1*.	a. Detail of *1*
b. This is a detail of *1*.	b. Detail of *1*
2. This is a detail of *A*.	2. Detail of *A*
B. This is a subpoint of *I*.	B. Subpoint of *I*
II. This is another main point.	II. Main point

Writing letters

1. Personal letters are usually handwritten in indented form (the first line of paragraphs, each line of the heading, the complimentary close, and the signature are indented). Business letters are usually typewritten in block or semiblock form. Block form contains no indents; semiblock form indents the heading, the complimentary close, and the signature.

2. The five parts of a personal letter are the heading (the writer's address and the date), the salutation (greeting), the body (message), the complimentary close (such as "Yours truly"), and the signature (the writer's name). The business letter has the same parts and also includes an inside address (the recipient's address).

PERSONAL LETTER   BUSINESS LETTER

Heading

Salutation

Body

Complimentary Close

Signature

Heading

Inside Address

Salutation

Body

Complimentary Close

Signature

3. Reveal your personality and imagination in colorful personal letters. Keep business letters brief, clear, and courteous.

4. **Personal letters** include letters to friends and family members. **Thank-you notes** and **invitations** are personal letters that may be either formal or informal in style.

5. Use a **letter of complaint** to convey a concern. Begin the letter by telling what happened. Then use supporting details as evidence. Complete the letter by explaining what you want done. Avoid insults and threats, and make reasonable requests. Use a **letter of request** to ask for information or to place an order of purchase. Be concise, yet give all the details necessary for your request to be fulfilled. Keep the tone of your letter courteous and be generous in allotting time for a response.

6. Use an **opinion letter** to take a firm stand on an issue. Make the letter clear, firm, rational, and purposeful. Be aware of your audience, their attitude, how informed they are, and their possible reactions to your opinion. Support your statements of opinion with facts.

7. Use a **résumé** to summarize your work experience, school experience, talents, and interests. Be clear, concise, and expressive. Use a consistent form. You do not need to write in complete sentences, but use as many action verbs as possible.

8. Use a **cover letter** as a brief introduction accompanying your résumé.

*T*roubleshooter

• •

Sentence Fragments

PROBLEM 1

Fragment that lacks a subject

frag	Ali baked a chocolate cake. (Took it to the party.)
frag	Maria thought the comedian was funny. (Laughed at his jokes.)

SOLUTION

Ali baked a chocolate cake. He took it to the party.
Maria thought the comedian was funny. She laughed at his jokes.

Make a complete sentence by adding a subject to the fragment.

PROBLEM 2

Fragment that lacks a complete verb

frag	Helen is a photographer. (She becoming well-known for her work.)
frag	Alicia has a new computer. (It very powerful.)

SOLUTION A

Helen is a photographer. She is becoming well-known for her work.
Alicia has a new computer. It is very powerful.

Make a complete sentence by adding a complete verb or a helping verb.

SOLUTION B

Helen is a photographer and is becoming well-known for her work.
Alicia has a new computer, which is very powerful.

Combine the fragment with another sentence.

PROBLEM 3

Fragment that is a subordinate clause

frag   Akira repaired the old boat. Because it was beautiful.

frag   Jennifer has two race car magazines. Which she bought at the store.

SOLUTION A

Akira repaired the old boat because it was beautiful.

Jennifer has two race car magazines, which she bought at the store.

Combine the fragment with another sentence.

SOLUTION B

Akira repaired the old boat. It was beautiful.

Jennifer has two race car magazines. She bought them at the store.

Make the fragment a complete sentence by removing the subordinating conjunction or the relative pronoun and adding a subject or other words necessary to make a complete thought.

PROBLEM 4

Fragment that lacks both subject and verb

frag   The soft rustle of the trees makes me sleepy. In the afternoon.

frag   The next morning. We talked about our adventure.

SOLUTION

The soft rustle of the trees makes me sleepy in the afternoon.

The next morning, we talked about our adventure.

Make the fragment part of a sentence.

Need More Help? *More help in avoiding sentence fragments is available in Lesson 30.*

Run-on Sentences

Problem 1

Comma splice—two main clauses separated only by a comma

run-on (I don't know where the oil paints are, they were over by the easel.)

Solution A

I don't know where the oil paints are. They were over by the easel.

Make two sentences by separating the first clause from the second with end punctuation, such as a period or a question mark, and start the second sentence with a capital letter.

Solution B

I don't know where the oil paints are; they were over by the easel.

Place a semicolon between the main clauses of the sentence.

Solution C

I don't know where the oil paints are, but they were over by the easel.

Add a coordinating conjunction after the comma.

Problem 2

No punctuation between two main clauses

run-on (Deelra ran the hurdles in record time Shawna placed second.)

Solution A

Deelra ran the hurdles in record time. Shawna placed second.

Make two sentences out of the run-on sentence.

SOLUTION B

Deelra ran the hurdles in record time; Shawna placed second.

Separate the main clauses with a semicolon.

SOLUTION C

Deelra ran the hurdles in record time, but Shawna placed second.

Add a comma and a coordinating conjunction between the main clauses.

PROBLEM 3

Two main clauses without a comma before the coordinating conjunction

run-on The robins usually arrive in the spring and they start building nests at once.

run-on Emily won the scholarship last year but she decided not to accept it.

SOLUTION

The robins usually arrive in the spring, and they start building nests at once.

Emily won the scholarship last year, but she decided not to accept it.

Separate the main clauses by adding a comma before the coordinating conjunction.

Need More Help? *More help in avoiding run-on sentences is available in Lesson 31.*

Lack of Subject-Verb Agreement

PROBLEM 1

A prepositional phrase between a subject and its verb

agr   The arrangement of those colorful pictures (make) a vivid, exciting combination.

agr   One of those big, gray seagulls (have perched) on the roof.

SOLUTION

The arrangement of those colorful pictures makes a vivid, exciting combination.

One of those big, gray seagulls has perched on the roof.

Make the verb agree with the subject, not with the object of the preposition.

PROBLEM 2

A predicate nominative differing in number from the subject

agr   Fast-paced adventure movies (was) always Jenny's choice.

SOLUTION

Fast-paced adventure movies were always Jenny's choice.

Make the verb agree with the subject, not with the predicate nominative.

PROBLEM 3

A subject following the verb

agr   On the sun deck there (was) several chairs and a table.

agr   Here (comes) the rain clouds and the heavy, slanting rain.

SOLUTION

On the sun deck there were several chairs and a table.

Here come the rain clouds and the heavy, slanting rain.

Look for the subject after the verb in an inverted sentence. Make sure that the verb agrees with the subject.

PROBLEM 4

Collective nouns as subjects

agr   The crowd really like the music, doesn't it?

agr   Margaret's company arrives tomorrow by bus and by train.

SOLUTION A

The crowd really likes the music, doesn't it?

Use a singular verb if the collective noun refers to a group as a whole.

SOLUTION B

Margaret's company arrive tomorrow by bus and by train.

Use a plural verb if the collective noun refers to each member of a group individually.

PROBLEM 5

A noun of amount as the subject

agr   The past two days seems like a week.

agr   One thousand millimeters equal a meter.

SOLUTION

The past two days seem like a week.

One thousand millimeters equals a meter.

A noun of amount that refers to one unit is singular. A noun of amount that refers to a number of individual units is plural.

PROBLEM 6

Compound subject joined by and

> agr   A clear day and a light breeze (brightens) a summer afternoon.
>
> agr   Pop and pizza (are) a common meal.

SOLUTION A

A clear day and a light breeze brighten a summer afternoon.

Use a plural verb if the parts of the compound subject do not belong to one unit or if they refer to different people or things.

SOLUTION B

Pop and pizza is a common meal.

Use a singular verb if the parts of the compound subject belong to one unit or if they refer to the same person or thing.

PROBLEM 7

Compound subject joined by or *or* nor

> agr   Neither Yuri nor Sarah (like) the menu.

SOLUTION

Neither Yuri nor Sarah likes the menu.

Make your verb agree with the subject closer to it.

PROBLEM 8

Compound subject preceded by many a, every, *or* each

> agr   Many a brush and tube of paint (were scattered) around the studio.

SOLUTION

Many a brush and tube of paint was scattered across the studio.

The subject is considered singular when *many a, each,* or *every* precedes a compound subject.

PROBLEM 9

Subjects separated from the verb by an intervening expression

agr   Jamal's new sculpture, in addition to his other recent works, (reflect) his abiding love of nature.

SOLUTION

Jamal's new sculpture, in addition to his other recent works, reflects his abiding love of nature.

Expressions that begin with *as well as, in addition to,* and *together with,* do not change the number of the subject. Make the verb agree with its subject, not with the intervening expression.

PROBLEM 10

Indefinite pronouns as subjects

agr   Each of the trees along the old canal (have) different colors in the fall.

SOLUTION

Each of the trees along the old canal has different colors in the fall.

Some indefinite pronouns are singular, some are plural, and some can be either singular or plural depending on the noun they refer to. (A list of indefinite pronouns is on page 54.)

More help with subject-verb agreement is available in Lessons 44–52.

Lack of Agreement Between Pronoun and Antecedent

PROBLEM 1

A singular antecedent that can be either male or female

> ant   A great coach inspires (his) athletes to be their best on or off the field.

Traditionally, masculine pronouns referred to antecedents that might have been either male or female.

SOLUTION A

A great coach inspires his or her athletes to be their best on or off the field.

Use *he or she, him or her,* and so on, to reword the sentence.

SOLUTION B

Great coaches inspire their athletes to be their best on or off the field.

Make both the antecedent and the pronoun plural.

SOLUTION C

Great coaches inspire athletes to be their best on or off the field.

Eliminate the pronoun.

PROBLEM 2

A second-person pronoun that refers to a third-person antecedent

> ant   Mary and Jodi prefer the new bridle trail because (you) get long stretches for galloping.

Do not use the second-person pronoun *you* to refer to an antecedent in the third person.

SOLUTION A

Mary and Jodi prefer the new bridle trail because they get long stretches for galloping.

Replace *you* with the appropriate third-person pronoun.

SOLUTION B

Mary and Jodi prefer the new bridle trail because the horses have long stretches for galloping.

Replace *you* with an appropriate noun.

PROBLEM 3

Singular indefinite pronouns as antecedents

ant   Each of the women in the boat received a rowing medal for (their) victory.

SOLUTION

Each of the women in the boat received a rowing medal for her victory.

Determine whether the antecedent is singular or plural, and make the personal pronoun agree with it.

 More help with pronoun-antecedent agreement is available in Lessons 57–59.

Unclear Pronoun References

PROBLEM 1

Unclear antecedent

> ref   The wind was fair and the water calm, and (that) made sailing across the bay an absolute pleasure.
>
> ref   The traffic was snarled, (which) was caused by an accident.

SOLUTION A

The wind was fair and the water calm, and those conditions made sailing across the bay an absolute pleasure.

Substitute a noun for the pronoun.

SOLUTION B

The traffic was snarled in a massive tie-up, which was caused by an accident.

Rewrite the sentence, adding a clear antecedent for the pronoun.

PROBLEM 2

A pronoun that refers to more than one antecedent

> ref   The team captain told Karen to take (her) guard position.
>
> ref   The buses came early for the students, but (they) were not ready.

SOLUTION A

The team captain told Karen to take the captain's guard position.

Substitute a noun for the pronoun.

SOLUTION B

Because the buses came early, the students were not ready.

Rewrite the sentence, eliminating the pronoun.

PROBLEM 3

Indefinite uses of you *or* they

ref   In those hills (you) rarely see mountain lions.

ref   In some movies (they) have too much violence.

SOLUTION A

In those hills hikers rarely see mountain lions.

Substitute a noun for the pronoun.

SOLUTION B

Some movies have too much violence.

Eliminate the pronoun entirely.

*More help in making clear
pronoun references is available
in Lesson 60.*

PROBLEM 1

Incorrect shift in person between two pronouns

> pro   They went to the stadium for the game, but you could not find a place to park.
>
> pro   One needs to remember to always keep their study time free from other commitments.
>
> pro   We were on the hill at dawn, and you could see the most wondrous sunrise.

Incorrect pronoun shifts occur when a writer or speaker uses a pronoun in one person and then illogically shifts to a pronoun in another person.

SOLUTION A

They went to the stadium for the game, but they could not find a place to park.

One needs to remember to always keep one's study time free from other commitments.

Replace the incorrect pronoun with a pronoun that agrees with its antecedent.

SOLUTION B

We were on the hill at dawn, and Mary and I could see the most wondrous sunrise.

Replace the incorrect pronoun with an appropriate noun.

More help in eliminating incorrect pronoun shifts is available in Lesson 58.

Shift in Verb Tenses

PROBLEM 1

Unnecessary shifts in tense

shift t   Akira waits for the bus and (worked) on the computer.

shift t   Jenny hit the home run and (runs) around the bases.

Two or more events occurring at the same time must have the same verb tense.

SOLUTION

Akira waits for the bus and works on the computer.
Jenny hit the home run and ran around the bases.

Use the same tense for both verbs.

PROBLEM 2

Tenses do not indicate that one event precedes or succeeds another

shift t   By the time the movie finally started, we (waited) impatiently
           through ten minutes of commercials.

If events being described occurred at different times, shift tenses to show that one event precedes or follows another.

SOLUTION

By the time the movie finally started, we had waited impatiently through ten minutes of commercials.

Use the past perfect tense for the earlier of two actions to indicate that one action began and ended before another action began.

 More help with shifts in verb tenses is available in Lessons 37–39 and 41.

Incorrect Verb Tenses or Forms

PROBLEM 1

Incorrect or missing verb endings

tense	Ricardo said it (snow) last night.
tense	Karen and her family (travel) to Costa Rica last year.

SOLUTION

Ricardo said it snowed last night.

Karen and her family traveled to Costa Rica last year.

Regular verbs form the past tense and the past participle by adding *-ed*.

PROBLEM 2

Improper formation of irregular verbs

tense	The sun (rised) out of scarlet clouds into a clear, blue sky.

SOLUTION

The sun rose out of scarlet clouds into a clear, blue sky.

An irregular verb forms its past tense and past participle in some way other than by adding *-ed*.

PROBLEM 3

Confusion between the past form of the verb and the past participle

tense	The horses (have ate) their feed already.
tense	The coach (has wore) the old team jacket to every graduation.

SOLUTION

The horses have eaten their feed already.

The coach has worn the old team jacket to every graduation.

When you use the auxiliary verb *have*, use the past participle form of an irregular verb, not its simple past form.

PROBLEM 4

Improper use of the past participle

tense   Deemee (drawn) the winning ticket for the door prize at the dance.

tense   The old rowboat (sunk) just below the surface of the lake.

       Past participles of irregular verbs cannot stand alone as verbs. They must be used in conjunction with a form of the auxiliary verb *have*.

SOLUTION A

Deemee had drawn the winning ticket for the door prize at the dance.

The old rowboat had sunk just below the surface of the lake.

Form a complete verb by adding a form of the auxiliary verb *have* to the past participle.

SOLUTION B

Deemee drew the winning ticket for the door prize at the dance.

The old rowboat sank just below the surface of the lake.

Use the simple past form of the verb instead of the past participle.

More help with correct verb forms is available in Lessons 35, 36, and 40.

Misplaced or Dangling Modifiers

PROBLEM 1

Misplaced modifier

mod	(Untended and overgrown since last summer,) Marlene helped Keshia in her garden.
mod	Sarah won the jumping contest with her mother's horse, (wearing western riding gear.)

A misplaced modifier appears to modify the wrong word or group of words.

SOLUTION

Marlene helped Keshia in her garden, untended and overgrown since last summer.

Wearing western riding gear, Sarah won the jumping contest with her mother's horse.

Place the modifying phrase as close as possible to the word or words it modifies.

PROBLEM 2

Misplacing the adverb only

mod	Akiko (only) runs hurdles in track.

SOLUTION

Only Akiko runs hurdles in track.

Akiko runs only hurdles in track.

Akiko runs hurdles only in track.

Each time *only* is moved in the sentence, the meaning of the sentence changes. Place the adverb immediately before the word or group of words it is to modify.

PROBLEM 3

Dangling modifiers

mod   (Branches swaying in the breeze,) we rested in the shade.

mod   (Trying out the new exercise equipment,) the new gym is a great improvement over the old one.

A dangling modifier does not modify any word in the sentence.

SOLUTION

Branches swaying in the breeze, the tree provided us with shade.

Trying out the new exercise equipment, Mary said the new gym is a great improvement over the old one.

Add a noun to which the dangling phrase clearly refers. You might have to add or change other words, as well.

Need More Help?

More help with misplaced or dangling modifiers is available in Lesson 66.

Misplaced or Missing Possessive Apostrophes

PROBLEM 1

Singular nouns

poss   (Charles) car is the white one, but (Jamals) is the red convertible.

SOLUTION

Charles's car is the white one, but Jamal's is the red convertible.

To form the possessive of a singular noun, even one that ends in *-s*, use an apostrophe and an *-s* at the end of the word.

PROBLEM 2

Plural nouns that end in -s

poss   The seven maple (trees) cool, delicious shade is the best in the park.

SOLUTION

The seven maple trees' cool, delicious shade is the best in the park.

To form the possessive of a plural noun that ends in *-s*, use an apostrophe by itself after the final *-s*.

PROBLEM 3

Plural nouns that do not end in -s

poss   The (childrens) movies are on that rack next to the nature films.

SOLUTION

The children's movies are on that rack next to the nature films.

Form the possessive of a plural noun that does not end in *-s* by using an apostrophe and *-s* at the end of the word.

PROBLEM 4

Pronouns

poss	That painting cannot be just (anybodys) work.
poss	(Their's) is the trophy in the center of the display case.

SOLUTION A

That painting cannot be just anybody's work.

Form the possessive of a singular indefinite pronoun by adding an apostrophe and -*s* to it.

SOLUTION B

Theirs is the trophy in the center of the display case.

With any of the possessive personal pronouns, do not use an apostrophe.

PROBLEM 5

Confusing its *with* it's

poss	The computer is booting up; I see (it's) power light blinking.
poss	(Its) going to be a great victory party.

SOLUTION

The computer is booting up; I see its power light blinking.
It's going to be a great victory party.

It's is the contraction of *it is*, not the possessive of *it*.

More help with apostrophes and possessives is available in Lessons 3 and 92.

Missing Commas with Nonessential Elements

PROBLEM 1

Missing commas with nonessential participles, infinitives, and their phrases

com	Lois scowling fiercely turned her back on Clark.
com	The detective mystified by the fresh clue scratched his head in bewilderment.
com	Television to tell the truth just doesn't interest me.

SOLUTION

Lois, scowling fiercely, turned her back on Clark.

The detective, mystified by the fresh clue, scratched his head in bewilderment.

Television, to tell the truth, just doesn't interest me.

If the participle, infinitive, or phrase is not essential to the meaning of the sentence, set off the phrase with commas.

PROBLEM 2

Missing commas with nonessential adjective clauses

com	The sailboat which looked like a toy in the storm rounded the point into the breakwater.

SOLUTION

The sailboat, which looked like a toy in the storm, rounded the point into the breakwater.

If the clause is not essential to the meaning of the sentence, set it off with commas.

PROBLEM 3

Missing commas with nonessential appositives

com   The palomino a beautiful horse with almost golden hair is often seen in parades.

SOLUTION

The palomino, a beautiful horse with almost golden hair, is often seen in parades.

If the appositive is not essential to the meaning of the sentence, set it off with commas.

PROBLEM 4

Missing commas with interjections and parenthetical expressions

com   Wow did you see that falling star?

com   I would have told you by the way but you weren't home.

SOLUTION

Wow, did you see that falling star?
I would have told you, by the way, but you weren't home.

Set off the interjection or parenthetical expression with commas.

 More help with commas and nonessential elements is available in Lesson 80.

Missing Commas in a Series

PROBLEM 1

Commas missing in a series of words, phrases, or clauses

s com   Mona said that Amy Tan James Baldwin and Charles Dickens were her favorite authors.

s com   Sailing on the Great Lakes can be as challenging adventurous and rewarding as sailing on the ocean.

s com   Our forensics team practiced hard did their research and used all their wit and intelligence to win the championship.

s com   The wind shifted the clouds parted and the sunlight streamed down.

SOLUTION

Mona said that Amy Tan, James Baldwin, and Charles Dickens were her favorite authors.

Sailing on the Great Lakes can be as challenging, adventurous, and rewarding as sailing on the ocean.

Our forensics team practiced hard, did their research, and used all their wit and intelligence to win the championship.

The wind shifted, the clouds parted, and the sunlight streamed down.

Use a comma after each item in a series except the last.

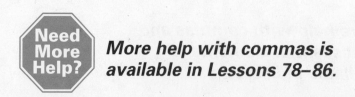

More help with commas is available in Lessons 78–86.

Grammar

Unit 1: Parts of Speech

Lesson 1

Nouns: Singular, Plural, Possessive, Concrete, and Abstract

A noun names a person, place, thing, or idea.

A singular noun names one person, place, thing, or idea. A plural noun names more than one.

	SINGULAR	PLURAL
Person:	poet, sister	poets, sisters
Place:	hill, biology lab	hills, biology labs
Thing:	wind, hairbrush	winds, hairbrushes
Idea:	love, belief	loves, beliefs

The possessive form of a noun shows possession, ownership, or the relationship between two nouns.

	SINGULAR POSSESSIVE	PLURAL POSSESSIVE
Possession:	writer's story	writers' stories
Ownership:	Samantha Winthrop's car	the Winthrops' cars
Relationship:	the cat's color	the cats' colors

▶ **Exercise 1** Write *S* above each singular noun, *P* above each plural noun, and *poss.* above each possessive noun.

       P   poss.   S
The breezes carried the nightingale's song.

1. Kamaria's family gave me a tour of their house yesterday.

2. Bill fulfilled his obligations to the charity through his generous donations.

3. When will Martha's mom find out whether the doctor recommends an operation?

4. Brad is studying to be a legal assistant, while Beth's plans include a career as a nurse.

5. Lightning and thunder don't frighten me as they did during my childhood.

6. The freshly mown grass will please my parents when they return from work.

7. Sharon explained Ted's faults to him throughout lunch.

8. Zahara, may I introduce to you my friends Scott, Kevin, and Paul?

9. I enjoy the wind's steady rushing sound on a long, windy afternoon in March.

10. The debater from the other team proved a point against our squad just before the buzzer.

11. After the prom, our friends breakfasted at the local diner on Main Street.

12. The instructor corrected Frank's misunderstanding about that particular chemical reaction.

13. The Nile River flows for a longer distance than any other of the world's rivers.

14. Camilla will sing both classical and popular songs during her audition.

15. Carrying heavy loads burdened the poor donkey all of his life.

16. Carl seized on this idea when his friends' suggestions did not work out.

17. Not only will I attend the girls' volleyball match, but I intend to root heartily.

18. I hope the long-awaited letter gladdens Ron's heavy heart.

A concrete noun names an object that occupies space or that can be recognized by any of the senses.

ocean   lightning   monk   pecan   pie   star   aroma

An abstract noun names an idea, quality, or characteristic.

truth   honor   beauty   justice   wisdom

▶ Exercise 2 Write *con.* for concrete or *abst.* for abstract above each italicized noun.

    abst.   con.

The *splendor* of the ruins inspired me to write a short *poem.*

1. All free people should cherish their *liberty.*

2. Tiffany explicitly believed everything the *advertisement* claimed for its product.

3. Priscilla said that it will take an *eternity* for us to finish this *job.*

4. Jimmy's dad has kept a close *watch* on his *health* ever since the heart attack.

5. The limpid stream winds through the dark *forest* for many miles.

6. The general *elegance* of the old mansion profoundly impressed me.

7. Only when we stood closer to the railing did the *depth* of the canyon surprise us.

8. I finally found the book under a *pile* of old newspapers and magazines.

9. César said he never thought that I would take *astronomy* seriously enough to buy a telescope.

10. The dark green bottle and the brown mandolin made a nice *subject* for the painting.

11. My *mother* was suprised at the *cleanliness* of my room.

12. The *job* well done brought Raul great *satisfaction.*

Lesson 2
Nouns: Proper, Common, and Collective

A **proper noun** names a specific person, place, or thing. Capitalize proper nouns.
A **common noun** refers to people, places, or things in general.

	PROPER NOUNS	COMMON NOUNS
Person:	Douglas MacArthur	general
Place:	Maryland	state
Thing:	Rover	dog
Idea:	Scholasticism	philosophy

A **collective noun** names a group. A collective noun is singular if it refers to the group as a whole, and plural if it refers to individual members of a group.

The **team is** winning.   The **team pack** up their equipment.

▶ **Exercise 1** Write *prop.* above each proper noun, *com.* above each common noun, and *col.* above each collective noun. Assume the collective nouns are also common nouns.

```
        prop.     com.              com.                        col.      com.
```
General Chow, my cat, rarely accepts newcomers into his exclusive fraternity of friends.

1. The milling crowd slowly dispersed after Sheriff Stone asked them to leave.

2. Mrs. Paulus told my mom that you have the chicken pox.

3. The crew on the boat relaxed after they anchored their vessel in the harbor.

4. Did you hear that the Thompsons are moving from Springfield to Indianapolis?

5. The entire community rejoiced to hear that the arsonist had at last been caught.

6. Of all the American presidents, I'd say my favorite is Theodore Roosevelt.

7. After only an hour, the jury returned its much anticipated verdict to Judge Eason.

8. The Western Tennis Association congratulated the Adams High School tennis team for winning the league championship.

9. I have a picture of a squadron of rare airplanes flying side by side.

10. If I ever created a periodical, I'd call it *The American Mercury*, after a magazine of long ago.

11. We studied about Fyodor Dostoevsky, a Russian writer of the nineteenth century.

12. The company my father works for has asked him to relocate to Alaska.

13. Mr. Todd asked me to paint his house with two gallons of paint.

14. Who could have believed that a speaker could have swayed so vast a multitude?

15. The inspector asked Detective Smythe to bring him the records of the latest case.

16. Waves on the Atlantic Ocean made me feel somewhat sick but not enough to affect my appetite.

17. I myself exercise at the Workout Gym every Wednesday and Friday.

18. We left the harbor with the flotilla of other craft, including sailboats and freighters.

19. Benny left his thesaurus at the library yesterday.

20. The council has passed a new law about riding bikes on sidewalks.

21. Did Jenny go with you to Smith's Department Store for the interview?

22. The solitary elm stood in the middle of Bader Field until the windstorm knocked it down.

23. The legislature is going to adjourn on Saturday for Christmas.

24. The Sahara, the largest desert, stretches across the north of Africa.

25. Noah Webster composed the first American dictionary.

26. Karen, the president of the class, has great plans for our trip.

27. Uncle Steve and Aunt Margaret are going to visit their son Tommy at the university.

28. James Monroe formulated an important plan for foreign policy known as the Monroe Doctrine.

29. Our team travels to Junction City to play for the championship.

30. The rain fell throughout the night and into the morning on Thursday.

31. The school newspaper, *The Cheerleader,* has a new editor, Sarah Hwan.

32. The board meets to elect its new president within a week.

33. A special committee exists for just that sort of investigation, Mr. Bentley.

34. I just could not mow that part of the yard because of all the beautiful violets.

35. Tammy found this wonderful old book on the lowest shelf.

36. When will our chorus get to practice again, Mrs. Rivera?

37. In the late evening, I often see rabbits at the edge of my yard.

38. This poem about life by Li Po is really very lovely, Mrs. Jefferson.

39. Our family goes out of its way so that all of us can share dinner together.

40. Franklin wants to be a sculptor, and he has already crafted interesting pieces.

Lesson 3
Pronouns: Personal, Possessive, Reflexive, and Intensive

A pronoun takes the place of a noun, a group of words acting as a noun, or another pronoun. We call the word or group of words that a pronoun refers to its antecedent

A personal pronoun refers to a specific person or thing by indicating the person speaking (the first person), the person being addressed (the second person), or any other person or thing being discussed (the third person).

	SINGULAR	PLURAL
First Person:	I, me	we, us
Second Person:	you	you
Third Person:	he, him, she, her, it	they, them

A possessive pronoun shows possession or control. It takes the place of a possessive noun.

	SINGULAR	PLURAL
First Person:	my, mine	our, ours
Second Person:	your, yours	your, yours
Third Person:	his, her, hers, its	their, theirs

▶ **Exercise 1** Draw one line under each personal pronoun and two lines under each possessive pronoun.

They made a float to represent their club in the village parade.

1. With her new shoes, she ran faster than she had before.

2. My floral arrangement won me first prize at the flower show on the fairgrounds.

3. Benny and Tara landscaped our yard for us before they did theirs.

4. When Akira returned from the hike, his ragged appearance made me frown.

5. Their vacation turned out to be the much-needed rest they wanted.

6. His manager gave him a bonus for his extra work over the busy holiday.

7. We noticed how playful our lambs are this morning.

8. Our newspaper carrier delivered the paper on her new bike this morning.

9. We left the house keys hanging in our garage on a nail behind the light switch.

10. Their new textbooks arrived after ours did.

11. His friends always make light of our efforts on the practice field.

12. I dropped my video machine off at the shop this morning; could I borrow yours?

13. It remains a puzzle how the jewel thief got past all of our electronic devices.

14. Those papers are theirs; ours are lying on top of your cabinet.

15. Seán's dad is a tailor, and he made Seán his new checkered coat.

16. They made sand castles on the beach, but waves soon washed away their work.

17. He raked the leaves, but the sudden wind scattered them all over our yard.

18. Your new puppy looks as if it will turn out to be a beautiful, large dog.

19. Our gardener gave the flower garden his special attention this morning.

20. My history teacher took us on a tour of her favorite places in the museum.

A **reflexive pronoun** refers to a noun or another pronoun and indicates that the same person or thing is involved. An **intensive pronoun** adds emphasis to a noun or another pronoun. Reflexive and intensive pronouns look alike. Their usage reveals the difference.

Otto reminded **himself** not to forget the party. (reflexive)
Otto **himself** told me he was coming to the party. (intensive)

▶ **Exercise 2** Write *ref.* above each reflexive pronoun and *int.* above each intensive pronoun.

                       ref.
The poet believed in himself and his work enough to send his poems to a publisher.

1. The chorus dancer dressed herself for her part in the Greek play.

2. Ron put himself to sleep with the music he composed for relaxation.

3. When you run in the practice heats, pace yourself with this stopwatch.

4. They bought themselves a new truck and traded in their old jalopy.

5. The grass itself is too wet for me to mow this morning, Mrs. Smith.

6. Kwaku gave himself a break after football practice.

7. The heavy rain itself doesn't frighten me; I myself am more scared of the lightning and thunder.

8. Why do you think they blamed themselves for the loss to Central?

9. The old house itself served as an inn before our family bought it twenty years ago.

10. I told myself again and again not to forget those keys!

Lesson 4
Pronouns: Interrogative, Relative, Demonstrative, and Indefinite

Grammar

Use an **interrogative pronoun** to form questions. Interrogative pronouns are *who, whom, whose, what,* and *which.* Other interrogative pronouns are *whoever, whomever, whatever,* and *whichever.*

Whatever gave you that absurd notion?

Use a **relative pronoun** to begin a subject-verb word group called a subordinate clause.

The last senator **who** stabbed Caesar was his friend Brutus.

RELATIVE PRONOUNS

who	whom	what	which	that
whoever	whomever	whatever	whichever	whose

▶ **Exercise 1** **Draw one line under each interrogative pronoun and two lines under each relative pronoun.**

Who would have imagined how some of the famous car designers started out?

1. Frederick Henry Royce, who as a boy served as an apprentice on the Great Northern Railroad, later started his own company.

2. Royce Limited, a company that manufactured electric cranes and dynamos, did not make cars.

3. The industrialist, whose origins had been in poverty, achieved considerable success with his cranes by the age of forty.

4. What interested Royce about the possibility of making a car?

5. We do not know for certain what Royce's answer to that question would have been.

6. Whatever his dreams were, the fact is that the former rail shop worker had developed poor health.

7. His friends encouraged him to buy an automobile, which they hoped would get his mind off his condition.

8. In those early days all autos, which were fascinating to almost everyone, delighted engineers prone to tinkering, adjusting, and improving.

9. By 1904 Royce had built three cars that greatly improved on the one he had bought himself.

10. An aristocrat, racing driver, and aeronaut whose attention had been attracted by Royce's new cars then became Royce's business partner.

11. Whoever was this eccentric individual?

12. He was the other person for whom the cars came to be named—Charles Stewart Rolls.

A **demonstrative pronoun** points out specific persons, places, things, or ideas.

That is a great idea, Charley.

DEMONSTRATIVE PRONOUNS

Singular: this   that
Plural: these   those

An **indefinite pronoun** refers to persons, places, or things in a more general way than does a noun or a personal pronoun.

Each of the winners chose his or her own prize.

INDEFINITE PRONOUNS

all	both	everything	none	some
another	each	few	nothing	somebody
any	either	many	one	someone
anybody	enough	most	other	something
anyone	everybody	neither	others	
anything	everyone	nobody	several	

▶ **Exercise 2** Write *ind.* above each indefinite pronoun and *dem.* above each demonstrative pronoun.

ind.
One of the great continental European automotive designers was Ettore Bugatti.

1. Of the world's famous carmakers, few, if any, approached Ettore Bugatti in excellence and genius.

2. Everyone who knew him considered him unique in the automotive world.

3. Many in his old and honored family had achieved acclaim as well-known artists.

4. These thought Ettore also possessed the skill and talent to become a great artist.

5. That appears to have been the reason they sent him to study sculpture.

6. Something came between the young Bugatti and a famous artistic career.

7. This was his love of automobiles.

8. He became an apprentice to one of Milan's world-renowned engineering firms.

Grammar

Lesson 5
Verbs: Action

A **verb** expresses action or a state of being and is necessary to make a statement. An **action verb** tells what someone or something does. Action verbs can express either physical or mental action. An action verb that is followed by a word that answers the question *what?* or *whom?* is called a **transitive verb.** An action verb that is not followed by a word that answers the question *what?* or *whom?* is called an **intransitive verb.**

Sally **made** the pie (transitive)
Sally **bakes** very well. (intransitive)

Some verbs can be either transitive or intransitive, depending on their use.

Bob **called** Tom. (transitive)   Bob **called** for a pizza. (intransitive)

▶ **Exercise 1 Draw two lines under each action verb. Write *T* in the blank if the verb is transitive and *I* if it is intransitive.**

___T, I___   Fina <u>sold</u> my sister that special flour she <u>uses</u> in those tasty cakes.

_____ 1. The car struck the fence before it went into the ditch.

_____ 2. The birds ate the cherries off the tree in our front yard.

_____ 3. Sam rested on the sofa under the bay window all day.

_____ 4. The trolley car rattled noisily along the busy street in front of the stores.

_____ 5. Sheila set the noisy radio on the kitchen table.

_____ 6. Aisha opened the cupboard above the oven.

_____ 7. I set the alarm clock to 6 A.M. because of the field trip tomorrow.

_____ 8. When you connect the telephone line, please inform the landlord.

_____ 9. My dog, Arfie, blundered into the party and knocked over the card table.

_____ 10. Tiffany prepared for the cross-country meet with time trials around the golf course.

_____ 11. Murray lent his favorite book to Karen for the long trip.

_____ 12. I heard the new CD last night before I went to the party.

_____ 13. Brad and Doralina found the old chest in the attic yesterday afternoon.

_____ 14. Billy scattered the grass seed over Mrs. Svenson's yard this morning.

_____ 15. We expect rain tomorrow for the family reunion at the park.

_____ 16. I returned without any more insights than when I left.

Grammar

_____ 17. Ed ran through the new gym and out past the parking lot.

_____ 18. Mark brought his dog a new water dish, a porcelain one.

_____ 19. We believed her promises until she finally confessed her real intentions.

_____ 20. Bobby, close the car door gently when you get out.

_____ 21. I always boil my potatoes, but Micah microwaves his.

_____ 22. She drinks this brand of soft drink instead of that other kind.

_____ 23. Kara's pitch flew very close to the batter, who shouted in anger.

_____ 24. Pioneers built a church on this site before they erected any other buildings.

_____ 25. Jamal's car stalled at the traffic light at Sixth and Wilson.

_____ 26. Mom smelled the pie and took it out of the oven.

_____ 27. That cat of yours meowed until I opened the refrigerator door.

_____ 28. The heavy porcelain vase fell off the shelf and onto the couch.

_____ 29. Roger, assist Casey with her homework, please.

_____ 30. For Carey, the world revolves around her kitten, Tinker Bell.

_____ 31. The adventurers discovered the lost city on the edge of a high plateau.

_____ 32. The scent of those beautiful flowers fills the room with a whiff of Tahiti.

_____ 33. I wish for good weather for the track meet tomorrow.

_____ 34. Paul sang the words to Tricia's favorite tune while she played it on her piano.

_____ 35. Please load Priscilla's van, and I will load Ron's car.

_____ 36. The famous detective investigated every lead, no matter how elusive.

_____ 37. Yoshio, I advise against any such course of action.

_____ 38. We escorted them at the honor ceremony in the gym.

▶ **Writing Link** **Write two sentences that use transitive action verbs and two sentences that use intransitive action verbs.**

_____

_____

_____

_____

_____

_____

Lesson 6
Verbs: Linking

A linking verb links, or joins, the subject of a sentence with a word that identifies or describes the subject. The most common linking verbs are forms of *be*. Some examples are *am, is, are, was, were, will be, has been,* and *was being.*

OTHER VERBS THAT CAN BE LINKING VERBS

appear	feel	look	seem	smell
become	grow	remain	sound	taste

▶ **Exercise 1** Underline each verb, and write *LV* in the blank if the verb is a linking verb and *AV* if the verb is an action verb.

_____LV_____ The English language <u>is</u> a relative of many other tongues.

_____ 1. Sir William Jones was a British jurist in India in the 1780s.

_____ 2. He was a learned eighteenth-century man; he became familiar with Latin and Greek in school.

_____ 3. At one point, Sir William studied Sanskrit, the ancient language of India.

_____ 4. Records in Sanskrit contained many legal tracts and other items of interest for him.

_____ 5. Therefore, Sir William felt a strong curiosity about this important scholastic language.

_____ 6. A surprise awaited Sir William, however.

_____ 7. Sanskrit, Latin, and Greek had many things in common.

_____ 8. The Sanskrit, Latin, and Greek words for *three* were similar.

_____ 9. The Latin *tres* and the Greek *trias* resembled the Sanskrit *trayas.*

_____ 10. Sanskrit *panca,* "five," was similar to the Greek for *five, pente.*

_____ 11. He also noted the similarity between the Latin words *rex* and *regem* and the Sanskrit word for king, *rajan.*

_____ 12. Many other parallels between Sanskrit words and Latin and Greek words were curiosities to Sir William.

Grammar

_____ **13.** The British jurist grew more and more certain of a direct relationship between these words.

_____ **14.** His linguistic studies finally led him to a surprising conclusion about these languages.

_____ **15.** On February 2, 1786, Sir William spoke to the Asiatic Society of Calcutta.

_____ **16.** Sir William made a bold statement that Greek, Latin, and Sanskrit were linguistic cousins.

_____ **17.** Everyone felt speechless at this news, and many doubted it.

_____ **18.** Sanskrit was also probably a linguistic relative of the Teutonic and Celtic tongues.

_____ **19.** Because of his Welsh origin, Sir William added the comment about Celtic.

_____ **20.** The Welsh people speak a Celtic language to this very day.

_____ **21.** Sir William also spoke English, of course; English is a Germanic language.

_____ **22.** Immigrants to Britain from northern Germany and Holland brought an early version of English with them long ago.

_____ **23.** Sir William, of course, was quite familiar with all this information.

_____ **24.** Ever since his presentation, scholars have talked about the Indo-European family of languages.

_____ **25.** They call it Indo-European; most of its languages originated in the regions of India and Europe.

_____ **26.** Numerous languages constitute this family of languages.

_____ **27.** Linguists count Russian and all the Slavic languages as members.

_____ **28.** Other Slavic languages include Polish, Bulgarian, and Croatian.

_____ **29.** Another relative in the family tree is Iranian.

_____ **30.** The Celtic section has a number of modern languages.

_____ **31.** Irish Gaelic is the language of Ireland, and it has a lot of wonderful literature.

_____ **32.** Many people in Scotland speak Scottish Gaelic as well.

Lesson 7
Verb Phrases

The verb in a sentence may consist of more than one word. We call the words that accompany the main verb auxiliary, or helping, verbs. A verb phrase consists of a main verb and all its auxiliary verbs.

I **am apologizing** because I **have arrived** so late.   **Do** you still **have** time?

AUXILIARY VERBS

Forms of *be:*	am, is, are, was, were, being, been
Forms of *have:*	has, have, had, having
Other helping verbs:	can, could, do, does, did, may, might, must, shall, should, will, would

I **could have arrived** on time if I **had planned** my day better.

▶ **Exercise 1** **Draw one line under each main verb and two lines under each auxiliary verb.**

Tom has been feeling much better since his visit to the doctor.

1. The new checks should be arriving today by airmail.

2. We all must work together on the class project.

3. The team's fans were happily celebrating the big championship win.

4. The artist has done all his work in a comfortable garret.

5. Tomorrow morning many veterans will march in the victory parade.

6. The farmer had held an auction of his livestock last week.

7. The highway was being widened for the increase in traffic from the city.

8. The children were being taken to the zoo in the newest school bus.

9. Our library will be training new volunteers.

10. Those students would have merited the scholarship by the first of June.

11. Your spring flowers will bloom in time for our May Day celebration.

12. Our guest might arrive in time for the dinner presentation at noon.

13. The neighborhood grocery does carry fresh fruit the entire year.

14. Many of my friends will exhibit their science projects at the county fair.

15. Grandmother had met me in time for the lecture.

16. The cows were being milked at the same time every morning.

Grammar

17. That old dictionary of yours might hold the answer to this puzzle.

18. The bank will announce new hours as early as tomorrow.

19. The weary jury must decide the verdict of this long trial.

20. Butter has added a more delicious taste to these cookies.

21. The cool spring rain should bring a wonderful bounty of flowers.

22. Custodians were cleaning the lion cages.

23. The graduates are having a dance in the gymnasium this afternoon.

24. You must cook those fresh eggs for that kind of special salad.

25. The lilac bush is displaying beautiful, sweet blossoms this spring.

26. Surely this hotel must have security for its many guests!

27. All drivers should have valid licenses in their possession.

28. The delightful storybook has been shown to all the children present.

29. One must practice many hours for that excellent band instructor.

30. The newspaper should report all the news accurately and in a timely fashion.

31. Beautiful huskies were pulling the fastest dogsled in that last race.

32. Karen's birthday cake had been decorated in pink roses and candles.

33. The earnest players had rehearsed all the acts in the play many times.

34. The school buses have been inspected for safety.

35. The student pictures have been selected for the yearbook by the staff.

36. The lumber company might make the fence for our garden next week.

37. Mary's mother will make cookies for the choir picnic on Saturday.

38. Our dance teacher has planned a ballet-like play for our parents.

39. The school band will play for the big game.

40. The circus should be ready for business at the county fairgrounds by tomorrow.

▶ **Writing Link** **Write a brief paragraph about what you might do after school today. Be sure to use auxiliary verbs along with main verbs.**

_____

_____

_____

_____

Lesson 8
Adjectives

An **adjective** modifies a noun or a pronoun by limiting its meaning. Adjectives include the articles *a, an,* and *the. A* and *an* are **indefinite** articles; *the* is a **definite** article. Because they modify nouns, possessive nouns and some possessive pronouns are considered adjectives as well.

The raging river roars through **this narrow** gorge.   **Al's used** car resembles **my** car.

A **proper adjective** is formed from a proper noun and begins with a capital letter. Proper adjectives are often created by using the following suffixes: *-an, -ian, -n, -ese,* and *-ish.*

Americ**an**   Chin**ese**   Engl**ish**

Many adjectives have different forms to indicate their degree of comparison.

POSITIVE	COMPARATIVE	SUPERLATIVE
big	bigger	biggest (regular forms of comparison)
little	less	least (Some adjectives have irregular forms of comparison.)

▶ **Exercise 1** Underline each adjective in the following sentences. Include articles and possessive nouns and pronouns.

<u>Ancient</u> mariners traveled to <u>far</u> places.

1. In 120 B.C., a nearly drowned sailor washed ashore on an Egyptian beach.

2. The local authorities taught him the Greek language, as they had little luck in understanding his speech.

3. They found out that the foreign mariner had come farther than any of them imagined.

4. He had sailed from remote India, and he maintained he could prove this amazing statement.

5. He offered to show the Egyptians the secret way back to his distant homeland.

6. The Egyptian leaders knew that India possessed fabulous wealth.

7. Indian and Arab sailors knew, however, an important secret about the sailing route.

8. Certain winds, monsoons, would blow toward India for half of the year.

9. These monsoons would then blow the other way for the second half of the year.

10. Thus, a sea captain could sail the handy monsoons on an outward voyage and then sail them back home a few months later.

11. A Greek sea captain, Eudoxius of Cyzicus, a famous explorer, took the Indian sailor back to India.

Grammar

12. Eudoxius made two successful trips to the eastern world, but the Egyptian tax collectors took all of his profit.

13. Eudoxius finally tired of this heavy taxation and made thorough plans to sail the other way around Africa, just to avoid the government officials.

14. He sailed past towering Gibraltar and into the mighty Atlantic, never to be heard of again.

15. Learned people of the ancient world knew the Earth was round.

16. Eratosthenes, a great geographer of the third century B.C., said that intrepid mariners could sail from Spain to India.

17. However, he also thought the distance too great for such a perilous endeavor.

18. According to old legend, bold Phoenicians had circumnavigated Africa about 600 B.C.

19. Much farther to the east than India, however, lay the wondrous land of China.

20. Bold travelers pioneered overland routes to China a very long time ago.

21. Once in a while, important ideas or inventions would slowly move eastward or westward.

22. The art of writing began in Mesopotamia, the modern country of Iraq, a millennium and a half before it appeared in China.

23. Western experts believe that traders carried it into ancient China.

24. Sharp debate still continues as to whether the first chariots came into China from western peoples.

25. We know that early Mesopotamians developed war chariots in their area around 3,000 B.C.

26. Archeologists now believe that the craft of metallurgy first started in what is now Thailand.

27. For a long time, they thought it had started in the Mesopotamian area.

28. But recent discoveries definitely point to the eastern nation of Thailand.

29. After they learned the important skill of making bronze from tin and copper, they did it very well.

30. The Chinese always produced the best bronze items to be found in the ancient world.

31. As for iron, the Chinese always used cast iron instead of wrought iron.

32. Researchers believe that the ancient Chinese smiths learned how to cast both bronze and iron from the fine craftspeople who practiced the art of ceramics.

Lesson 9
Adverbs

An adverb modifies a verb, an adjective, or another adverb by making its meaning more specific. Adverbs answer the questions *how? when? where?* and *to what degree?* When modifying a verb, an adverb may appear in various positions in a sentence. If modifying an adjective or another adverb, an adverb appears directly before the modified word.

Shani said she really wanted to meet the very famous actor backstage yesterday.

The negatives *no* and *not* and the contraction *-n't* are adverbs. Other negative words, such as *nowhere, hardly,* and *never,* can function as adverbs of time, place, and degree.

My dad never loses his temper.   **Haven't you chosen the menu yet?**

▶ **Exercise 1** Underline each adverb, and draw an arrow from each adverb to the word it modifies.

The old city trolley rumbled steadily down the street.

1. My little sister regularly skips rope after school.

2. Corn harvest begins after the milk in the kernel finally becomes hard and the fodder is dried.

3. The week after a forest fire, when the earth cools down, is often the best time to plant tree

   seedlings.

4. The grandchildren gleefully hunted Easter eggs scattered throughout the yard.

5. The company actually installed neon signs for the new cafe.

6. Manufacturers often fill baked pie shells with fruit topped with meringue.

7. Any list of good reptile pets almost always includes snakes, turtles, and iguanas.

8. Many people are severely allergic to poisonous plants such as ivy, hemlock, and pokeweed.

9. The artist dexterously displayed many styles of painting.

10. Nature deftly forms seashells in many colors, forms, and sizes.

11. The earthworm is very beneficial to the fertility of the land.

12. Tom could not wait to tour the tropical forest when he visited Brazil.

13. As the runners jogged along the country road, they suddenly saw a handsome team of Belgian

    horses.

Grammar

14. While walking slowly along the seashore, Jake found a blue mussel.

15. If you ever travel through the western states, you might see many Prairie dogs.

16. Razor-backed hogs wander freely through some national forests.

17. Several hunters gathered at the end of the woods as they hastily planned the hunt.

18. The young graduate looked very relaxed in his photo.

19. After the argument, Bob and Tom quietly settled their differences.

20. To produce their fine silk, silkworms feed chiefly on mulberry leaves.

21. Early settlers in the West often diligently mined silver and gold.

22. The discussion became terribly loud when the mayor suggested new taxes.

23. The old home had been newly decorated for the young couple.

24. A new deck and green shrubs certainly enhanced the old brick home.

25. Many beautiful butterflies instinctively fly south before winter arrives.

26. Someone generously filled the fruit basket with tropical fruit.

27. Grandmother attentively used her sewing scissors to trim the lace ruffles.

28. The tall ship smoothly sailed into the harbor as the very attentive spectators cheered.

29. The Saint Bernard dog is lovingly trained to hunt for lost travelers.

30. A small child innocently smeared her face with jelly.

31. The high wind mercilessly bent the spindly ash tree completely over.

32. The swallows flew swiftly into the old barn where they vigilantly guarded their nests.

33. The police continuously directed traffic during the heavy downpour.

34. Violets and jack-in-the-pulpit grow abundantly in the large woods.

35. Its favorite person's mood often affects a cat's behavior.

36. Delicious fragrance from the fully open apple blossoms quietly filled me with a sense of peace.

Lesson 10
Prepositions

A **preposition** shows the relationship of a noun or a pronoun to some other word in the sentence.

The salesclerk waited **by** the telephone.

COMMON PREPOSITIONS

aboard	as	but (except)	inside	outside	toward
about	at	by	into	over	under
above	before	despite	like	past	underneath
across	behind	down	near	pending	until
after	below	during	of	regarding	unto
against	beneath	except	off	since	up
along	beside	excepting	on	than	upon
amid	besides	for	onto	through	with
among	between	from	opposite	throughout	within
around	beyond	in	out	to	without

A **compound preposition** is a preposition that is made up of more than one word.

I put my backpack **on top of** the kitchen table.

COMMON COMPOUND PREPOSITIONS

according to	apart from	because of	in front of	next to	out of
ahead of	aside from	by means of	in spite of	on account of	owing to
along with	as to	in addition to	instead of	on top of	

Phrases that begin with a preposition usually end with a noun or a pronoun called the **object of the preposition**

The baron rode **into** his private **forest**.

▶ **Exercise 1** Underline each preposition and circle the object of each preposition.

The Renaissance music echoed <u>along</u> the (hallway) <u>of</u> the (palazzo).

1. We happily boarded the cruise ship from the passenger waiting room.

2. Tom found this little kitten out on the sidewalk.

3. The letter concerned an event that happened before last week.

4. Your idea, Bill, is really beyond my comprehension.

5. Wanjiru told us all about it as we stood within the dugout.

6. Do you like living near the ocean, Francis?

Grammar

7. I am still waiting for an answer to the question I posed yesterday.

8. How can you expect success without serious practice, Samantha?

9. Tammy parked in the driveway behind your dad's car.

10. To Robert, there seems nothing of importance next to his personal goals.

11. The excited fans pointed beyond the outfield fence when Mattingly hit the home run.

12. Harold and Ellen offered assistance to the last person, who declined it.

13. I was sure I had placed the box of cookies inside the grocery sack.

14. I'll try anything except a high dive; I am afraid of that.

15. Take the path that runs between the trees, Jonathan.

16. The emperor sat on his horse among the kings, dukes, counts, and barons.

17. Look beneath the tree and see if your present still awaits you.

18. Regarding your story, we liked it, but we can't use it for the school paper.

19. In spite of her misgivings, Emma told Marjorie about the broken punch bowl.

20. I think I left the magazine on top of the desk in the front room.

21. Your words flow, Tricia, like a clear brook through a sunny woodland at noon.

22. Besides the spice rack, Jamie, what did you make in shop class this year?

23. According to that notion, we'd all have to choose Africa instead of Europe.

24. The job fair is downtown, opposite the courthouse.

25. Travel past the supermarket; then turn left onto Chestnut Street.

26. I laid the broom against the goldfish bowl, and that must have tipped it over.

27. Next to the bank and behind the hardware store, you'll find the old curiosity shop.

28. Try solving the problem by means of this other variable, and I think you'll have it.

29. We finished our assignment three weeks ahead of the due date.

30. Upon her arrival, everyone stopped talking and stared at her.

31. I left my pocket recorder on the porch, along with my radio.

32. Working through the weekend at the senior citizen center was an eye-opening experience.

Lesson 11
Conjunctions: Coordinating, Correlative, and Subordinating

A conjunction joins single words or groups of words. A coordinating conjunction joins words or groups of words that have equal grammatical importance. Coordinating conjunctions include *and, but, or, nor, for, so,* and *yet.*

I flipped the light switch, **yet** nothing happened.

Correlative conjunctions work in pairs to join words and groups of words of equal importance. Correlative conjunctions include *both...and, just as...so, not only...but also, either...or, neither...nor,* and *whether...or.*

Either the rain will stop by noon, **or** we'll reschedule the picnic.

A subordinating conjunction joins a dependent idea or clause to a main clause.

COMMON SUBORDINATING CONJUNCTIONS

after	as though	provided (that)	until
although	because	since	when
as	before	so long as	whenever
as far as	considering (that)	so that	where
as if	if	than	whereas
as long as	inasmuch as	though	wherever
as soon as	in order that	unless	while

I will split the phone bill with them, **provided** each pays for her own long-distance calls.

▶ **Exercise 1** Circle each coordinating, correlative, and subordinating conjunction. Write *coord.* in the blank if the conjunction is coordinating, *corr.* if correlative, or *sub.* if subordinating.

_____sub._____ The rider rode by (as if) he were the wind itself.

_____ 1. The baron and the countess found each other at last, and the rest of the story is poetry.

_____ 2. Just as tadpoles become frogs, so this caterpillar will become a moth.

_____ 3. I will remember that beautiful story as long as I live.

_____ 4. Whenever the moon shines, we marvel at the simple beauty of the natural world.

_____ 5. I know him better than I know her, but I know neither well.

_____ 6. We will go where you like.

Grammar

_____ **7.** Both Mike and Paula discussed it, and Joe and Sheila considered it, too.

_____ **8.** The rhythm of this music is delightful, inasmuch as it has a special tempo.

_____ **9.** Whether we take the chance or not, we'll always appreciate your offer.

_____ **10.** We played the game again and again until we wore out, but it remained beyond

our skill.

_____ **11.** Just as it snowed on our last outing, so it will probably rain on this one.

_____ **12.** Whereas it is true that I said that, it is not true that I meant it.

_____ **13.** It is a lovely story, for everything worked out in the end.

_____ **14.** The rocket soared higher and higher into the wide blue sky, as if it were an

arrow from a mighty bow.

_____ **15.** The whale swam near our boat and then raised a flipper out of the water.

_____ **16.** I couldn't remember her name, nor could anyone else.

_____ **17.** The horses ran across the field, but the colt stayed near its mother.

_____ **18.** Belinda and Jennifer saw the movie, and neither of them liked it.

_____ **19.** Either that is the solution to the mystery, or there is none.

_____ **20.** I will let the cat out as soon as I finish the matzo balls.

_____ **21.** We waited for you, though you had probably forgotten about us.

_____ **22.** Not only did Bob get me a birthday present, but also Karen gave me a card.

_____ **23.** As far as I am concerned, we should try again.

_____ **24.** Talia told us everything, yet somehow something is still missing.

_____ **25.** If you go to the soccer match, may I have a ride?

_____ **26.** So that we might expedite this process, could you fill out this form again?

_____ **27.** Before you say anything, Nina, count slowly to ten.

_____ **28.** Either the king calls a new parliament, or he faces the possibility of a rebellion.

_____ **29.** Cole played the tennis match as though the championship were at stake.

_____ **30.** Robert stopped to tell us the news, for we had not heard it.

Lesson 12
Conjunctive Adverbs and Interjections

A **conjunctive adverb** is used to clarify the relationship between clauses of equal weight in a sentence.

I left the keys in the house; **consequently,** I was locked out.

CONJUNCTIVE ADVERBS

again	further	indeed	nevertheless	still
also	furthermore	instead	nonetheless	then
besides	hence	likewise	otherwise	therefore
consequently	however	moreover	similarly	thus

An **interjection** is a word or phrase that expresses emotion or exclamation. An interjection has no grammatical connection to other words. Commas follow mild interjections; exclamation points follow stronger ones. Common interjections include *oh; oh, my; good grief; my heavens; darn; drat; gee whiz;* and *well.*

▶ **Exercise 1 Draw a line under each conjunctive adverb, and circle each interjection.**

(Oh, no) the wind blew my favorite tree down in the park!

1. Linda won't be a hairdresser; instead, she'll be a manicurist.

2. Soto was late for class; moreover, he forgot his homework.

3. The club gave the donation for the tree; then, the town designated the plot for it.

4. The china shop is raffling off a lovely tea set at an open house; however, you need not be present to win.

5. The teacher stood watching the class; indeed, she seemed lost in thought.

6. The evening was late; still, she lingered at the party.

7. Jean's mother preferred the pink jacket; however, Jean picked the checkered one.

8. Gee, she went shopping for a blouse; instead, she bought me this nice sport coat.

9. The police officer stopped Henry, who argued his case; nonetheless, he got a ticket.

10. The farmer plowed, fertilized, and planted good seed; consequently, he reaped a bountiful crop.

11. Darn it! George painted the wrong desk white.

12. Priscilla used oil paint for the woodwork; therefore, she had to use paint remover to clean the brush.

13. Good grief! The cattle broke the fence and are milling about in the field.

Grammar

14. Television is boring; instead, listen to the radio and enjoy good music.

15. Oh, blast! The post office closed at 4:00 P.M., and now it is ten after!

16. We have many differences of opinion; nevertheless, we remain the best of friends.

17. Sally waited for the clearance sale; thus, she saved money.

18. Good gracious, I hardly knew you with your long hair and beard, Alphonso.

19. Jason passed his medical exam; therefore, he is still in the running for the scholarship.

20. Wow! The fragrance from those lilacs is delightful!

21. Oh, no! The rabbits have destroyed my lettuce and cabbage patch.

22. Bill dieted on advice of the doctor; otherwise, he would have been too heavy for the weight class.

23. Rats! I forgot the book, the homework, and my house keys!

24. Grandma made pies for the harvesters; then, she baked cookies for the children.

25. Whoops! She lost the heel off her brand-new shoe.

26. Gathering black walnuts is fun; however, they always stain my hands.

27. Impossible! There she goes, sliding down the banister again!

28. Riding a horse bare back is fun; still, it is wiser to use a saddle.

29. Listening to old records today brought back memories; otherwise, I might have forgotten them completely.

30. Oh, dear, the horse broke gait and is out of the competition.

31. The greedy show pig grew too fat; thus, it lost first place at the fair.

32. The grand marshall spoke for over an hour; then, the band played a lively tune, and everyone woke up.

33. She made a dress for the street festival; nevertheless, we see her wearing jeans and a sweater.

34. Dad baked the turkey to a golden brown; likewise, he did the same to the duck and the roast.

35. When building a home, don't forget a nice porch; otherwise, how can one enjoy the summer evenings?

36. Take photos on your vacation; then, you will have memories to view again.

37. Great day in the morning! The fish are biting, and Grandpa nearly fell out of his new boat!

38. Ouch! That hurt! Watch where you leave your toys, Tommy.

39. The porch needs painting; besides, the fence needs repair.

40. Oh, oh, here comes the neighbor, and she doesn't look too happy with us.

Unit 1 **Review**

▶ **Exercise 1** Write the part of speech above each italicized word or words: *N* for noun, *P* for pronoun, *V* for verb, *adj.* for adjective, *adv.* for adverb, *prep.* for preposition, or *conj.* for conjunction.

     adj.   adv.   prep.
The wind blew *fiercely against* the rigging of the sailboats.

1. Your glass *of* water *sat* on the table *all* day, Harley.

2. How can you *even* think *sad* thoughts on a day like *today?*

3. *That* is an *absolutely* wonderful painting you *have* on your wall.

4. Jack *belongs* to the French Club; *however,* he is *not* able to speak the language yet.

5. The old *gray* elephant shuffled slowly along, *as if* it were deep in sad *thoughts.*

6. The *April* sky shines *with* a blue so *wonderful* that you cannot forget *it.*

7. A large moth, *brilliantly* colored, perched on a *windowsill* on the sunny side *of* the house.

8. *The* computer printer hummed *along,* laying out page *after* page of document.

9. The waves *rolled* onto the *beach* in a *permanently* wet whisper.

10. Oh, look, *Lake Michigan* stretches to the *horizon,* and it is *so* blue!

11. Angie told *me* her cat sleeps *daily* on the windowsill *in* their family room.

12. When will your *older* brother Dennis *return* from his hike *along* the Appalachian Trail?

13. Ron's car is *newer* than the *one* Carol drives, but Carol's is newer than *mine.*

14. Gerard Manley Hopkins *definitely* is my favorite poet, *and* I think *he* should be more

    widely read.

15. I've *never* been to *a* rock concert as *energetic* as *that!*

16. *Both* the mayor *and* they *will assemble* a town meeting for *public* discussion of the *problem.*

17. I know *practical* jokes *can be* funny, but they *usually* don't turn out that way.

18. *Never* take up smoking, and *you* won't have to be trying to quit all the *time.*

19. *Beth* makes a real *effort* to read the local paper *every* day.

20. I can't imagine why Molly and Steve are late; *maybe* the car broke *down?*

21. Your grass is *so* very green, *Mrs. Cortez,* and it *grows* too *quickly* for just a *weekly* mowing.

22. Mr. Winthrop has a *grape* arbor over there, and over here *he* has a *pumpkin* patch.

Cumulative Review: Unit 1

▶ **Exercise 1** Write the part of speech above each italicized word: *N* for noun, *P* for pronoun, *V* for verb, *adj.* for adjective, *adv.* for adverb, *prep.* for preposition, *int.* for interjection, or *conj.* for conjunction.

      adv.   V   N

The *very* cute little chicks *pranced* around like so many fuzzy toy *ostriches*.

1. Are *you* ready for the *big* street festival next week, my *friends?*

2. *Wow!* The circus paraded right *through* the *center* of town *and* past my house.

3. The *wide* green pasture stretched down *the* hillside.

4. The park *and* the playground *have been closed* for *renovations*.

5. I *simply* cannot find *that* coffee cup, and I've looked *everywhere*.

6. *Oh, no,* the alarm clock didn't go off, and I *will be late* for work!

7. *A* thesaurus is absolutely *essential* for a student to have.

8. The *young* tree has developed *only* a few leaves, and they don't look *very* healthy.

9. *I* have a long drive *to* work every day, *but* the radio makes the *trip* pleasant.

10. *Observe* the *glacier* moving down the mountainside, destroying *everything* in its path.

11. *I* bought that green *fern* for my desk; I call it Kermit.

12. The distant hills *look* purple *from* this vantage point, don't *they?*

13. My *computer* has more than *enough* memory *but* not enough RAM *for* my needs.

14. Are the works of *J.R.R. Tolkien the* only twentieth-century writings *that* will be read

    a thousand years from now?

15. The girls' *basketball* team *does* much *better* than the boys' team each *year*.

16. *Ah, do* you *hear* the coyote *pups* yipping *in* the morning for their *mother?*

17. There's *a* rainbow—a *real,* complete, fantastic rainbow—arching *across* the sky.

18. My cousin *tells* fascinating *traditional* stories about my family's ethnic *heritage*.

19. I'd love the *summer unreservedly* if it weren't *for* the mosquitoes.

20. *The* music I *most* enjoy is *Gregorian* chants.

21. Regina *is* a whiz at these card games, *but* I *never* really understood them.

22. Do *you* know when the recycling truck *will come again?*

Unit 2: Parts of the Sentence

Lesson 13
Subjects and Predicates

Every sentence has a subject and a predicate. A simple subject is the key noun or pronoun (or group of words acting as a noun) that tells what the sentence is about. A simple predicate is the verb or verb phrase that expresses the essential thought about the subject.

Mr. Cline shuffled the papers on his desk. (*Mr. Cline* is the simple subject; *shuffled* is the simple predicate.)

▶ **Exercise 1   Draw one line under each simple subject and two lines under each simple predicate.**

The hummingbird fluttered around the red flowers in the backyard.

1. A winding path led to hidden treasure in the forest.

2. Tracy spurned Mick's attempts at apology.

3. The bride walked slowly and majestically down the aisle.

4. My grandmother has taught me a few basic quilt patterns.

5. That store sells everything from anise cookies to zinnia seeds.

6. The gale-strength winds uprooted the old oak.

7. Barb's graduation pictures look great!

8. The early morning sky dripped with dew.

9. Good news is always welcome.

10. Hot embers glowed in the bottom of an old garbage barrel.

11. Linda's collection of china dolls is awesome.

12. The light of dawn brightened gradually into full day.

13. Those rocks are home to several badgers.

14. The trail guide sat astride a spirited roan.

15. My neighbor Chan let me drive his '57 Chevy in the Memorial Day parade.

Grammar

The complete subject includes the simple subject and any words that modify it.

The constant drip of rain frazzled my nerves.

The complete predicate includes the simple predicate and any words that modify or complete it.

Selma **distributed blankets at the downtown homeless shelter.**

▶ Exercise 2 **Draw a vertical line (|) between the complete subject and the complete predicate.**
David| tried to tune in an all-news station.

1. The ice cream truck was surrounded by eager customers.

2. Howard knows something about everything!

3. Carlos divided the popcorn among the three of us.

4. Ginny teaches set dancing at the Police Athletic League gym.

5. Rows of bric-a-brac filled the tiny bookcase.

6. Large, colorful pillows adorned the otherwise sparse living room.

7. The soup boiled over onto the bottom of the microwave oven.

8. My favorite teacher dares to treat others with dignity and respect.

9. Marshall and Sylvia are in charge of candy sales.

10. I always look forward to spring.

11. This computer program is stuck in a loop!

12. We could paint Mr. Henry's front porch for him.

13. The hibiscus blossom unfolded a little more each day.

14. They will set the booth close to the front door.

15. Darien rented a tandem bike for Saturday's picnic.

▶ Writing Link **Write a sentence with a long complete subject and a short complete predicate, and then write one with a short subject and a long predicate.**

_____

_____

_____

_____

_____

Lesson 14
Compound Subjects and Predicates

A **compound subject** has two or more simple subjects that are joined by a conjunction and that share the same verb. A **compound predicate** (or compound verb) has two or more verbs or verb phrases that are joined by a conjunction. They share the same subject.

Compound subject: **Jerry** and **Jeri,** best friends since first grade, enjoy the confusion caused by their first names.

Compound predicate: They **drew** near to the nest and **discovered** inside a bird with a broken wing.

▶ **Exercise 1** Write *S* above each simple subject and *V* above each simple verb.

      S   V   V

The juggler caught and held my attention.

1. Susie and Cindy are my sister's black and white miniature poodles.

2. The patient coughed and wheezed.

3. Derri, Aleta, and Juan mulched and pruned the yew bushes near the student union.

4. Math and Asian History are my best subjects this year.

5. The conscientious librarian catalogued and shelved the shipment of new books.

6. Soda or tea would taste good right now.

7. Mrs. Cleary's art class collected used items and made them into colláges.

8. Lek found and bagged twenty specimens for his biology assignment.

9. Marilyn or Bonnie mowed and raked that big yard.

10. Near and far, people traveled to the new amusement park and paid exorbitant prices to get in.

11. Hillsburger and fried mushrooms is the best meal on the menu.

12. Francesca washes and waxes her neighbor's car every month.

13. Jackie typed and printed her report on the Inuit of Alaska.

14. I painted and decorated my bedroom over summer break.

15. The stroke of midnight brought remembrance of her instructions and, unfortunately, ended the night's magic.

▶ **Exercise 2** **Draw a vertical line between the subject and predicate. Write in the blank *CS* if the subject is compound, *CP* if the predicate is compound, or *B* if both are compound.**

__CS__		Hair rollers and bobby pins|were strewn about Marsha's bedroom.
_____	1.	I listened carefully and took notes my first day at work.
_____	2.	Gary and Larry disagree and fight over practically everything.
_____	3.	My old car engine chugged and smoked all the way home.
_____	4.	Nina, Robert, and Victor worked hard to complete their project before the science fair.
_____	5.	Jean washed and styled my hair today.
_____	6.	Trees and bushes now fill the old runway.
_____	7.	Casy and Jeanette entered and won a local talent contest.
_____	8.	Percy or Sharon has the latest draft of our research paper.
_____	9.	Stacks of papers and books clutter and almost hide my desk.
_____	10.	Rose or purple would accent and define the upper portion of your painting.
_____	11.	Roger scrimped and saved for a more dependable car.
_____	12.	Jim, Chip, and Martin ate some of Bruce's homemade chili.

▶ **Writing Link** **Write several sentences describing two people who live in your neighborhood. Use at least one compound subject and one compound predicate in your sentences.**

_____

_____

_____

_____

_____

_____

_____

_____

_____

_____

_____

_____

Lesson 15
Order of Subject and Predicate

In most sentences, the subject comes before the predicate. In a sentence written in inverted order, the predicate comes before the subject.

Some sentences are written in inverted order for variety or special emphasis.

                PREDICATE   SUBJECT
Near the downed airplane **stands** the injured **pilot**.

The subject also follows the predicate in sentences that begin with *there* or *here*.

PREDICATE SUBJECT   PREDICATE   SUBJECT
There **is** a **convertible** in the driveway.   Here on the desk **are** your car **keys**.

When the subject *you* is understood, the predicate appears without a subject.

UNDERSTOOD SUBJECT   PREDICATE
(You)   **Read** the novel.

▶ **Exercise 1** **Draw one line under each simple subject and two lines under each simple predicate. Circle the number of any item that contains the understood subject *you*.**

In that valley stands a series of Adena mounds and earthworks.

1. There sit your books on the dining room table.

2. On the runway waits the jetliner.

3. Listen to the new Mary Black CD before noon, please.

4. Observe the animals in their own habitat.

5. To her appeared three angels.

6. On the porch, right by the door, sat a huge spotted toad.

7. Sing us again that beautiful ballad about the cup and the tree and the windswept hill.

8. There still remain many ruins from ancient Rome and Greece.

9. In your aquarium, Benito, swim some pretty, colorful tropical fish.

10. Into the sunset rode the weary travelers.

11. For Christopher Columbus, beyond the ocean lay an exciting, mysterious adventure.

12. Within the enclosure stands the statue in warm, quiet sunlight.

13. Deep within the sea lives that amazing titan, the giant squid.

14. How absolutely beautiful grows your flower garden this year, Mrs. Crow!

15. Up and down the lagoon swam the shark in search of prey.

16. Through the night echoed the yips and cries of the lonely coyote pups.

17. On the Fourth of July, 1776, appeared the Declaration of Independence for the Continental Congress's approval.

18. Across the Irish bog drifted the exquisite, heartrending music of the uilleann pipes, those lovely Irish bagpipes.

19. High on the dizzy mountain heights live the white mountain sheep.

20. All through the night danced the crowd in the ballroom near the moonlit beach.

▶ **Exercise 2** **Write *U* beside each sentence that has *you* as its understood subject. Write *I* beside each sentence that is in inverted order. If the sentence is in inverted order, draw one line under the subject and two lines under each simple predicate.**

_____I_____ At the bottom of the old well lay many coins, trinkets, and other items.

_____ **1.** There lived a man in an old cottage out on the headland.

_____ **2.** Mow the lawn this morning, Ron.

_____ **3.** Sound asleep, after the long, wearying day on the trail, were all of the cowboys.

_____ **4.** Remember the lesson, Kevin.

_____ **5.** Forget about it, Paul.

_____ **6.** Inside a trunk in the attic were hidden an old wedding dress, photo albums of unknown people, and a family Bible in a foreign language.

_____ **7.** Work on this assignment until noon, Carlos.

_____ **8.** Under the large elms and chestnuts sat the Union soldiers, weary and sad after the battle.

_____ **9.** Over the outfield wall sailed the ball.

_____ **10.** Put that trampoline away, please.

_____ **11.** There will be an exchange student with us next month.

_____ **12.** Lift the boxes carefully.

_____ **13.** Trim the hedges, Harley.

_____ **14.** Here were the Hopewell earthworks and mounds at one time.

_____ **15.** In the castle on the crest of the hill lived an ancient, noble family.

_____ **16.** Here slept George Washington on the night of April 16, 1779.

Lesson 16
Direct and Indirect Objects

A complement is a word or a phrase that completes the meaning of a verb. A direct object is one type of complement. It answers the question *what?* or *whom?* after an action verb.

Alex built a model airplane. (*Airplane* answers the question *Alex built what?*)

An indirect object is also a complement. It answers the question *to whom? for whom? to what?* or *for what?* after an action verb.

Alex gave me a model airplane for my birthday. (*Me* answers the question *Alex gave a model airplane to whom?*)

▶ **Exercise 1** Draw two lines under each verb. Circle each direct object.

Not one member of the Flowers family <u>had</u> a green (thumb.)

1. Spread the good news far and wide.

2. Richard the Lionhearted ruled England for only ten years.

3. Perhaps Ginny could locate the missing set of keys.

4. Jill hung her clothes outside in the sunshine.

5. The rescue worker wouldn't leave the building without the little boy.

6. Ted McElwee teaches shop classes at the local high school.

7. The uncapped pen leaked ink all over the desktop.

8. After days out on the sea, Martin welcomed the sight of land.

9. Eenie colored the Easter eggs a myriad of bright shades and patterns.

10. Devona gave the old car a complete tune-up.

11. Rose plays the harp and the harmonica, but (thankfully) not at the same time.

12. These new shoes are pinching my feet.

13. Henry raked the leaves and stuffed them into garbage bags.

14. You, too, can write mystery plots.

15. The ocean sounds lulled Patti.

▶ **Exercise 2** Circle each direct object. Draw one line under each indirect object if there is one.

Could you give <u>me</u> a (hand) with this, Carly?

1. Aunt Sue sent the manufacturer a letter of complaint about her broken Handy-Dandy machine.

2. I bowled a 125 in the tournament.

Grammar

3. Don't give Tully a hard time.

4. The disc jockey announced an hour of uninterrupted music.

5. You could do him a favor in return for his kindness.

6. The class gave their teacher a *bon voyage* gift.

7. Please pay us the remainder of your bill.

8. Dad and Jim are playing golf at Snowhill today.

9. Mr. Larramore assigned the class a term-long project.

10. Lyn left a trail of mud from the front door to the kitchen.

11. A telegrapher sent them news of the ship's distress.

12. Midge, clean the cookie dough off the walls, please.

13. The strong gale winds bowed the trees almost to the ground.

14. The catalog offered shoppers a plethora of useless items.

15. Kent expected the surprise party after all.

16. Give me enough time to think this over.

17. A pot of heather graced the window ledge.

18. This new television show has no commercial breaks.

19. Michael raked the leaves for his brother.

20. Nikita designs and makes her own paper dolls.

▶ Writing Link **Write four or more sentences about a special gift that someone has given you. Use a direct object and indirect object in at least two of your sentences.**

_____

_____

_____

_____

_____

_____

_____

_____

_____

Lesson 17
Object and Subject Complements

An **object complement** is a noun, pronoun, or adjective that completes the meaning of a direct object by identifying or describing it.

Bob considers hamburgers his favorite **food**. (noun)
Ashley considers the CD **hers**. (pronoun)
Sheila finds it **useless**. (adjective)

Grammar

▶ **Exercise 1** Above each object complement, write *N* for noun, *P* for pronoun, or *adj.* for adjective.

                                                      adj.
Our math teacher Mrs. Ashton considers math important for everyone.

1. Everyone presumed her innocent at first.

2. The blacksmith found the horseshoe bent beyond repair.

3. Yes, Scott won; the board judged the winning entry his.

4. We made our opinions known.

5. The people of Dunwhich would reckon the monument theirs.

6. The officers of the court denoted the house a historical site.

7. The aspiring artist considered the statue his best work.

8. The troop of young, hopeful performers elected Jennifer director.

9. The composer called his composition "Summer Dawn."

10. The electrical discharge made the computer useless.

11. My dear Aunt Cassandra can make a simple story profound.

12. The senatorial commission appointed my aunt an ambassador.

13. How, James, could you ever think it the truth?

14. They thought the man a coward for leaving his post at that moment.

15. Without doubt, they will name their new boat "Charlie" after their uncle.

16. Xian has not proven the theory true.

17. Mrs. Pendelton, feel free to make my house home until the flood waters die down.

18. Admiral, I must report that I consider this ship unseaworthy.

19. No way, I believe it impossible.

20. You could not prove them false, no matter what you said.

Grammar

A **subject complement** follows a subject and a linking verb. It identifies or describes a subject. The two kinds of subject complements are predicate nominatives and predicate adjectives

A predicate nominative is a noun or pronoun that follows a linking verb and gives more information about the subject.

The two teams are **competitors.**

A predicate adjective is an adjective that follows a linking verb and gives more information about the subject.

The music sounded **mysterious.**

▶ **Exercise 2 Write *PN* above each predicate nominative and *PA* above each predicate adjective.**

PA
Fresh apples are delicious.

1. My cousin Tom is a professor of philosophy at Bracton College.

2. The Ambersons remain satisfied with our work on their house and garage.

3. Well, it seems a real tragedy, unfortunately.

4. The small sapling will become an oak tree.

5. My favorite cousin Tabitha will become a doctor of osteopathy soon.

6. Oh, Wanjiru, you suddenly look very ill.

7. The harvest moon appeared large and bright in the night sky.

8. My brother is the captain of the tennis team.

9. I grew full from eating so much pizza.

10. Helen might have been happy with that sort of vacation after all.

11. Mr. Newman may become the new track coach.

12. Napoleon was a general first and foremost.

13. This dish you made, Lisa, tastes salty.

14. The remote clang of the country church bell sounds clear in the evening stillness.

15. After many different jobs, Uncle Todd remains a factory foreman.

16. The person at the door might be the new neighbor.

17. The cat became friendly with me only slowly over a period of time.

18. The story line of this novel seems quite dull.

☑ Unit 2 **Review**

▶ **Exercise 1** Draw a vertical line between the subject and predicate. Write *DO* above each direct object and *IO* above each indirect object.

                IO   DO

Franklin|gave Tanya a copy of his favorite tape.

1. Cindy offered Wanda a free ticket to the concert.

2. Ernest made Beth a beautiful, multicolored cloak.

3. Bill suggested the idea to us yesterday after track practice.

4. The young, nervous, bright-eyed colt watched me intently.

5. Our student council presented Mr. Cortez, our principal, with a plaque.

6. The Cincinnati Reds played the Pittsburgh Pirates yesterday evening.

7. Roxanne read me her poems.

8. Eileen gave me her old copy of the book.

9. The Industrial Revolution brought the world material comforts.

10. The store guaranteed Steve his money back.

▶ **Exercise 2** Draw a line between the subject and the predicate. Above each italicized word, write *OC* for object complement, *PN* for predicate nominative, or *PA* for predicate adjective.

                          OC

Our class|voted Robert *president*.

1. Oh, the weather this morning appears *gorgeous*.

2. Carroll seems *unhappy* with the results of the test.

3. The student survey named Caroline most *talkative*.

4. The ancient Greeks were a powerfully curious *people*.

5. The delicious aroma of cherry pie renders me *weak* with hunger.

6. Zack felt absolutely *joyful* about the college acceptance letter.

7. Our good friend Al is a *man* with a mission—to teach.

8. Everything in the forest smelled *musty* and *wet* after the night of rain.

9. Many in my family consider me an *extrovert*.

10. Your new puppy really seems *timid*.

Unit 2, Parts of the Sentence **83**

Cumulative Review: Units 1–2

▶ **Exercise 1** Write *C* for concrete, *A* for abstract, or *col.* for collective above the simple subject of each sentence. Write *TR* for transitive or *int.* for intransitive above each simple predicate.

              C   int.
The little bear cub cried for its mother.

1. Conrad fenced in the yard last week.

2. Our team made the winning play in the last minute of the championship game.

3. Beauty comes through each one of Akira's many wonderful paintings.

4. A mighty lightning bolt struck the tall fir tree outside my window last night.

5. That idea originated in the mind of a nineteenth-century writer named Thomas Hardy.

6. Jamal bought his car in Cleveland from his Aunt Harriet.

7. The royal regiment parades daily in front of the queen's palace.

8. The assembly gathered everyone in our class together for the big announcement.

9. Wisdom finds a way through even life's most complicated difficulties.

10. Alice took Todd to the theater for a performance of Shakespeare's *Much Ado About Nothing*.

11. The snow shines brightly in the clear morning sunlight.

12. Yussuf explained everything clearly and without hesitation.

13. Our family enjoys this brand of cereal more than any other.

14. My foolishness embarrassed me yesterday in front of everyone in the acting class.

15. Daniel loves a hike through the state forest every once in a while.

16. Reason dictates a careful response to any form of aggression.

17. A jury must decide on many important questions.

18. The little chicks peeped loudly for some food.

19. The student confederation suggested a number of options for our consideration.

20. These old brick streets echo wonderfully under the car tires.

21. Our big dining room table seats twelve people.

22. I cracked my wristwatch against the doorpost this morning on my way out the door.

23. A true sense of peace wafted over Tricia slowly because of the sweet music.

24. The hot rod collection delighted many fans of the "muscle" cars.

25. The Roman senate passed a vote of thanks to the victorious general for saving the republic.

Unit 3: Phrases

Lesson 18
Prepositional Phrases

A **prepositional phrase** is a group of words that begins with a preposition and usually ends with a noun or a pronoun, called the **object of the preposition**. Adjectives and other modifiers may be placed between the preposition and its object. A preposition may have more than one object.

He put the note **into his pocket.** (*Pocket* is the object of the preposition *into.*)

Prepositional phrases may occur sequentially in a sentence.

He put the note **into the pocket of his shirt.**

A prepositional phrase is usually used as an adjective or an adverb. When it is used as an adjective, it modifies a noun or a pronoun. When it is used as an adverb, it modifies an adjective, a verb, or another adverb.

We read the book **about the West.** (adjective phrase modifying the noun *book*)

Who **around town** could help us hang posters? (adjective phrase modifying the pronoun *who*)

She parks her new car **in the garage.** (adverb phrase modifying the verb *parks*)

The job is easy **for you.** (adverb phrase modifying the adjective *easy*)

She reads well **for her age.** (adverb phrase modifying the adverb *well*)

▶ **Exercise 1** **Underline each prepositional phrase.**

Icarus flew high <u>before his fall</u>.

1. Our cat made her bed under the table in the kitchen.

2. One never knows what wonderful worlds might be found between the covers of a book.

3. Our flight took us over the Rocky Mountains and the Grand Canyon.

4. Please have this list of items in stock in time for the holiday season.

5. Before summer vacation be sure to complete the entire reading list for extra credit.

6. Reserve the small conference room for the morning of March 22 from nine until noon.

7. The room across the hall is the public relations office.

8. We will wait until this evening to do the grocery shopping.

9. The book I needed was beneath a stack of papers under my bed.

10. The telephones inside her office can be heard outside the building.

11. After my automobile accident, I placed a claim for damages to my car.

12. There was an ice storm yesterday followed by a snowstorm during the night.

13. The winning points were scored when the ball dropped through the hoop just before the final whistle.

14. We watched the eagle soar above the tree line on the mountain.

15. The man by her side is president of the company.

▶ **Exercise 2 Underline each prepositional phrase. Draw an arrow to the word it modifies.**

I read most of that story yesterday.

1. Quarrels among the four brothers were rare.

2. His rollerblades were behind the house.

3. Mother asked me if I would pick up the dry-cleaning before play practice.

4. My cousin from Duluth will visit us during spring break.

5. My best friend lives in the apartment complex behind our house.

6. Her comment about the time was totally off the subject of our conversation.

7. My decision depends upon the price he will quote for the work.

8. My favorite television program is about an American family who lives outside this country.

9. When you arrive at the airport, be sure to check your ticket at the gate.

10. The plane from Atlanta will land around midnight.

11. Some strange kind of weed began growing beneath the deck.

12. Periods of silence can be quite comfortable between good friends.

13. Over a period of several years, Grandmother has collected dolls from her travels in many countries.

14. Our team picnic will be held inside the shelter house.

15. The plumber found the problem with the pipes under the sink.

Lesson 19
Participles and Participial Phrases; Absolute Phrases

A participle is a verb form that can function as an adjective. It modifies a noun or a pronoun.

A **blooming** plant sat on the desk. (The participle *blooming* modifies the noun *plant*.)

Present participles end in *-ing*. Past participles usually end in *-ed*, although there are other forms. Many familiar adjectives are in fact participles.

In the **driving** snow, the world was invisible.   The **handwritten** text was hard to read.

When a participle is part of a verb phrase, it does not function as an adjective.

The **baked** chicken is ready to eat. (adjective)   The chicken **has been baked**. (verb)

A participle with its complements and modifiers is called a participial phrase. A participial phrase that begins a sentence is usually followed by a comma. A participial phrase that appears in the middle or at the end of a sentence is set off by commas only if it is not essential to the meaning of the sentence.

Charging with all his might, the quarterback plowed through the defense.
The quarterback **sporting the number 12** is my sister. (essential)
My sister, **playing for the home team,** never misses a football game. (nonessential)

▶ **Exercise 1** Underline each participle, participial phrase, or verb phrase. Write *adj.* if it functions as an adjective or *V* if it functions as a verb.

adj.   A <u>soaring</u> bird is a glorious sight.

_____ **1.** We collected used clothing for the local American Red Cross drive.

_____ **2.** She said the concert had impressed her.

_____ **3.** My aunt had gone before I arrived at my mother's house.

_____ **4.** An embarrassed Mrs. Gonzel apologized for the intrusion.

_____ **5.** Her new coat was made of dyed wool.

_____ **6.** The waiting room in the doctor's office was full of sick people.

_____ **7.** The attorney had been elected to the town council.

_____ **8.** My answering machine does not record long messages.

_____ **9.** He has spoken to exceptionally large groups on the subject of environmental protection.

_____ **10.** I had looked everywhere for my baseball glove.

_____ **11.** The struggling artist cheerfully sold her painting.

_____ **12.** The advertised price is higher than my limit.

_____ 13. Mr. Munson has studied the stock market for several years.

_____ 14. The written word is a powerful tool.

_____ 15. At your request, I have investigated possible locations for our annual company party.

An **absolute phrase** consists of a noun or a pronoun that is modified by a participle or a participial phrase but has no grammatical relation to the rest of the sentence.

Computers having become common, manufacturers report fewer typewriter sales. (The participial phrase *having become common* modifies the noun *computers.*)

The race (being) over, the runners sat in the shade to cool down. (The participle *being* is often understood rather than stated.)

▶ Exercise 2 **Underline each absolute phrase.**

The young writer having sold her first story, her mentor decided to throw her a party.

1. The adventurer having just climbed Mt. Everest, his book became a best-seller.

2. Mike's salary was lower, but his take-home pay was higher than at his old job, the insurance premium being paid by his new employer.

3. We are constantly alert for forest fires, the weather being unusually dry.

4. The early hours being excepted, I love my job at the radio station.

5. The trip having been strenuous and exhausting, I wanted to sleep for days.

6. The game over, we gathered for a party at Coach's home.

7. Karl being trained in nursing, his application for school security guard was approved.

8. We fought the traffic at rush hour, the appliance store being expected to close at six.

9. The commuter plane having flown over nine hundred miles, the mechanic gave it a thorough checkup.

10. Father says we must postpone buying a new car, inflation being its worst in years.

11. His hero having succeeded so well, Pedro worked long hours to earn his own degree.

12. We plan to move to a larger city, career opportunities being rare here.

13. His story phoned in, the reporter prepared to enjoy the rest of the evening.

14. The politician having been accused of accepting a bribe, his bank records were subpoenaed.

15. Many species of herbs having become well established in wastelands, we drove there to study them.

Grammar

Lesson 20
Gerunds and Gerund Phrases; Appositives and Appositive Phrases

A gerund is a verb form that ends in -*ing* and functions as a noun in the sentence.

Racing is his greatest love. (gerund used as subject)
He loves **racing**. (gerund used as direct object)
He is very good at **racing**. (gerund used as object of preposition)
His love is **racing**. (gerund used as predicate nominative)

A gerund phrase is a gerund plus any complements and modifiers.

Stock car racing is his greatest love.

▶ Exercise 1 **Underline each gerund and gerund phrase.**

Astronauts enjoy exploring outerspace.

1. Obtaining a degree in engineering, science, or a medical field is how several of my classmates plan to enter the space industry.

2. Terra believes that as an astronaut she could combine her two great loves—flying and science.

3. Becoming an astronaut requires a college education and many months of special study.

4. Becoming an astronaut is not in William's plans; he wants to pursue a career in rocketry.

5. His dream is building a nuclear-powered starship that will travel many times faster than today's chemical rockets.

6. Scientists are excited about designing a spacecraft to go on a proposed mission to our nearest star, Barnard's Star.

7. Reaching Barnard's Star in fifty years or less now seems possible.

8. Plans for the mission include using robots.

9. The robots will be used for grabbing satellites and bringing them inside the shuttle for repair.

10. Studying the type of life support systems needed to live in space is Lon's plan for the future.

11. Creating artificial gravity is only one problem already solved of the many potential problems.

12. Space colonies will have special areas for raising food crops.

13. Zero gravity conditions are good for producing some medicines and other products.

14. The National Aeronautics and Space Administration, or NASA, has responsibility for exploring space for peaceful purposes.

15. Working with NASA is certain to become a reality for several of my classmates.

An **appositive** is a noun or pronoun that is placed next to another noun or pronoun to identify it or give additional information about it.

My brother **Frank** has red hair. (*Frank* identifies *brother.*)

An **appositive phrase** is an appositive plus any words that modify it. Commas should be used to set off an appositive or appositive phrase that is not essential to the meaning of the sentence.

Mrs. Robinson, **a woman of humble origins,** now owns a large retail chain. (*A woman of humble origins* gives additional information about Mrs. Robinson. It is not essential to the meaning of the sentence.)

▶ **Exercise 2** **Underline each appositive and appositive phrase.**

Robert H. Goddard, <u>a pioneer in American rocketry,</u> was first to use gasoline and liquid oxygen instead of gunpowder as fuel.

1. In 1957 a Soviet rocket launched Earth's first artificial satellite, *Sputnik I.*

2. Satellite pictures, exact maps of Earth, can pinpoint the spread of plant diseases.

3. Meteorologists, scientists who study weather, can predict dangerous storms using radio waves converted to pictures.

4. Communication satellites, receivers and transmitters of radio waves, make communication possible from continent to continent.

5. Geostationary satellites, satellites that orbit at the same speed as Earth's rotation, are used for telecommunications, weather forecasting, and even spying.

6. Space probes, satellites that travel close to other worlds, were first launched in 1959 when the first probe raced past the moon.

7. In 1974 the *Mariner 10* came within 203 miles of Mercury, the planet closest to the sun.

8. Probes of Mars, the planet most like Earth, help us understand our own planet.

9. *Voyager 1* and *Voyager 2* were probes that photographed the planet Jupiter.

10. Few countries have launch sites, points from which a rocket can carry a satellite into space.

Lesson 21
Infinitives and Infinitive Phrases

An infinitive is a verb form that is preceded by the word *to* and is used as a noun, an adjective, or an adverb. If *to* precedes the base form of the verb, it is part of an infinitive, not a preposition.

To fly in my own plane is one of the greatest thrills I have known. (infinitive as subject)

My father loves **to drive** through the country. (infinitive as direct object)

Our goal is **to build** twenty birdhouses by the end of the week. (infinitive as predicate nominative.)

Are you ready **to go?** (infinitive as adverb)

An infinitive with its complements and modifiers is called an infinitive phrase

To write with great clarity has been my goal for many years.

▶ **Exercise 1** Underline each infinitive and infinitive phrase.

Jamal goes to the lab to study botany because he wants to know about the formation and growth of plants.

1. If we pause to consider the smallest algae and the giant sequoia, we realize how important plants are to our world.

2. Jamal is interested in plant structure and how plants are equipped to fight disease.

3. Kara's interest seems to be the role of plants in the food chain.

4. She hopes to expand her knowledge of nutrition and agronomy.

5. Su Lin's desire to enter the National Park Service often takes her to the woods to indulge her interest in wild plants.

6. She asked me to notice the difference in the growth patterns of trees.

7. Maple trees, to name one example, do not usually grow in mountainous areas because they cannot find enough room to place their roots.

8. Many pines, on the other hand, tend to thrive in the mountains, for they are anchored by a tap root, a single, thick root that extends into the ground a distance equal to the height of the tree.

9. Willow trees may send roots several hundred feet to find water and will not flourish in arid places.

10. Ancient people knew that many plants growing wild in the United States are good to eat.

11. They were forced to depend on nature to supply their food, and although we have learned to control nature to a great extent, ultimately we are still dependent on it to produce our food.

12. William has a contract to write a book about edible wild plants.

13. One thing he wants to point out to his readers is the importance of learning to identify properly any plant included in your diet.

14. For example, Queen Anne's lace, which has also come to be known as wild carrot, has a lacy leaf similar to that of poison hemlock.

15. Two sure ways to tell the difference are that the stalks of Queen Anne's lace are hairy and the roots are certain to smell like carrots.

16. Every spring we searched the woods and fields for the common morel, a delicious edible mushroom that my mother loved to sauté in butter.

17. A poisonous false morel, a mushroom that is convoluted instead of pitted, is known to have a skirt on the stem.

18. Wild rice, sunflower, lamb's-quarters, and cane can all be found when we go to the wild to find seeds to eat as cereal.

19. My cousin, who is a chef in a large restaurant, is able to serve fresh herbs because he grows them in a flower box.

20. His sister gathers herbs to send to a pharmaceutical company that will use them to make medicines.

21. People have spent millions of dollars to destroy the dandelion.

22. Early colonists were eager to bring this little flowering plant to North America because of its many beneficial properties.

23. Dandelions, able to bloom for a long season, provided a good food source for the honey bees that the colonists wanted to keep.

24. Native Americans came to see the dandelion as a healing herb.

25. The Mohicans used the leaves to make a tonic, and other tribes used the roots to relieve heartburn.

26. My cousin uses the leaves to create gourmet salads, which are also quite nutritious.

Lesson 22
Distinguishing Participial, Gerund, and Infinitive Phrases

Grammar

Participles, gerunds, and infinitives are called verbals because they are verb forms that function in other ways in a sentence.

A participle is a verb form that functions as an adjective. Present participles end in -ing. Past participles usually end in -ed. A participial phrase is a participle plus any complements and modifiers. For examples of participles and participial phrases, see Lesson 19.

A gerund is a verb form that ends in -ing and functions as a noun in the sentence. A gerund phrase is a gerund plus any complements and modifiers. For examples of gerunds and gerund phrases, see Lesson 20.

An infinitive is made from the base form of the verb, which is nearly always preceded by the word to. An infinitive phrase is an infinitive plus any complements and modifiers. For examples of infinitives and infinitive phrases, see Lesson 21.

▶ **Exercise 1** **Identify the italicized word or phrase. Write *P* for participle, *G* for gerund, or *I* for infinitive.**

___G___　　*Swimming* is exercise.

_____ 1. *Driving beyond the state park with several friends,* we explored the countryside.

_____ 2. *Attending the concert* was the highlight of our week.

_____ 3. Space science is an *ever-expanding* field of study.

_____ 4. We drove to the mall *to buy our new furniture.*

_____ 5. Each summer our library gives a prize to the person *reading the most books.*

_____ 6. *Parking in the drive in front of the school* is restricted.

_____ 7. They have closed the street *to repair the railroad crossing.*

_____ 8. *Elected to the position of county auditor,* he has purchased a home closer to his new office.

_____ 9. *Breaking the light barrier* is simply not a possibility.

_____ 10. I am planning *to pay all my bills by June.*

_____ 11. *Beginning Friday,* there will be a huge inventory reduction sale.

_____ 12. *Overwhelmed by calculus,* I rearranged my schedule to take geometry instead.

_____ 13. The high school awards banquet, *followed by a dance,* will be held at the American Legion Hall this year.

_____ **14.** *Bass fishing in Smith Lake* is my father's favorite pastime.

_____ **15.** Last night's sunset seemed *to color the sky with pinks, purples, and reds.*

_____ **16.** I have special shoes for *running the marathon.*

_____ **17.** My sister loves *cleaning the house on Saturday.*

_____ **18.** *Feeding the homing pigeons on the roof* is my sister's favorite chore.

_____ **19.** *Searching for unusual paperweights for our collection,* we visited a number of stores during our stay in Florida.

_____ **20.** My brother was asked *to drive my aunt to Texas.*

_____ **21.** When my homework is done, I love *reading novels.*

_____ **22.** We were relieved *to settle the dispute out of court.*

_____ **23.** *Recycling our newspapers* is the least we can do to help the environment.

_____ **24.** The photograph *mounted in the silver frame* was my mom's favorite birthday present.

_____ **25.** The dog *running toward us* seems to be limping.

_____ **26.** My favorite pastime is *cross-country skiing.*

_____ **27.** We hope *to persuade Mr. Lee to postpone the test.*

_____ **28.** Jeremiah, *wanting a higher grade,* did an extra-credit report.

_____ **29.** A free throw results from *fouling another player.*

_____ **30.** The woman *acting concerned* is my aunt.

▶ Writing Link **Write five or six sentences about your choice of career. Use verbals in each sentence.**

_____

_____

_____

_____

_____

_____

_____

_____

Grammar

✓ Unit 3 **Review**

▶ **Exercise 1** Identify each italicized word or phrase. Above it write *P* for participle, *prep.* for preposition, *G* for gerund, or *I* for infinitive.

       G
    Singing is a beautiful art.

1. The two men *walking* down the street were tall and handsome.

2. Hard work is the best way *to impress an employer.*

3. *Inviting my friends to visit my home* was the highlight of last week.

4. *Yelling loudly,* the children *on the playground* watched the dog *chasing the cat.*

5. Doria decided *to find and visit her ancestral home.*

6. *Before dark,* Lucy's mother sent her *on an errand.*

7. Marco and I held a consultation *to determine our next move.*

8. What sports do you play *besides hockey?*

9. *Winning* the debate this morning puts the senior team in first place.

10. *Using a Clearview microscope* is different from using any other type.

11. *Recycling* becomes a way of life.

12. We said good-bye and promised *to meet at the rink tomorrow.*

13. *To invest in real estate* requires *taking a financial risk.*

14. I like *to participate* in games rather than just watch.

15. *Picking wildflowers* is prohibited by law.

16. My best suggestion is *to take the tollway.*

17. Darnel has one serious fault, *overeating.*

18. Michael says his hobby is *skiing.*

19. Let's plan *to visit* the museum together.

20. *Needing* money for the trip, Luis took a part-time job *at a furniture store.*

21. *Reading* about flying cannot compare *to soaring* above the earth.

22. George, *hoping* to master several business machines, is already an excellent typist.

23. *Dancing into the night,* Mary and Liam were oblivious to the time.

24. Xian is our best sprinter in *running the hundred-yard dash.*

Cumulative Review: Units 1–3

▶ **Exercise 1** Draw one line under each simple subject. Draw two lines under each simple predicate. Circle each phrase used as a modifier.

The trees (on the hill) rustled mysteriously (in the breeze).

1. Neither of t6he reports will be prepared before tomorrow.

2. The man in the brown derby looks like my uncle.

3. Having all the facts makes it easier to choose the best classes.

4. Hard-working and conscientious, Ellen had no trouble with the promotion.

5. Volunteering at the local day-care center is excellent preparation for a career

   in early childhood education.

6. Paul got his information from reading books and talking to people.

7. Mutual funds provide higher yields and offer reasonable security.

8. People who, on a daily basis, ride the subway witness its continuing expansion.

9. I bought the gift, costing a mere $10.99, at a large department store.

10. Employees throughout the company were curious about the executive board meeting.

11. Gathered around the water cooler, we wondered why the president was so nervous.

12. A college education is planned by most of my friends.

13. The day started with the ringing telephone.

14. Wandering around the showroom, I tried to study the new models.

15. What would you do if you were faced with someone having a heart attack?

16. We should take the excellent CPR training offered here in the school.

17. Currently, Lydia's new firm is deeply involved in municipal improvement.

18. What does a species extinction mean to the world?

Unit 4: Clauses and Sentence Structure

Lesson 23
Main and Subordinate Clauses

A main clause is a group of words that contains a complete subject and a complete predicate. Also known as an independent clause, a main clause can stand alone as a complete sentence.

Many people wait on the bus.

A subordinate clause also contains a subject and a predicate but cannot stand alone. Because it depends on a main clause to make sense, it is also known as a dependent clause. Usually, a subordinating conjunction introduces a subordinate clause, although it may begin with a relative pronoun (such as *who, whose, whom, which, that,* or *what*) or a relative adverb (such as *when, where,* or *why*). In some subordinate clauses, the connecting word also serves as the subject of the clause.

Many people wait on the bus **while the driver repairs it.**
Will the gentleman **who paged Mrs. Trotter** please pick up the courtesy phone? (The relative pronoun *who,* which connects the clauses, is the subject of the subordinate clause.)

SUBORDINATING CONJUNCTIONS

Time:	after, as, as soon as, before, since, until, when, whenever, while
Place:	where, wherever
Manner:	as, as if, as though
Cause:	as, because, inasmuch as, since, so that
Concession:	although, even though, though
Condition:	if, unless

▶ **Exercise 1** Check (✔) the blank before each sentence that contains a subordinate clause.

__✔__ Where the wind blows steadily, one can imagine the possibilities of wind power.

_____ 1. The tribe that lived here erected many wonderful earthworks and ceremonial mounds.

_____ 2. Stacey, who tried out for the Olympic team, has a number of scholarship opportunities for college.

_____ 3. After the heavy snow, we had to spend the morning shoveling out the car.

_____ 4. As far as I can tell, there aren't many choices for us to consider.

_____ 5. Reckless behavior impresses no one and may easily endanger one's health.

_____ 6. The comedians bravely acted on while the audience booed their efforts.

_____ 7. Mrs. Chin believes the story because you said it was true.

_____ 8. Mike won the bike race inasmuch as my bike lost a tire a mile from the finish line.

_____ 9. Whenever did the Ramsey twins paint their parents' house?

_____ 10. The championship game dragged on until everyone knew we had lost.

_____ 11. Braxton, my dog, loves ice cream, a food that he should not have, of course.

_____ 12. For the longest time Clint hiked on the old trail every weekend.

_____ 13. The powerful ocean waves struck the sea wall that had been erected to protect the tidal basin.

_____ 14. Beneath the peaceful valley flows a mighty underground river.

_____ 15. If you talk to her, Hernando, please tell her about the senior class party next Friday after school.

_____ 16. General Robert E. Lee, who was born in Virginia, hated slavery and opposed it.

_____ 17. Relax, but do try to finish the project by the end of the day, please.

_____ 18. She looked at me as if I had insulted her.

_____ 19. Perhaps you will remember it as soon as I play a few bars on the piano, Frank.

_____ 20. Excellent music and good friends make for a wonderful evening.

_____ 21. Although Sheila ran hurdles last year, this year she participated only in the dash and the relay.

_____ 22. The library card on the counter belongs to the woman at the computer terminal.

_____ 23. My hope remains strong, even though the doctor seems quite downcast.

_____ 24. The leaves on the trees turned a tawny, deep lavender red during the past week.

_____ 25. The moon, which is in its first quarter, produced little light to interfere with our stargazing.

▶ Writing Link **Write a brief paragraph about your favorite season of the year. Use at least two subordinate clauses.**

_____

_____

_____

_____

_____

_____

_____

Lesson 24
Simple and Compound Sentences

A simple sentence has one complete subject and one complete predicate. The subject, the predicate, or both, may be compound.

SUBJECT	PREDICATE
Long **strands** of pearls	**were looped** around the door wreath.
Pansies and **lilacs**	**filled** the flower boxes.
Several **dogs**	**sniffed** and **searched** through the loose garbage.

Two or more simple sentences, each considered a main clause, comprise a compound sentence. Main clauses can be joined to build a compound sentence by using a comma followed by a conjunction, such as *or, and,* or *but.* However, a conjunction is not necessary to form a compound sentence. A semicolon may be used to join two main clauses without a conjunction. A semicolon is also used before a conjunctive adverb, such as *moreover.*

Spring arrived late this year, **but** Mona's garden was as beautiful as ever.
Spring arrived late this year; Mona's garden was as beautiful as ever.
Spring arrived late this year; **however,** Mona's garden was as beautiful as ever.

▶ Exercise 1   Write in the blank whether the sentence is *simple* or *compound.*

compound   Jeremy likes to cook, but he isn't very good at it.

_____ 1. That song always reminds me of you.

_____ 2. Tell me more about your experiences in China.

_____ 3. Geoff ran into Mr. Gaines last week.

_____ 4. Mary may seem nervous during rehearsals, but she becomes quite calm during her turn on the stage.

_____ 5. Glenna will arrive today, but Carl won't be here until Saturday.

_____ 6. Darkness blanketed the countryside, and stars twinkled into sight.

_____ 7. Music blared forth from the tiny pocket radio.

_____ 8. Neil and Alvin walked in the Muscular Dystrophy Walk-a-thon.

_____ 9. Suzanne practices ventriloquism every afternoon.

_____ 10. The old tractor was still the most dependable of the lot.

_____ 11. Last year Joyce sewed her school wardrobe; moreover, she made several of the accessories.

_____ 12. Nadine needs help with the laundry today; morever, she wants help on a regular basis.

_____ **13.** Cass will draw either a lion's head or a ram's head for our door plaque.

_____ **14.** Lauren is sweeping the dugout, and Kat is cleaning the bases.

_____ **15.** Mums lined the sidewalk, the side of the house, and even the outer rim of the yard.

_____ **16.** The Astronomy Club is selling magazines to earn a trip to Washington, D.C., but they will probably pay most of the expenses themselves.

_____ **17.** The Lincoln High School Bobcats won the state finals.

_____ **18.** Brad Pitt is Claire's favorite actor, but Barbie prefers Michael J. Fox.

_____ **19.** Dr. Stark presented the puzzle, and Dr. Yee showed us the solution.

_____ **20.** Clean the cat hairs off the couch, please.

▶ **Exercise 2** **Underline each main clause. If there is more than one main clause in a sentence, add a comma or a semicolon as needed.**

Our school colors are scarlet and white.

1. Young hopefuls lined the waiting room but no one noticed them.

2. Gardenias grew near the elm tree and columbine grew beside the driveway.

3. Carolina is wearing her velvet jacket but Sammy has on jeans and a t-shirt.

4. Walk over to the outlet store or use some of the money to take a taxi.

5. Whales shouldered the waves and dripped rivers.

6. White orchids graced Lynette's prom dress.

7. The trees glowed in the bright sunlight my eyes could barely stand the strain of looking at them.

8. The local cable station aired my story but they mispronounced my name.

9. The novel's ending intrigued me.

10. Lisa hung pictures of Beatrix Potter characters in her little sister's bedroom.

11. Joanna has never been beaten at chess.

12. Parker edited the yearbooks and they will be available in a few weeks.

13. I bought honey cake for after dinner tonight and I can't wait to eat it!

14. The three main characters in the play constantly bickered, yelled, or argued.

15. Our baseball team holds the season record for most home runs.

Lesson 25
Complex and Compound-Complex Sentences

A **complex sentence** contains a main clause and one or more subordinate clauses.

    MAIN CLAUSE   SUBORDINATE CLAUSE
We read stories by candlelight   when the lights went out.

Do not be confused by the element *the lights went out,* which is a complete sentence. The complete subordinate clause is *when the lights went out,* which cannot stand alone as a sentence.

A **compound-complex sentence** has more than one main clause and one or more subordinate clauses.

    MAIN CLAUSE   SUBORDINATE CLAUSE   MAIN CLAUSE
We were sailing on the lake   when the storm hit,   so we immediately headed for shore.

▶ **Exercise 1** Draw one line under the main clause and two lines under the subordinate clause. Write *C* in the blank if the sentence is complex and *CC* if it is compound-complex.

__C__   Emily laughs heartily whenever she watches a Chevy Chase movie.

_____ **1.** Whenever the road is slippery, drive more cautiously.

_____ **2.** After I heard the bell choir perform, I decided to join it myself, so I signed up the next day.

_____ **3.** Link is leaving next Wednesday if he can take time off from work.

_____ **4.** As long as I have been writing, I don't remember ever seeing a story quite like this one.

_____ **5.** After I had typed the document, I found some misspelled words, so I looked them up and changed them.

_____ **6.** After he spilled chili on his favorite chair, Bruce admitted that he should have sat at the table to eat.

_____ **7.** Although June is a long month, its sunny days can never be long enough.

_____ **8.** Unless I am mistaken, the first door on the left is the entrance to the art room; however, it may be another door farther along.

_____ **9.** We'll go horseback riding tonight if we can be back home before the Pattersons arrive.

_____ **10.** After I had seen that Kenneth Branagh movie (*Henry V*), I was hooked!

_____ **11.** If you hold the door open too long, the alarm will sound.

_____ **12.** So that he could gain control of his time, Arnelle mapped out a weekly schedule.

_____ **13.** If you have never been to the Smithsonian Institution, you may be surprised at its myriad of treasures.

_____ **14.** Mom says that I can't go with you until I get my homework done.

_____ **15.** Elise wants to rent a carpet shampooer so that she can fix up her room before the slumber party.

_____ **16.** When the graduating class gave a talent show, some of the students performed; others, of course, held behind-the-scenes jobs.

_____ **17.** While the clock ticked methodically, the contestant struggled to answer quickly the remaining trivia questions.

_____ **18.** Could I help you with anything so that you can finish on time?

_____ **19.** After the writers' workshop was over, Lila and Glen decided to stop for hamburgers.

_____ **20.** We should tell Graham about the change in assignments before he starts writing his report.

_____ **21.** Here is the spot where I had my accident.

_____ **22.** When Louise and Yvette went shopping at the mall, they walked through many stores, but they never found an appropriate gift.

_____ **23.** Although she is only four feet tall, ten-year-old Bethany can jump over five feet.

_____ **24.** When the elevator stopped between floors, an alarm sounded.

_____ **25.** Although she never hosts any herself, Cin plans parties for a living.

_____ **26.** Whenever Clark has a serious problem, he consults Lois; similarly, Lois shares her troubles with Clark.

_____ **27.** Since that man doesn't look familiar to you, why should he look familiar to me?

_____ **28.** Because our club needs more money, Jack has planned several fund raisers, and he has appointed a committee to review the plans.

_____ **29.** Beth Ann will help us with Kiddie Week if she is allowed to miss some work.

_____ **30.** When the call finally came, Zack was asleep in the den, and no one could find him.

Lesson 26
Adjective Clauses

An **adjective clause** is a subordinate clause that modifies a noun or a pronoun. It usually follows the word it modifies.

I decided to keep for myself the present **that I had bought for Ron's birthday.** (modifies the noun *present*)

She visited Paris, **where she had been born.** (modifies the noun *Paris*)

An adjective clause usually begins with a relative pronoun, although it may also begin with *when* or *where*. Sometimes the introductory word is omitted altogether.

The writing group **she started** meets every Monday evening. (The relative pronoun *that* was omitted.)

RELATIVE PRONOUNS

that	whom	whomever
which	whose	what
who	whoever	whatever

▶ **Exercise 1** Underline each adjective clause. Circle each relative pronoun that is given, and write in the blank those that have been omitted.

_____that_____ The song Mr. Quatman is promoting has beautiful lyrics.

_____ 1. The sweater, which was thick and wooly, kept Margaret warm on her long walk home.

_____ 2. Al decided on a college that was near his hometown.

_____ 3. Would you like to see the spot where the tornado touched down?

_____ 4. They are the kind of books I would like to read again.

_____ 5. The woman whose hat seemed twenty stories high sat a row ahead of me.

_____ 6. Care of the newborn pups, which was Barry's sole responsibility, was a full-time job.

_____ 7. Micah, who spoke to us during halftime, was able to make it to the game after all.

_____ 8. The stereo Judy wants to buy includes a five-disc CD player.

_____ 9. The review sessions the chemistry teacher provided made a big difference.

_____ 10. Was Mr. Farnsworth the representative whom you contacted?

_____ 11. The fish Linda chose was vividly colored black and purple and yellow.

_____ 12. The cabinet Kent built was hung in the industrial arts room.

_____ **13.** The flutist whose solo you applauded is my sister.

_____ **14.** The nest, which looks like a wren's work, rests atop the fuse box.

_____ **15.** Tom looked forward to the day when he could buy a car of his own.

Adjective clauses may be either essential or nonessential. Essential (or restrictive) clauses are necessary to make the meaning of a sentence clear. A clause beginning with *that* is essential. Nonessential (or nonrestrictive) clauses add interesting information but are not necessary for the meaning of a sentence. A clause beginning with *which* is usually nonessential. Use commas to set off nonessential clauses from the rest of the sentence.

Georgia has a talent **that is hard to match.** (essential clause)
My uncle, **who was born in New York,** moved to California when he was twelve. (nonessential clause)

▶ **Exercise 2** **Underline each adjective clause in the sentences below. Write *E* (essential) or *non.* (nonessential) in the space provided to identify the type of clause.**

___E___ Aunt Agatha has a zest for living that few can match.

_____ **1.** Those players who steal bases make baseball fun to watch.

_____ **2.** The trail guide showed us the path that led to a ghost town.

_____ **3.** My brother, who is in the service, writes to me at least once a month.

_____ **4.** Our poster, which is over seven feet tall, hangs just inside the front door of the school.

_____ **5.** The moment when the last winner is announced will be Jordan's cue to return to the stage.

_____ **6.** Are you the person whose car is parked in the loading zone?

_____ **7.** The algebra exam that was scheduled for next Tuesday has been postponed.

_____ **8.** The green and pink teapot, which had been a present from Gail, served as a vase.

_____ **9.** One of the seamstresses who had sewn the bridesmaids' dresses was commissioned to make the bride's gown.

_____ **10.** Swiftly approaching is the moment when the winners are announced.

_____ **11.** The reading club, which met last Thursday, is trying to recruit more members.

_____ **12.** A lone lilac bush, which protruded through the fence, supplied an unexpected splash of color in the alley.

_____ **13.** Tom's role model is Jeeves, the fictional butler who can solve any problem.

_____ **14.** Kim and Kelly went to the restaurant that has tableside musicians.

Lesson 27
Adverb Clauses

An **adverb clause** is a subordinate clause that modifies a verb, an adjective, or an adverb. It is used to tell *when, where, why, how, to what extent,* or *under what conditions.* An adverb clause is usually introduced by a subordinating conjunction.

I cry **whenever I see a sad movie.** (The adverb clause modifies the verb *cry.* It tells when.)

An adverb clause that seems to have missing words is called **elliptical**. The word or words that are left out are understood in the clause.

Steve runs faster **than I** [run].

▶ **Exercise 1 Underline the adverb clause in each sentence.**

When they arrived at Space Camp, the aspiring astronauts grew nervous.

1. After I finished doing the dishes, I helped my dad mow the lawn.

2. The little girl was upset because her puppy was lost.

3. That old house looked spookier than a haunted house in a nightmare would look.

4. Jeremy left for the football game before I could offer him a ride.

5. Jennifer will go on the retreat unless it rains.

6. Dino ran the 100-yard dash much faster than I did.

7. Because the sweaters were on sale, Stuart bought three.

8. Eve was more interested in geography than her brother was.

9. Will you wait in the car until it's time to leave for school?

10. Alex waxed the car until it looked brand new.

11. We met where his street intersects mine.

12. I heard a strange noise when I turned on the computer.

13. While it was snowing outside, Simon was daydreaming about sunny beaches.

14. The band began a food drive so that we could help the hungry.

15. Since she couldn't find an opener, Sandy didn't open the can.

16. Whenever I go to that restaurant, I run into someone from the old days.

17. I dropped my wallet as I was crossing the street.

18. You will see a gas station wherever you look in that city.

19. The crowd roared as the team ran onto the field.

20. We sat in the dark and shivered because the power was out.

21. The charity event would be a success as long as it didn't rain.

22. Whenever we ice-skate, we put on our mittens.

23. He will go away unless you apologize.

24. Wherever we went, we put up flyers announcing the play.

25. If we understood the rules, we would be able to play the game.

26. We walked slowly away from the barking dog, because we weren't sure of its intentions.

27. Because he is a fine athlete, Terry will compete for a scholarship.

28. Tim has been driving everywhere since he got his driver's license.

29. Rosa grew taller than her older sister.

30. While we were on the plane to Hawaii, I dreamed of flying.

31. We rode the bus because the car was being serviced.

32. After Sabine went back to France, we promised to write letters every week.

33. Sean is a better cook than I.

34. You will do well on the essay questions as long as you answer each question completely.

35. Grandpa bought the telescope because my brother loves to look at the stars.

36. I like to exercise soon after I get up each morning.

37. Those chemicals are not dangerous unless they are combined.

38. After they left the theater, John and Kim went out to dinner.

39. Whenever I get a cold, I feel miserable.

40. We will stick to the schedule as long as there are no objections.

41. My muscles ached after I had completed the exercises.

42. Though he was in no immediate danger, we were still concerned.

43. The audience was restless until the performance began.

44. We had a substitute teacher because our regular teacher was ill.

45. Sherry has a heavier southern accent than I have.

Lesson 28
Noun Clauses

A **noun clause** is a subordinate clause that is used as a noun. A noun clause may be used as a subject, a direct object, an object of a preposition, or a predicate nominative.

A noun clause usually begins with one of these words: *how, that, what, whatever, when, where, which, whichever, who, whom, whoever, whose,* or *why.*

direct object
Cindy did not know **where the beakers were kept.**

subject
What makes them different is their ability to change colors to blend with their environment.

▶ **Exercise 1** **Circle each sentence that contains a noun clause.**

(Whenever we choose to leave for the game is fine with them.)

1. The board proposed that all residents be required to recycle.

2. Whatever you choose is fine with me.

3. Mike defended his position on the issue.

4. The community college offers a course in fencing.

5. The teacher predicted how the chemicals might react.

6. Ted should have been at the swim meet an hour ago.

7. The rest of the group arrived later.

8. You may take whichever puppy you want.

9. The raccoons eat whatever they can find.

10. The spilled soda did not stain the carpet.

11. What the majority wants usually becomes the law.

12. Onlookers were disappointed when the shuttle lift-off was delayed.

13. Marla was encouraged to enter her poems in a contest.

14. Many people believe that they can do anything in the world.

15. Melissa thought that her test was marked incorrectly.

16. Whatever we give will be appreciated by the charity.

17. Ethan started his own business at the age of thirteen.

Grammar

Name _____ Class _____ Date _____

18. Your opinion of the show was what I thought, also.

19. The little boy mimicked whatever Kirk did.

20. I did not hear what Brenda said.

▶ **Exercise 2** **Underline the noun clause or clauses in each sentence.**

I do not know <u>which route we take to the cabin.</u>

 1. Sam did not know where the art exhibit was.

 2. I do not know why Tonya chose to go with them instead of us.

 3. I dreamed that I was the president of the United States.

 4. What makes them so special is their ability to see the good in everyone.

 5. When Mom came in with bags of groceries, she was happy for whatever help we could give her.

 6. Historians disagree about why wars start.

 7. Whoever was in charge of that experiment made it easy to understand.

 8. That the boys had nothing in common became apparent.

 9. Brent's patience and understanding were what we appreciated most.

10. Chantal was not interested in what the others wanted to do.

11. Whoever can play the piano will be the first on the list.

12. Kyle always felt that he'd like to live in Australia.

13. Ron said that there were no seats left in the auditorium.

14. Why Jay left the party early was a mystery to everyone.

15. How anyone could dislike homemade bread amazes me!

16. How well the task is done is an important issue.

17. The principal told me that the band show was a great success.

18. Holly's explanation, that she had run out of gas, was true.

19. What we didn't know was that the surprise was waiting for us outside.

20. Florence's goal, that she could be an Olympic champion, was realized.

21. Cheryl hears only what she wants to hear.

22. I cannot understand how this invention works.

23. We gave a ticket to the dress rehearsal to whoever asked for one.

24. What Carl does not realize is that he has a great career ahead of him.

Lesson 29
Kinds of Sentences

A declarative sentence makes a statement and usually ends with a period.

Diet soda is my favorite drink.

An imperative sentence gives a command or makes a request. The subject "you" is understood.

(You) Report any safety violations to the supervisor.

An interrogative sentence asks a question and ends with a question mark.

Are your allergies bothering you?

An exclamatory sentence shows strong or sudden feeling. It ends with an exclamation point.

We won the game!

▶ **Exercise 1** Label each sentence as *dec.* for declarative, *imp.* for imperative, *int.* for interrogative, or *exc.* for exclamatory.

_____imp._____ Always wear eye protection in the laboratory.

_____ 1. The backyard was flooded after the strong rains.

_____ 2. Watch out for the falling rocks!

_____ 3. Is this the place where Lee surrendered?

_____ 4. The spaghetti was cold by the time we sat down to eat.

_____ 5. My glasses were bent after my little sister sat on them.

_____ 6. The drugstore was closed by the time I arrived there.

_____ 7. Don't spill your drink!

_____ 8. My throat was sore after I had my tonsils taken out.

_____ 9. Send a letter to your representative if you have a complaint.

_____ 10. Please wash my white shirt by Monday.

_____ 11. Do you like sugar in your tea?

_____ 12. We've lived in the same house since I was born.

_____ 13. An isosceles triangle has two equal sides.

_____ 14. Have faith in my abilities, and I will do well.

_____ 15. Would you pick up some eggs at the store?

_____ 16. The tent is too small for the whole family to use.

_____ 17. When Tuesday comes, take out the trash.

_____ 18. I won first-chair violin!

_____ 19. Antonio was the best gymnast at the competition.

_____ 20. Remind me to return my library books.

_____ 21. The family that moved in next door is very nice.

_____ 22. Stay away from that wild horse.

_____ 23. Which station do you listen to the most?

_____ 24. Take Mel to see the penguins.

_____ 25. Science fiction has never interested me.

_____ 26. Eduardo always reads the comics first.

_____ 27. Gather your belongings and come with me.

_____ 28. Violin music makes me sleepy.

_____ 29. Lock the door on your way out.

_____ 30. My science textbook had been lost all year.

_____ 31. Linda loves to watch old westerns on television.

_____ 32. Please wear your seat belt in my car.

_____ 33. Stay in the hospital until you feel well.

_____ 34. We saw *The Nutcracker* at the theater downtown.

_____ 35. Hold on to my hand until I can skate by myself.

_____ 36. We played board games until midnight.

_____ 37. Donna grew up on a farm.

_____ 38. Was our team defeated last night?

_____ 39. What will happen if I change my mind?

_____ 40. I can't believe he missed that shot!

_____ 41. Don't touch the freshly painted walls.

_____ 42. Hurry, or we'll be late!

_____ 43. Read all about it in the newspaper today.

_____ 44. The photos made me remember my childhood.

_____ 45. Inform the guidance counselor whenever you need extra help.

Grammar

Lesson 30
Sentence Fragments

A **sentence fragment** is an incomplete sentence. It may lack a subject, a verb, or both. Alternatively, it may be a subordinate clause that cannot stand alone. Correct it by adding the missing phrase or words.

Although the road stops. (fragment)
Although the road stops here, we can travel farther on foot. (sentence)

▶ **Exercise 1** Write *frag.* next to each sentence fragment. Write *S* next to each complete sentence.

frag.   In the event of a disaster.

_____   **1.** Samuel Clemens became one of the best-loved American storytellers.

_____   **2.** Because Misha had an innovative style.

_____   **3.** Works from charcoals to watercolors to pastels.

_____   **4.** Nancy, feeling that her ideas were unpopular, kept them to herself.

_____   **5.** By distancing herself from historians, biographers, and critics.

_____   **6.** In his paintings, David has developed a very individual style.

_____   **7.** A concept that became apparent in 1915.

_____   **8.** I'd like to study at the Art Institute of Chicago or the Arts Students League in New York.

_____   **9.** Willie Stieglitz, a promoter and art exhibitor.

_____ **10.** Come in.

_____ **11.** Whom he later called to apologize.

_____ **12.** Myriads of flowers, some from her well-manicured gardens.

_____ **13.** Appeared in the mid-1920s.

_____ **14.** Many clothing designs have been influenced by the American Southwest landscape.

_____ **15.** Where they first visited in 1995.

_____ **16.** Establishing herself as the authority on short story writing.

_____ **17.** Just give it a tweak and it'll come on.

_____ **18.** Long-stemmed purple irises rising from their beds.

_____ **19.** Her perfume lingered in the air, revealing her recent presence.

<u>frag.</u> **20.** Until we meet again!

▶ **Exercise 2 Tell whether you would add a subject (S), a verb (V), or a main clause (M) to form a complete sentence.**

<u>V</u>   A gaggle of geese honking their displeasure.

_____ **1.** As if he were the team's only athlete.

_____ **2.** Each year thousands of socks lost in dryers around the world.

_____ **3.** How to forget Ginny's parting words.

_____ **4.** Mentioned the risks associated with eating fatty foods.

_____ **5.** A doctor for the emotions.

_____ **6.** Free to the first fifty customers.

_____ **7.** Since I forgot my essay.

_____ **8.** The influence of a large crowd.

_____ **9.** Which appeared in the local paper.

_____ **10.** Officials from the city zoo arriving this afternoon for a special assembly.

_____ **11.** Tried to warn Tisha about taking on too many activities.

_____ **12.** Are living in Alabama near the Space Center.

_____ **13.** A foghorn sounding through the heavy mist.

_____ **14.** Presents an additional opportunity.

_____ **15.** Because I cannot do two things at once.

_____ **16.** An ice cream bar melting in the sun.

_____ **17.** Every year walks in the Merchant's Parade.

_____ **18.** Although I thought I had the bases covered.

_____ **19.** Requires extra time to prepare.

_____ **20.** Sweeping the deck clean.

_____ **21.** Sifts through the leftovers and other trash.

_____ **22.** Mr. Ashby counting the orange crates.

_____ **23.** Grow along the riverbank.

_____ **24.** Hammering for all she's worth.

Lesson 31
Run-on Sentences

A run-on sentence contains two or more complete sentences written as one. To correct a run-on sentence, separate the main clauses with either an end mark, a semicolon, or a comma and a coordinating conjunction.

Incorrect: There was a mistake on our bill, the server took care of it. (two main clauses separated by just a comma)

Incorrect: There was a mistake on our bill the server took care of it. (two main clauses with no punctuation between them)

Correct: There was a mistake on our bill. The server took care of it.

Correct: There was a mistake on our bill; the server took care of it.

Correct: There was a mistake on our bill, but the server took care of it.

▶ **Exercise 1** Write *run-on* next to each run-on sentence.

_____run-on_____   Robert is ready now, please take him to his soccer game.

_____   1. The performance left the audience cold and several asked for a ticket refund.

_____   2. The Pulitzer awards were established by the powerful publisher Joseph Pulitzer.

_____   3. Garnet owned several first-edition books she bought one in a yard sale.

_____   4. A severe financial panic and depression hit the United States in 1837.

_____   5. Do you think rust protection for a new car is worth the added expense?

_____   6. Communication involves sending and receiving information.

_____   7. Wireless TV systems are competing with cable systems and I say it's about time that we have a choice.

_____   8. Scientists from Japan, Italy, and the United States designed the particle accelerator used at the Fermi National Accelerator Laboratory in Illinois.

_____   9. I think we should do something about the overgrown playground on Third Street it presents a danger to the community.

_____ 10. Look at this fossil I bought at the gift shop in the Museum of Natural History.

_____ 11. Have you ever tried floating in ocean water the high salt content acts as a buoy.

_____ 12. Boston's Tremont House, built in the 1800s, is credited by some as the first modern hotel.

_____ 13. Samuel Morse is known for his contribution to telegraphy but did you know that he also was the first U.S. citizen to own a camera, an 1839 daguerreotype from Paris?

_____ **14.** Babe Ruth and Ty Cobb were both inducted into baseball's Hall of Fame in 1936.

_____ **15.** We have fifteen minutes to complete the tests; Howard's class has another hour.

_____ **16.** I have been working on this jacket for two weeks now, and I still have not finished it.

_____ **17.** The Wilsons thoroughly planned their weekend outing and felt comfortable leaving.

_____ **18.** Joan went to the bank Chris waited at home.

_____ **19.** Barbie's dog, a teacup poodle named Susie, bites its nails and hitches rides on top of my foot.

_____ **20.** His smile started as a barely visible upturn in the corners of his mouth and from there grew ever wider.

_____ **21.** Ken checked my addition and he found an error.

_____ **22.** Janice directed several committees at once, the refreshments committee, the elections committee, and the cleanup committee.

_____ **23.** Leaping into the waiting sports car, the movie hero dashed to the rescue.

_____ **24.** Pearl Buck wrote many stories about Chinese life, she did not achieve success until 1931 when *The Good Earth* was published.

_____ **25.** Sharon brought cheesecake to the class reunion, Marla brought brownies.

_____ **26.** A baseball scout showed up unexpectedly at our last home game.

_____ **27.** Mom showed us how to make taffy but she never warned us that it would be a messy process.

_____ **28.** The harassed receptionist worked amid a pile of papers and empty coffee cups.

▶ **Writing Link** **Describe the kind of job you would like to have. Use and punctuate correctly at least two compound sentences in your description.**

_____

_____

_____

_____

_____

_____

_____

_____

_____

Unit 4 **Review**

▶ **Exercise 1** **Label the sentences below with *imp.* for imperative, *int.* for interrogative, *dec.* for declarative, or *exc.* for exclamatory.**

<u> dec. </u>   Kristi's red hair was streaked with gold.

_____   **1.** Leave the details to us.

_____   **2.** What class does Ms. Hargrove teach?

_____   **3.** Does that old vending machine still work?

_____   **4.** Two dogs sat in the window and barked at passersby.

_____   **5.** My attention was arrested by a low, groaning sound.

_____   **6.** That's the silliest thing I've ever heard!

_____   **7.** We're never going to try driving that far again.

_____   **8.** Don't slam the door!

_____   **9.** Drive carefully.

_____ **10.** Could you take this casserole over to Grandma's?

_____ **11.** The ground was moss-covered.

_____ **12.** What do you think about the rule against wearing jeans?

_____ **13.** Bring me some ribbons, and I'll decorate that sweatshirt for you.

_____ **14.** Who ordered a pizza with anchovies?

_____ **15.** Watch out for that car!

_____ **16.** Mr. Greer is my favorite teacher.

_____ **17.** Did you remember to feed the fish this morning?

_____ **18.** Hand me that wrench, please.

_____ **19.** That meal was incredible!

_____ **20.** The wind was blowing stronger; a storm was on its way.

_____ **21.** Allow the plaster fifteen minutes to set.

_____ **22.** What happened to my backpack?

_____ **23.** The impromptu performance drew an enthusiastic crowd.

_____ **24.** Batten down the hatches!

Cumulative Review: Units 1–4

Grammar (sidebar)

▶ **Exercise 1** Draw one line under each simple subject and two lines under each simple predicate. In the blank identify the kind of sentence by writing *dec.* (declarative), *imp.* (imperative), *int.* (interrogative), or *exc.* (exclamatory).

exc.   How cold this <u>winter</u> <u><u>has been</u></u>!

_____ 1. The store sent the customer the wrong package.

_____ 2. Show me your hall pass.

_____ 3. The captain and the crew of the starship *Enterprise* were very experienced.

_____ 4. How much did you pay for that dress?

_____ 5. There is smoke coming from under that door!

_____ 6. Susan went to the library to gather information for her report.

_____ 7. Please don't cut in front of the line.

_____ 8. Does anyone know where his office is located?

_____ 9. Our senator campaigned to become president.

_____ 10. Their new house withstood the hurricane better than the last one.

▶ **Exercise 2** Underline the subordinate clause in each sentence. Write *adj.* (adjective), *adv.* (adverb), or *N* (noun) in the blank to tell what kind of clause it is.

adj.   Students <u>who sing in the choir</u> are dismissed early.

_____ 1. We arrived at the theater after the movie had begun.

_____ 2. My problem is how I can finish this lengthy book in one week.

_____ 3. The stylish woman to whom I spoke is the founder of the local department store.

_____ 4. There will be a quiz after we watch the film on the battles of the Civil War.

_____ 5. Sarah was worried about whether she had made the basketball team.

_____ 6. The realtor who sold us this house designed it himself.

_____ 7. We were fortunate to arrive home before the snowstorm hit.

_____ 8. Shall I wait for you at your locker while you go to the office?

_____ 9. No one could understand what the foreign exchange student was trying to say.

_____ 10. The classical music that Mrs. Griffin likes the best is by Beethoven.

Name _____ Class _____ Date _____

▶ **Exercise 3** **Write *frag.* next to each sentence fragment. Write *S* next to each complete sentence.**

_____frag._____   The towels that Marcia used.

_____   **1.** Elbow grease, elbow grease!

_____   **2.** A lone bird floated high above us.

_____   **3.** Where the other chemicals are stored.

_____   **4.** Until we meet again!

_____   **5.** Whenever you are ready to go.

_____   **6.** Oh, just run of the mill.

_____   **7.** The woman with the big hat.

_____   **8.** The story *Mondays are Murder* by P. L. Rhoades is funny and mysterious.

_____   **9.** If all of us can.

_____ **10.** Gladys is feeling better today.

_____ **11.** The dog went bananas at the sight of a Crispy Treat.

_____ **12.** Said to tell you about it.

_____ **13.** The moon is shining brightly tonight.

_____ **14.** Mom would like to have a van, too.

_____ **15.** The young man sitting alone on the bench.

_____ **16.** Is that a sentence?

_____ **17.** A kind of milky white?

_____ **18.** Long, loose folds of a gossamer material.

_____ **19.** Do they know you are doing this?

_____ **20.** Beside the desk blotter, on the mouse pad.

_____ **21.** Linda's work requires a lot of attention.

_____ **22.** My sister always says, "I don't know anything about it!"

_____ **23.** How are you today, Jenifer?

_____ **24.** Probably didn't listen very closely.

_____ **25.** Under and through it all.

▶ **Exercise 4** **Add a subject, verb, or a main clause to form a complete sentence.** Answers will vary.

Under the rose bush. <u>Under the rose bush lay a broken robin's egg.</u>

_____

_____

1. Was rolling down the sidewalk. _____

_____

_____

2. The children or the bluejay in the tree. _____

_____

_____

3. I think the T'ang dynasty greatest in Chinese history. _____

_____

4. In from the cold weather. _____

_____

5. Located near Lake Huron. _____

_____

_____

6. Fell out of the sack. _____

_____

_____

7. Into the water. _____

_____

_____

8. Next to the mossy boulders. _____

_____

9. Sitting by the statue. _____

_____

10. Until tomorrow. _____

_____

_____

Unit 5: Diagraming Sentences

Lesson 32
Diagraming Simple Sentences

Diagraming is a method of showing the relationship of various words and parts of a sentence to the sentence as a whole. Use the following models as a guide in diagraming simple sentences with adjectives and adverbs, direct objects and indirect objects, object complements, and subject complements.

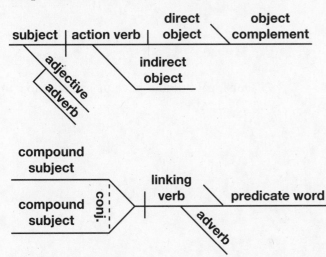

Grammar

▶ **Exercise1 Diagram each sentence.**

1. Tall giraffes stalked the game preserve.

2. The king and queen considered the knight noble.

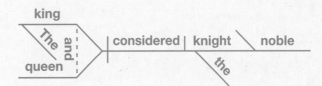

3. The answer was the least obvious choice.

6. The Renaissance was an important era.

4. Her heavy eyelids eventually closed.

7. Our local butcher gave us extra lamb chops.

8. Clara thought the speaker's anecdotes inspiring.

5. The short story was stimulating and melancholy.

Grammar

Lesson 33
Diagraming Simple Sentences with Phrases

Use the following models as a guide in diagraming simple sentences with prepositional phrases, appositives and appositive phrases, participles and participial phrases, gerunds and gerund phrases, infinitives and infinitive phrases, and absolute phrases.

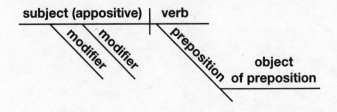

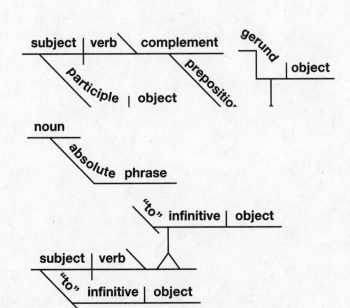

Grammar

▶ **Exercise 1 Diagram each sentence.**

1. Looking sharp, the drill team marched ahead of the band.

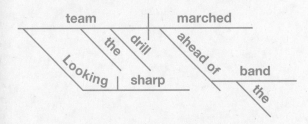

2. Yawning is a good way of stretching the vocal chords.

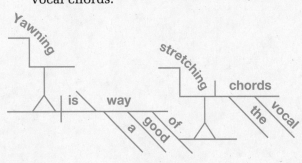

Grammar

3. To cruise across the ocean would be my ideal vacation.

6. The young volunteer, a senior at Chatfield, distributed blankets to the flood victims.

4. Leading the cheers was fun for Ashley.

7. Seeing the congestion on the interstate, I took the freeway.

5. One of the boxes to unpack holds my collection of children's books.

8. My notes having been written, I was ready to make an outline.

Lesson 34
Diagraming Sentences with Clauses

Use the following models as a guide in diagraming compound sentences and complex sentences with adjective, adverb, and noun clauses.

Crop hybridization has been used to improve crop yields, and more grain is being exported world-wide. (compound sentence)

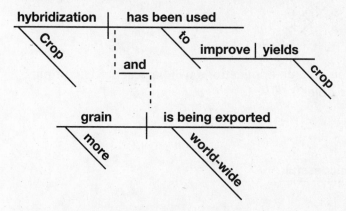

Our mother has a dog that barks constantly. (complex sentence with adjective clause)

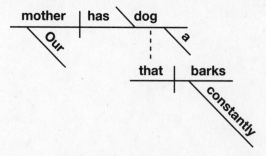

If you want healthy rosebushes, you should apply liquid manure in the spring. (complex sentence with adverb clause)

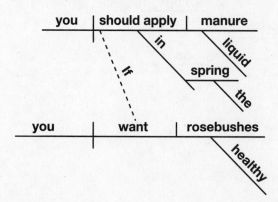

Which of many traits are desirable is an important decision. (complex sentence with noun clause as subject)

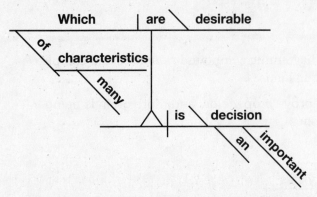

Twelfth-grade students hope that their college applications will be accepted. (complex sentence with noun clauses as direct object)

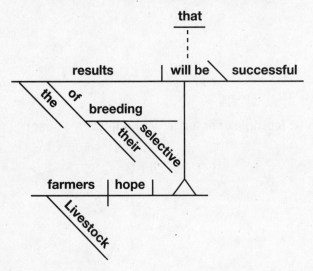

Here is a printout of what we are requesting. (complex sentence with noun clause as object of preposition)

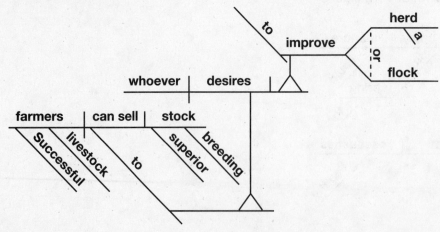

▶ **Exercise 1 Diagram each sentence.**

1. You should choose whomever you want for class president.

2. That Joshua was having to search for the solution made the game more fun.

3. Whenever Miles mows the yard, the lawnmower breaks.

4. Although the votes were already validated, Miles asked for a recount.

5. Give a donation to whoever represents the local church.

7. Not every person who heard the speaker was impressed, but most wanted to hear more.

6. The driver who hit my car did not see me.

8. How we are to sleep tonight is a mystery to me.

✓ Unit 5 **Review**

▶ **Exercise 1 Diagram each sentence.**

1. The student council and the Pep Club elected Scott mascot.

4. Shirley, my oldest cousin, is a ballerina.

2. The last black cloud having disappeared from the sky, the players hurried onto the field.

5. Whether Lily chooses to attend the meeting is important to whoever is in charge.

3. Reacting quickly, Anita darted past the runaway bus.

6. Winning the match means that she will move to the finals.

Cumulative Review: Units 1–5

▶ **Exercise 1** Write *trans.* in the blank if the action verb is transitive or *intr.* if the action verb is intransitive.

<u>trans.</u>   We heaped the stones in a pile by the door.

_____ **1.** The twins sang at the top of their lungs.

_____ **2.** Surely they have investigated the cause of the accident by now.

_____ **3.** I couldn't believe my eyes!

_____ **4.** Where are we going tonight?

_____ **5.** The wind whipped through my too-thin jacket.

_____ **6.** Milan answered the phone with a gruff, "What?"

_____ **7.** Joshua collected the discarded pizza boxes.

_____ **8.** Mrs. Glimsher wrote me a letter about Kyle's broken wrist.

_____ **9.** Mary Lou paints like Picasso.

_____ **10.** Did anyone tell the Mozzels about the block party?

▶ **Exercise 2** Add an adjective clause or an adverb clause to each sentence.

The man had a phone in his car.

The man who talked incessantly had a phone in his car. _____

1. Howard has written a book. _____

_____

_____

_____

2. The lampshade was shaped like a lily. _____

_____

_____

_____

3. The sky was clear. _____

_____

_____

Grammar

4. Why don't we play a board game? _____

_____

_____

_____

5. The hotel lacked all but the barest necessities. _____

_____

_____

_____

6. More people attended this year's home show. _____

_____

_____

_____

7. Joe missed his cue. _____

_____

_____

_____

8. You'll have to replace that pitcher. _____

_____

_____

_____

9. That clarinetist is my sister. _____

_____

_____

_____

10. Someday I'd like to visit Aberdeen, Scotland. _____

_____

_____

_____

Grammar

▶ **Exercise 3** **Read the two italicized sentences. Using these sentences, write at least one example of the word, phrase, or clause described.**

Our general policy is to give the customer whatever she wants.

Thinking of something special that I can do for each of my friends has been fun, but it has taken a lot of my time.

1. possessive pronoun _____

2. adjective _____

3. noun _____

4. linking verb _____

5. infinitive phrase _____

6. gerund phrase _____

7. indirect object _____

8. preposition _____

9. complete subject _____

10. complete predicate _____

_____

11. prepositional phrase _____

12. simple subject _____

13. simple predicate _____

14. infinitive _____

15. adjective clause _____

16. pronoun _____

17. predicate adjective _____

18. noun clause _____

19. conjunction _____

20. direct object _____

21. definite article _____

22. gerund _____

23. indefinite article _____

24. personal pronoun _____

Unit 6: Verb Tenses, Voice, and Mood

Lesson 35
Regular Verbs: Principal Parts

Verbs have four main parts—a base form, a present participle, a simple past, and a past participle. A regular verb forms its past and past participle by adding *–ed* or *–d* to the base form. A verb forms its present participle by adding *–ing* to the base form. Both the present and past participles require a helping verb.

Base Form:	The children **ask** for a snack.
Present Participle:	The children **are asking** for a snack.
Past:	The children **asked** for a snack.
Past Participle:	The children have **asked** for a snack.

▶ **Exercise 1** **Complete each sentence by writing the form of the verb indicated in parentheses.**

We all _____live_____ in the same neighborhood. (base form of *live*)

1. Mr. Ramirez _____ onto our street two years ago. (past of *move*)

2. Sandra is _____ Russian in college. (present participle of *study*)

3. I _____ cello with a youth orchestra. (base form of *play*)

4. The art students are _____ pictures of buildings. (present participle of *sketch*)

5. I _____ for our dog to come home. (past of *yell*)

6. The store manager has _____ prices drastically. (past participle of *slash*)

7. The babies _____ as if they could use naps. (base form of *look*)

8. Dad is _____ spaghetti for dinner tonight. (present participle of *cook*)

9. I _____ to my mother about our spring break plans. (past of *talk*)

10. Tracy has _____ to go camping all summer. (past participle of *want*)

11. We _____ all of our reports on computer disks. (base form of *store*)

12. June is _____ her birthday presents. (present participle of *open*)

13. The Conlans _____ their phone calls while they work. (base form of *screen*)

14. I _____ all morning for my car keys. (past of *search*)

15. Shaun is _____ his collection for the valuable comic book.

    (present participle of *check*)

16. Greg and Chip _____ to dunk basketballs. (base form of *try*)

17. Patsy has _____ the yearbook for us again. (past participle of *edit*)

18. We _____ that school's team last year. (past of *debate*)

19. The Ignatowski family is _____ Boston. (present participle of *visit*)

20. Lola and Tim _____ for new tennis rackets every other spring. (base form of *shop*)

▶ **Exercise 2** **Write the form of the verb indicated.**

past participle of *clean*	cleaned
1. present participle of *post*	_____
2. past of *dry*	_____
3. past participle of *shell*	_____
4. base form of *clip*	_____
5. past participle of *brush*	_____
6. present participle of *donate*	_____
7. past of *stop*	_____
8. past of *dance*	_____
9. base form of *explode*	_____
10. present participle of *wonder*	_____
11. present participle of *pry*	_____
12. past participle of *starve*	_____
13. past of *plant*	_____
14. past participle of *harvest*	_____
15. base form of *work*	_____
16. past participle of *ship*	_____
17. present participle of *allude*	_____
18. past of *drop*	_____
19. past participle of *tick*	_____
20. past of *charge*	_____
21. present participle of *shake*	_____
22. past of *love*	_____
23. present participle of *bend*	_____
24. past participle of *look*	_____

Lesson 36
Irregular Verbs: Principal Parts

Irregular verbs form their past and past participle in ways different from the -ed addition used for regular verbs.

Present participle: He is **shaking** the politician's hand.
Past: The car **shook** at speeds higher than forty miles per hour.
Past participle: We have **shaken** the ingredients as the recipe specified.

PRINCIPAL PARTS OF SOME IRREGULAR VERBS

BASE FORM	PRESENT PARTICIPLE	PAST	PAST PARTICIPLE
teach	teaching	taught	taught
take	taking	took	taken
freeze	freezing	froze	frozen
sing	singing	sang	sung
become	becoming	became	become
grow	growing	grew	grown
burst	bursting	burst	burst
tear	tearing	tore	torn
write	writing	wrote	written
steal	stealing	stole	stolen
swim	swimming	swam	swum
buy	buying	bought	bought
bite	biting	bit	bitten
draw	drawing	drew	drawn
sleep	sleeping	slept	slept
stand	standing	stood	stood

▶ **Exercise 1** Underline the verb form in parentheses that best completes each sentence. Write whether the verb form is a base form, a past, a present participle, or a past participle.

___base form___ The girls (sleeping, sleep) less in the fall than they do in the winter.

_____ **1.** Stanley (drawn, drew) the winning number.

_____ **2.** The nervous juror (cast, casted) the deciding vote.

_____ **3.** The running back (torn, tore) through the defense.

_____ **4.** I have (flown, flew) in an airplane before.

_____ **5.** Elliot has (beat, beaten) enough eggs for the recipe.

_____ **6.** The child (is growing, grown) out of all his clothes.

_____ **7.** Who (chose, choosed) to rent this movie?

_____ 8. Maria (sneaking, sneaked) in through an open window.

_____ 9. The room was dark after I (blown, blew) out the candles.

_____ 10. The biologists have (frozen, froze) those specimens.

_____ 11. On weekends, I (teach, taught) piano and guitar in a local music shop.

_____ 12. Look what the dog (drug, dragged) in.

_____ 13. The boys (ate, eaten) all the pie.

_____ 14. Uncle Fletcher has (climbed, climb) that hill before.

_____ 15. For weeks, we have (knew, known) about the test.

_____ 16. In the second half, the referees (blew, blown) their whistles often.

_____ 17. Nick (runned, ran) for student council.

_____ 18. Monica has (drunk, drank) all the milk.

_____ 19. Annie (got, gotten) a raise after working six months.

_____ 20. I (bursted,) the balloon with a pin.

▶ **Exercise 2 Write in the blank the verb form indicated. Use a dictionary if necessary.**

past participle of *choose* __chosen__

1. past of *dive* _____

2. past participle of *teach* _____

3. past participle of *buy* _____

4. past of *lay* _____

5. past of *pay* _____

6. past participle of *preach* _____

7. past participle of *throw* _____

8. past of *grow* _____

9. past of *tow* _____

10. past participle of *sting* _____

11. past of *ride* _____

12. past of *bite* _____

13. past participle of *decide* _____

14. past of *speak* _____

15. past of *joke* _____

16. past participle of *spend* _____

17. past of *stand* _____

18. past of *snow* _____

19. past participle of *rise* _____

20. past participle of *seek* _____

Lesson 37
Tense of Verbs: Present, Past, and Future

The present tense expresses an action that is repeated, ongoing, or always true. It also expresses an action that is happening now. The present tense and the base form of a verb are the same, except for the third person singular (a singular noun or *he, she,* or *it*), which adds *-s* or *-es.* The verb *be* is an exception to this rule.

I **march** in the band at football games. (repeated action)
Stella **needs** some tape. (right now)
That store **is** on Main Street. (always true)

The past tense expresses an action that has already occurred. In regular verbs the past tense is formed by adding *-ed* to the base form. In irregular verbs the past tense takes a variety of forms. The verb *be* uses two past tense forms—*was* and *were.* The past tense is the same as the past.

Jerry **looked** at the geometry book. (regular)
Wanda **crept** through the dark hallway. (irregular)

The future tense expresses an action that will take place in the future. The future tense is formed by adding *will* or *shall* to the base form.

I **will attend** the game tomorrow afternoon.

▶ **Exercise 1** **Complete each sentence by writing the form of the verb indicated in parentheses.**

Whatever _____became_____ of your poetry project? (past tense of *become*)

1. The band _____ a tape of original songs. (past tense of *release*)

2. The whole team _____ sore after conditioning. (future tense of *feel*)

3. I _____ my favorite shirt on the trip. (past tense of *lose*)

4. Evan _____ to be alone when he studies. (present tense of *prefer*)

5. The dog _____ to stay in the yard. (future tense of *learn*)

6. The soldier _____ the burden of digging a long trench. (past tense of *bear*)

7. The horse _____ across the open field. (past tense of *trot*)

8. The dance troupe _____ the crowd with its performance. (present tense of *stun*)

9. Grandpa _____ his moustache for the wedding. (future tense of *shave*)

10. I almost _____ on the dry bread. (past tense of *choke*)

11. The amusement park always _____ last year's employees. (present tense of *rehire*)

12. The judge who _____ that case has an office downtown. (past tense of *try*)

Name _____ Class _____ Date _____

Grammar

13. Richard _____ a picture of the field hockey team. (past tense of *take*)

14. The turkey buzzards _____ in the barn. (future tense of *roost*)

15. Sandra and Bernice _____ in most school plays. (present tense of *act*)

16. The costumed man _____ his true identity. (past tense of *reveal*)

17. We _____ the Frisbee in the park. (future tense of *fling*)

18. I _____ my sister's hand as we walked through the crowd. (past tense of *hold*)

19. The hospital staff _____ a lot of coffee. (present tense of *consume*)

20. My brother and cousin _____ together at Ohio State. (present tense of *room*)

21. Mom and Dad _____ a deal with the real estate agent. (past tense of *strike*)

22. Alicia _____ us do the laundry. (future tense of *help*)

23. The hunter _____ the rabid beast. (past tense of *slay*)

24. Mr. Bailey _____ the championship game. (future tense of *umpire*)

25. The baby _____ to get what he wants. (present tense of *shriek*)

26. Ahmad _____ the lifesaving class. (future tense of *instruct*)

27. Through binoculars, Nate _____ a deer. (past tense of *spot*)

28. Veronica and Julie _____ steaks to the picnic. (past tense of *bring*)

29. The twins _____ to fool the babysitter. (future tense of *try*)

30. That movie _____ at the theater this week. (present tense of *open*)

31. The bikers _____ over rough mountain terrain. (past tense of *journey*)

32. Before dawn, the baker _____ doughnuts. (present tense of *glaze*)

33. The sun _____ Saturday afternoon. (future tense of *shine*)

34. The thief _____ open the safe. (past tense of *pry*)

35. The lost hikers _____ to the cleared path. (past tense of *retreat*)

36. The class _____ numbers in the raffle. (future tense of *draw*)

37. The famous novelist _____ the spotlight. (present tense of *shun*)

38. The interior decorator _____ the painting. (future tense of *hang*)

39. Don't tell me you _____ the party favors. (past tense of *forget*)

40. You _____ a fine flute player. (present tense of *be*)

Lesson 38
Perfect Tenses: Present, Past, and Future

The present perfect tense is used either to express an action that took place at some indefinite time in the past or to express an action that began in the past and continues in the present. The present perfect tense is formed with the past participle of the verb and the helping verb *has* or *have*. This tense often includes adverb phrases.

We **have met** our new neighbors.

The past perfect tense is used to show that one action in the past began and ended before another action in the past started. The past perfect tense is formed with the past participle of the verb and the helping verb *had*.

We **had eaten** the leftovers before Mom and Dad came home.

The future perfect tense is used to show that one action or condition in the future will begin and end before another event in the future starts. The future perfect tense is formed with the past participle of the verb and the helping verbs *will have.*

By tonight I **will have practiced** that piece several times.

▶ **Exercise 1** Underline each perfect–tense verb. Write whether the tense of the verb is *present perfect, past perfect,* or *future perfect.*

present perfect	I have explored that cave before.
_____	1. Ned has attended three high schools.
_____	2. By summer, I will have learned how to canoe.
_____	3. Before seeing the movie, Jimi had read the book.
_____	4. When we called back, Thea had already left.
_____	5. We will have driven five hundred miles by nightfall.
_____	6. The happy couple has adopted a baby girl.
_____	7. I have worked at the mall since December.
_____	8. Theresa will have finished her chores before the Simpsons arrive.
_____	9. Roone had never chopped wood before.
_____	10. The police had established a checkpoint by nightfall.
_____	11. We will have harvested the crops by October.
_____	12. I have mentioned these concerns of mine before.
_____	13. Mr. Jefferson has worked as an engineer for thirty years.
_____	14. If we win, we will have beaten that team three times.

_____ **15.** I had never received this many birthday gifts before.

_____ **16.** The crew had already laid the foundation for the house.

_____ **17.** I will have known her for ten years this June.

_____ **18.** Chrissie has dyed her hair several different colors.

_____ **19.** Popeye has taken all he can stand.

_____ **20.** By the time you read this, I will have departed.

▶ **Exercise 2** **Complete each sentence by writing the form of the verb indicated in parentheses.**

The cast _____had rehearsed_____ that scene countless times. (past perfect of *rehearse*)

1. Grandpa _____ that land for fifty years. (present perfect of *farm*)

2. The award proved that he _____ a prominent citizen. (past perfect of *become*)

3. By midmorning, the fog _____. (future perfect of *lift*)

4. We were too late; the guest of honor _____. (past perfect of *speak*)

5. Aunt Millie _____ to lend us the car. (present perfect of *agree*)

6. Hopefully, I _____ the lost dog by dusk. (future perfect of *find*)

7. Toria _____ the team in hitting all season. (present perfect of *lead*)

8. We reached South Carolina sooner than I _____. (past perfect of *think*)

9. If he is re-elected, he _____ that office three times. (future perfect of *win*)

10. Grandma _____ two pies for just such an occasion. (past perfect of *freeze*)

11. By the time we get to the bank, Joe _____ all of his money.
    (future perfect of *spend*)

12. Our cat Zippy _____ this house for years. (present perfect of *rule*)

13. The grocer _____ us all these turkeys. (present perfect of *give*)

14. The realtor _____ all the available houses. (future perfect of *show*)

15. Riding all day, my legs _____. (past perfect of *chafe*)

16. _____ he _____ the truth, he wouldn't have lied. (past perfect of *know*)

17. Otis _____ eggs all morning. (present perfect of *fry*)

18. _____ you _____ those old clothes away before the garage sale? (future
    perfect of *throw*)

19. _____ anyone _____ my little brother? (present perfect of *see*)

20. The adversaries _____ their differences aside. (past participle of *put*)

Lesson 39
Tenses of Verbs

In review:

VERB TENSE	EXPRESSES AN ACTION THAT	EXAMPLE
present	is repeated is always true is happening right now	Marta **carves** a miniature horse from a bar of soap.
past	has already occurred	The bird **stood** watch as the worm **crawled** out of its hole.
future	will take place in the future	Sharon **will total** your bill.
present perfect	took place sometime in the past began in the past and is still continuing	That man **has talked** all day!
past perfect	began and ended before another action (both actions in the past)	She **had** already **memorized** the stanza before I finished reading it.
future perfect	will begin and end before another action begins (both actions in the future)	I **will have sailed** to the Caribbean by the time you get this postcard.

▶ **Exercise 1** Draw two lines under each verb. Write the verb tense in the blank.

_____past_____ A group of friends <u>made</u> an important decision yesterday.

_____ **1.** Rocky Mountain National Park is a beautiful vacation spot.

_____ **2.** Many of their friends camp in the Rockies.

_____ **3.** By midnight, they had considered all possible campgrounds.

_____ **4.** At sunrise, they jumped into their cars and all-terrain vehicles.

_____ **5.** Once they were on the road, their thoughts of school and jobs

 had vanished.

_____ **6.** The group had driven five hundred miles by six o'clock that night.

_____ **7.** After a big dinner, Matt and Stephen talked for a while.

_____ **8.** They discussed the terrain and the wildlife of the Rockies.

_____ **9.** At some point, both noticed a trail map in the corner.

_____ **10.** An atmosphere of excitement filled the room.

_____ **11.** The map will be useful tomorrow for the hike.

Grammar

_____ **12.** By dawn, everyone in the group was ready to try the unfamiliar trails.

_____ **13.** Wendi and Beth slung their heavy backpacks over their shoulders.

_____ **14.** All had prepared well for this day.

_____ **15.** Across the sparkling creek and grassy knoll, they walked.

_____ **16.** "This is certainly a beautiful area," said Marlin.

_____ **17.** "You boys are too slow!" said one of the girls.

_____ **18.** After walking most of the afternoon, the group arrived at their campsite.

_____ **19.** They began setting up their tents.

_____ **20.** Once they pound the last stake, they will have built their campsite.

▶ **Exercise 2** **Write in the blank the tense of the verb indicated in parentheses.**

We ___will have ridden___. (future perfect of *ride*)

1. They _____. (future of *play*)
2. She _____. (past of *hear*)
3. We _____. (future perfect of *sing*)
4. It _____. (past perfect of *wobble*)
5. You _____. (present perfect of *shout*)
6. They _____. (future perfect of *play*)
7. I _____. (past of *think*)
8. We _____. (past perfect of *think*)
9. She _____. (present perfect of *write*)
10. She _____. (future of *act*)
11. She _____. (future perfect of *throw*)
12. He _____. (past of *throw*)
13. You _____. (future of *tune*)
14. I _____. (present of *be*)
15. She _____. (future perfect of *speak*)
16. He _____. (present perfect of *travel*)
17. He _____. (present of *run*)

Lesson 40
Verbs: Progressive and Emphatic Forms

Each of the six tenses of a verb has a progressive form that expresses a continuing action. The progressive form uses the present participle of the verb with the appropriate tense of the verb *be.*

Present Progressive	We **are running.**
Past Progressive	We **were running.**
Future Progressive	We **will be running.**
Present Perfect Progressive	We **have been running.**
Past Perfect Progressive	We **had been running.**
Future Perfect Progressive	We **will have been running.**

▶ **Exercise 1** **Write in the blank the verb form indicated in parentheses.**

We ___are singing___ in the choir tomorrow afternoon. (present progressive of *sing*)

1. They _____ about the funny movie they saw last week. (past progressive of *laugh*)

2. Todd _____ on the importance of recycling. (present progressive of *speak*)

3. The cat _____ all night, making it impossible to sleep.

   (past perfect progressive of *meow*)

4. The prince _____ our city sometime next month. (future progressive of *visit*)

5. The heavy rain _____ throughout the long night. (past perfect progressive of *fall*)

6. I certainly hope we _____ not _____ you with the music, Mrs. Philips.

   (past progressive of *disturb*)

7. Mr. Tamaka _____ this afternoon to see if you can paint his porch next week.

   (future progressive of *call*)

8. Talia and I _____ at the contest last night. (past perfect progressive of *dance*)

9. A big toad _____ across our deck. (present progressive of *hop*)

10. The pageantry knights _____ when the thunderstorm broke.

    (past perfect progressive of *joust*)

11. My archery instructor told me how I _____ incorrectly. (present progressive of *aim*)

12. These exercises _____ my physical constitution for the long hike this weekend.

    (present progressive of *fortify*)

13. The detective noticed that one of the suspects _____.

(past progressive of *tremble*)

14. Marvin _____ for a taste of the big pecan pie you made.

(future progressive of *long*)

15. Amy _____ Jean's phone number when the line suddenly went dead.

(past progressive of *dial*)

16. The Morris family _____ for three hours. (future perfect progressive of *fly*)

17. I _____ these boxes for the movers, John. (present progressive of *label*)

18. Those rabbits _____ your garden before you erected that fence.

(past progressive of *destroy*)

19. The big silver blimp _____ over the football stadium. (future progressive of *circle*)

20. I _____ to the premiere when the tire started making a hissing sound.

(past perfect progressive of *hurry*)

The emphatic form adds emphasis to the verb. It uses a form of the verb *do*.

Present Emphatic	We **do believe** the umpire made the wrong call.
	Sam **does listen** to that music group.
Past Emphatic	Well, they **did ask** us to the party after all.

▶ Exercise 2 **Write in the blank the emphatic form of the verb in parentheses.**

She ___does like___ those colorful, noisy birds that she keeps. (*like,* present emphatic)

1. You _____ a lot about your vacation plans, Searas. (*talk,* present emphatic)

2. They _____ the actual truth about what Edward said. (*suppress,* past emphatic)

3. Karl and Marilyn _____ from one diet to another. (*switch,* past emphatic)

4. The cheerleaders _____ a lot of energy, don't they? (*show,* present emphatic)

5. Gee, Ted _____ that game himself. (*program,* past emphatic)

6. Betty, you _____ all the way to Centerville last week. (*bicycle,* past emphatic)

7. Terri _____ on the piano now and then. (*perform,* present emphatic)

8. Chin _____ the Jensens' garden. (*weed,* past emphatic)

Lesson 41
Verbs: Compatibility of Tenses

Grammar

When two or more events take place at the same time in a sentence, the verb tenses must remain the same.

Incorrect: When April **appeared** in the doorway, she **gives** me a start.

This sentence is incorrect because while both events in the sentence took place in the past, the tense changes from past to present.

Correct: When April **appeared** in the doorway, she **gave** me a start.

Sometimes one event occurs before or after another event in a sentence. In these cases it is appropriate to shift tenses.

Incorrect: By the time Carlene **arrived**, Jason **walked** by.

This sentence is incorrect because the verbs are both past-tense forms and suggest that the two events took place at the same time.

Correct: By the time Carlene **arrived**, Jason **had walked** by.

Here the tense shifts from past (*arrived*) to past perfect (*had walked*) to show that Jason had walked by before Carlene arrived.

▶ **Exercise 1** **Write *C* in the blank before each sentence that contains compatible verb tenses.**

___C___   Lenny loved baseball, so he decided to read about it.

_____ 1. James loved college, but likes working, too.

_____ 2. She will have watched the children when she went to the park.

_____ 3. As the choir sang, the audience applauded several times.

_____ 4. The sun had already set by the time they started to eat.

_____ 5. The weather was nice today, so we play.

_____ 6. Julie arrived later and had turned off the radio.

_____ 7. The girls washed their cars while the guys painted the signs.

_____ 8. The dog barked while it has run through the door.

_____ 9. Melissa had left the room by the time Ryan started telling his jokes.

_____ 10. The snake hid under a rock while it sleeps.

_____ 11. The new band plays loudly and never made a mistake.

_____ 12. My mother made ice cream and asked me to try it.

Grammar

_____ 13. You will have eaten the cake by the time I arrive.

_____ 14. The cat sleeps on the chair while the dog prowled around the room.

_____ 15. Never go outside if the lightning had been severe.

_____ 16. While Vicki answered the phone, Robert opened the door.

_____ 17. Because Thomas had been running, he was hot.

_____ 18. The girls listened to the radio while it rains.

_____ 19. I will ignore the noise if you will ignore my mess.

_____ 20. Concerts are good if they started on time.

▶ **Exercise 2** **Write in the blank the correct tense of the verb given in parentheses.**

We stopped by your apartment, but you _____were_____ not home. (*be*)

1. Robert saw me, and he _____. (*wave*)

2. Beth _____ by the time William arrived. (*leave*)

3. Tracy found some antiques when she _____ her grandmother's house. (*visit*)

4. Whenever I stop by your house, you _____ never there. (*be*)

5. Once she sings the last song, she _____ for two hours. (*sing*)

6. Bobbi accepted the job when the manager _____ it to her. (*offer*)

7. We were planning to leave, but Kevin _____ us to wait. (*tell*)

8. She _____ for the earrings every day this week. (*look*)

9. While moving the piano yesterday, the movers _____ over a lamp. (*knock*)

10. I didn't know that you _____ at the assembly last week. (*speak*)

11. By the end of the show, the crowd _____. (*leave*)

12. Lisa studies every night, so I know she _____ the test. (*pass*)

13. I know that you like this group, so I _____ their album for you. (*buy*)

14. They _____ all their money before the fair closes. (*spend*)

15. Bryan _____ for his wallet in five places before he found it. (*look*)

16. By the time the tomatoes are ripe, the insects _____ them. (*eat*)

17. Buds are on the trees, so spring _____ on the way. (*be*)

18. The game was exciting, but the rain _____ our vision. (*obstruct*)

19. Patti was tired, so she _____ a nap. (*take*)

20. Because you don't understand computers, I _____ them to you. (*explain*)

Lesson 42
Voice of Verbs

Action verbs can be in the active voice or in the passive voice. A sentence has a verb in the active voice when the subject performs the action. A verb is in the passive voice when the action is performed on the subject. Although the passive voice can give variety to your writing, the active voice is more interesting and more direct than the passive voice, which makes for livelier writing. Form the passive voice by using the past participle of the verb with a form of the helping verb *be*.

Mr. Carter **played** the piano solo. (active voice)
The piano solo **was played** by Mr. Carter. (passive voice)

▶ **Exercise 1** Draw two lines under each verb or verb phrase. Write *A* above the verb if it is active and *P* if it is passive.

       P   A

We <u><u>were amazed</u></u> that our choir <u><u>won</u></u> first place.

1. The play will be performed by a local company.

2. The system software was updated last year.

3. He served the ball hard, but it was returned even harder.

4. The winning essay was written by a freshman.

5. The mail was delivered late because of the snowstorm.

6. Sharon's earrings were lost, but her English teacher found them.

7. Rafael planted his garden with the seeds he was given.

8. The charcoal for the barbecue was supplied by the park rangers.

9. The President threw the ceremonial first pitch of the World Series.

10. Zina would have been injured if she had climbed that cliff.

11. The basketball player was fouled, so he shot two free throws.

12. The Student Council meeting was held in the school auditorium.

13. Neal loves potato pancakes, but he never makes them himself.

14. Mi-Ling will paint houses as part of her community service project.

15. Dad repaired our fence after it was damaged by the strong winds.

16. Whales are being killed by hunters, so tougher laws are needed.

17. Tricia's house was filled with smoke, but not a sound came from her smoke detector.

18. Alexander Calder is known for his mobiles that move when they are pushed by the air.

19. Nutritionists study and develop new foods, such as those that are used by astronauts.

20. I lent my new CD to a friend, but it has not been returned.

▶ **Exercise 2** **Rewrite each active-voice sentence in the passive voice and each passive-voice sentence in the active voice.**

The book was read by everyone in the class. ___Everyone in the class read the book.___

1. The national anthem was sung by the school choir. _____

2. We drove the noisy car to the muffler shop. _____

3. Taro was puzzled by the meaning of the last scene. _____

4. Juan shut the window suddenly. _____

5. Did the cardinal endure the severe winter? _____

6. The coach will give the team a lecture after the match. _____

   _____

7. Reiko won the door prize at the dance. _____

8. The precious jewels were recovered by the police. _____

9. The prom decorations were chosen by the committee. _____

10. My parents gave me a treadmill for my birthday. _____

   _____

11. The ranchers had not noticed the runaway colt. _____

   _____

12. Chopin wrote sonatas, scherzos, mazurkas, and waltzes. _____

   _____

13. Water is not drunk by koala bears. _____

14. Our picture was taken by a photographer. _____

15. In New York City, Thanksgiving Day is marked by a big parade. _____

   _____

Grammar

Lesson 43
Mood of Verbs

Verbs express one of three moods—the indicative mood, the imperative mood, or the subjunctive mood.

The **indicative mood** makes a statement or asks a question. This is the mood most often used.

Ron **told** Sarah the news.

The **imperative mood** expresses a command or makes a request.

Tell Sarah the news, Ron.

The **subjunctive mood** is used mainly in formal English. It is used to express a demand, a recommendation, a suggestion, or a statement of necessity.

Ace recommended that the minutes **be** accepted. (*be* instead of *am, is,* or *are*)

The subjunctive mood may also be used to state a condition or a wish that is contrary to fact.

If he **were** sure of his facts, he would sign the affidavit. (*were* instead of *was*)

▶ **Exercise 1** Write *ind.* in the blank if the verb in italics is indicative, *imp.* if it is imperative, or *subj.* if it is subjunctive.

<u>ind.</u>   Steve *sold* his old car to Frances.

_____ **1.** Alexandra *said* she did believe the story after all.

_____ **2.** It is important that Carlos *speak* to Jane immediately.

_____ **3.** *Hold* that bolt securely.

_____ **5.** The artist *sculpted* a wonderful likeness of her mother.

_____ **6.** If only I *were* able to go with you to the Isle of Rhodes, I'd be happy.

_____ **7.** It is necessary that Don *be* here for the presentation.

_____ **8.** When will Hernando *report* on the charity collection?

_____ **9.** They wished she *were* on her way already.

_____ **10.** *Call* Muhammad and explain why the party was canceled.

_____ **11.** If he *were* to try it again, he might be successful.

_____ **12.** *Did* Scott *write* that story or did Brent?

_____ **13.** *Make* another one, and bake it according to the directions.

Name _____ Class _____ Date _____

_____ **14.** Katherine wishes she *were* here for the birthday celebration, Dad.

_____ **15.** I suggest he *rethink* that idea.

▶ **Exercise 2** **Complete each sentence with the indicative, imperative, or subjunctive form of the verb in parentheses.**

_____Display_____ your handiwork, Martha. (imperative of *display*)

1. If I _____ able, I would certainly attend the gathering. (subjunctive of *be*)

2. I suggest she _____ this new novel by my favorite author. (subjunctive of *read*)

3. Your new mower _____ you a lot of time, Ray. (indicative of *save*)

4. Angie _____ that movie about the rainforest. (indicative of *see*)

5. Try to write him a letter, Matt; he _____ one to you. (indicative of *write*)

6. It is crucial that you _____ here for the reception, Alsonso.
   (subjunctive of *be*)

7. _____ these books back on the shelf where they belong, Anna.
   (imperative of *place*)

8. Axel wishes he _____ more fluent in English than he actually is.
   (subjunctive of *be*)

9. The children _____ happily on the swings in the park. (indicative of *play*)

10. Her picture _____ on the mantle right next to the trophy. (indicative of *sit*)

11. If he _____ more hardworking, he might be successful. (subjunctive of *be*)

12. _____ one for your little brother, Edith. (imperative of *buy*)

13. The glider _____ easily, directed with a steady hand by Marcus.
    (indicative of *land*)

14. Elaine wishes she _____ in Florida. (subjunctive of *be*)

15. I am sorry if I _____ you, Uncle John. (indicative of *disturb*)

148 *Grammar and Language Workbook, Grade 12*

Unit 6 Review

▶ **Exercise 1** Draw two lines under each verb or verb phrase. Then write the verb tense in the blank before each sentence.

<u>present perfect</u>   Lance has thoroughly analyzed the steps of applying for admission to college.

_____   1. The reunion had disbanded by the time we found the park.

_____   2. Tanny turned to me and mumbled something inaudible.

_____   3. If you look to the left, you will see the Southern Cross constellation.

_____   4. Shannon will finish her painting in time for next week's art show.

_____   5. Voters questioned the mayoral candidates about the proposed waste-water treatment plant.

_____   6. The physics class is studying the flight ability of eagles.

_____   7. We have been leaving cat food by the back door to feed the strays.

_____   8. Our janitor was hoping for a trouble-free weekend.

_____   9. In another hour, she will have been biking long enough to secure the record.

_____   10. Chip will have written forty pages by Saturday.

_____   11. Hugh did see the comet discovered by the Russian astronomer.

_____   12. I will be eating breakfast in Oslo next week.

_____   13. My cousin Beth attends college in Sweden.

_____   14. Rochelle will arrange the bouquets for her brother Wayne's wedding.

_____   15. My friend Gloria does like to play practical jokes.

_____   16. Preparations for the come-as-you-are party had taken nearly an hour.

Grammar

Cumulative Review: Units 1–6

▶ **Exercise 1** Underline the simple subject. Identify the verbal or verbal phrase in each sentence by placing brackets ([ ]) around it. In the blank, write whether the verbal is a gerund, a participle, or an infinitive.

_____infinitive_____   The merry <u>carolers</u> tried [to sing together.]

_____   **1.** Reading the comics is one of Kevin's favorite pastimes.

_____   **2.** The heavy snowfall buried the abandoned truck.

_____   **3.** A man carrying a dozen red roses walked into Miss Carter's

     classroom.

_____   **4.** Many stuntmen were used in making this movie.

_____   **5.** Li Cheng forgot to register for the computer class.

_____   **6.** They hiked along the trail, over decaying logs

     and snarled underbrush.

_____   **7.** I saw many wildflowers growing along the country lanes.

_____   **8.** Skiing is anexciting winter sport.

_____   **9.** It takes courage to admit our mistakes.

_____   **10.** Aisha tried to wait patiently for the phone call.

_____   **11.** The best place for running is the Olentangy bike trail.

_____   **12.** Julie's brother is good at designing video games.

_____   **13.** We achieved a victory by scoring a basket in the last minute.

_____   **14.** The tuxedo was too expensive to buy.

_____   **15.** Peg woke to the aroma of frying bacon.

_____   **16.** Speaking before a large group isn't easy for many people.

_____   **17.** My mother insisted on returning the damaged goods.

_____   **18.** The homeless man discovered the deserted warehouse.

_____   **19.** The dream of the Wright brothers was to build the first successful

     airplane.

_____   **20.** The raging wind knocked down power lines and tree limbs.

▶ **Exercise 2** Label each participle *part.*, each gerund *ger.*, and each infinitive *inf.* Then write whether the sentence is *simple, compound, complex,* or *compound-complex.*

                                                                      inf

_____**complex**_____ Although I've always wanted to see Switzerland, I've never yet been there.

_____ 1. All those who wish to compete should gather by the judges' table.

_____ 2. Stretching warms Truman's muscles, and running strengthens them.

_____ 3. Rappelling is my favorite pastime in the summer.

_____ 4. Nita wants to be a singer, so she will study voice in college.

_____ 5. As the train pulled out of the station, Roberto took his seat, and his fidgeting younger brother walked up and down the aisle.

_____ 6. Unless it begins to snow, the ski resort will not be able to open.

_____ 7. The bell may ring, or the irritating buzzer may sound when time has expired.

_____ 8. We will hike to Mt. Healthy Park to do our stargazing.

_____ 9. If the weather is clear, Millicent will devote herself to gardening.

_____ 10. The glittering guests ascended the stairs to the awards ceremony.

_____ 11. Although Tammy studies acting, her sister studies voice.

_____ 12. Geoff's desire to win was great, yet he skipped practice for two days.

_____ 13. Helga was worried, but she did not want the frightened child to know it.

_____ 14. The flight that Ruth and Oliver wanted to take was canceled.

_____ 15. A pulsating beat accompanied the melody as Mike played the new song he had composed.

_____ 16. Since Jacques knows how to get to my house, he can bring Susan, and I will bring Kim.

_____ 17. Swimming can be a relaxing activity.

_____ 18. You need to decide what should be done, and we need to find willing helpers.

Name _____ Class _____ Date _____

▶ **Exercise 3** **Draw two lines under the verb or verb phrase in each sentence. Then write the tense of the verb.**

_____future_____ This little device will save us a bundle!

_____ 1. By next Sunday I will have worked four weekends in a row.

_____ 2. They have filled the major potholes on Main Street.

_____ 3. A good choice for your assistant is Ellen.

_____ 4. The speaker droned on endlessly about his trip to the Australian Outback.

_____ 5. My first book has already received some good reviews.

_____ 6. The streets were almost empty before rush hour.

_____ 7. Christy gave Stella an abalone-covered watchband.

_____ 8. His sudden appearance had startled me badly.

_____ 9. Martin Luther King Jr. spoke eloquently against violence as a means of change.

_____ 10. The marching band and the football team will travel in different buses to the game.

_____ 11. Suki has seen several lunar eclipses.

_____ 12. Lee takes pictures for the yearbook.

_____ 13. The tape is in the top drawer.

_____ 14. By ten o'clock I will have landed in New Guinea.

_____ 15. This is the employee who will replace Mr. Rogers.

_____ 16. By yesterday evening I had written thirteen letters of application for a summer job.

_____ 17. The caricaturist at the state fair drew a funny portrait of my family.

_____ 18. I have given you all I know on the subject.

_____ 19. Katrina scoffed at the ridiculous story.

_____ 20. The infielder has dropped the ball again.

_____ 21. Sonja types 120 words per minute!

_____ 22. Within an hour the rocket will have splashed down in the Pacific.

Unit 7: Subject-Verb Agreement

Lesson 44

Subject-Verb Agreement

A verb must agree with its subject in person and number. Most verbs change form to indicate agreement only in the present tense. For a third person singular subject an -*s* (or -*es*) is added to the base verb. The linking verb *be* changes form in both the present and the past tense. When *be, have,* and *do* are used as auxiliaries in verb phrases, their form changes to show agreement with third-person subjects.

SINGULAR	PLURAL
He **paints**.	They **paint**.
She **is** happy.	They **are** happy.
She **was** joyful.	They **were** joyful.
He **has** volunteered.	They **have** volunteered.
It **does** function.	They **do** function.

▶ **Exercise 1 Draw one line under the simple subject of each sentence and two lines under the verb in parentheses that agrees with the subject.**

Over lunch, <u>Celeste</u> (<u><u>tells</u></u>, tell) us about her trip to New Zealand.

1. I (knows, know) little about the country.

2. Celeste (explains, explain) that it consists of two main islands and several smaller ones.

3. New Zealand (is, are) slightly smaller than the state of Colorado.

4. Celeste's family (visits, visit) Wellington, the capital of the country, as well as Auckland, the largest city in New Zealand.

5. Though the temperature is mild most of the year, summer weather (remains, remain) the best.

6. In the summer, New Zealand (enjoys, enjoy) long periods of bright sunshine.

7. Celeste's parents (insists, insist) they have never seen such bright sunshine before.

8. Her sisters (admires, admire) the rolling green hills and evergreen forests.

9. During their visit, they (discovers, discover) that the population is quite diverse.

10. The majority (traces, trace) their roots to Europe, but there are also significant numbers of persons from Polynesia, China, and India.

11. Most persons (speaks, speak) English, although some speak Samoan.

Grammar

12. Immigrants generally (adopts, adopt) the European lifestyle, but Celeste's family observed some traditional customs of the Pacific Islanders who have settled in New Zealand.

13. Celeste (learns, learn) that short-story writer Katherine Mansfield and poet R.A.K. Mason lived and worked here.

14. Professional theatre groups (thrives, thrive) in the larger cities, particularly the Downstage in Wellington and the Mercury Theatre in Auckland.

15. Celeste (was, were) able to see a play and an opera during her visit.

16. Now she (realizes, realize) what an interesting country New Zealand is.

▶ **Exercise 2** **Write in the blank the form of the verb in parentheses that agrees with the subject.**

Planning a vacation _____requires_____ patience and organization. (*require*)

1. With so many fascinating places to visit, choosing a destination _____ difficult. (*become*)

2. Even after a person decides where to go, he or she _____ much work to do. (*have*)

3. A traveler _____ a plane reservation, a hotel reservation, and sometimes a reservation for a rental car. (*make*)

4. If the traveler intends to stay in more than one city, additional reservations _____ necessary. (*be*)

5. Sometimes travelers _____ the knowledge or skill to get the best accommodations. (*lack*)

6. This is one of the reasons many persons _____ travel agencies. (*use*)

7. A travel agent _____ everything, often arranging for the best rates available. (*schedule*)

8. Even so, many decisions _____ to be made by the individual who is taking the trip. (*need*)

9. How one travels _____ his or her enjoyment of the vacation. (*affect*)

10. Careful plans _____ to fun trips. (*lead*)

Lesson 45
Subject-Verb Agreement and Intervening Prepositional Phrases

The subject of a sentence never appears within a prepositional phrase. Be sure that the verb agrees with the actual subject of the sentence and not with the object of a preposition.

The **gifts** on the table **are** for Maria.

In the sentence above, the verb *are* agrees with the subject, *gifts,* not the object of the preposition *table.*

▶ **Exercise 1 Place a check (✔) in the blank in front of each sentence in which the subject and verb agree.**

_____✔_____ The flowers in Tammy's garden bloom each spring.

_____ 1. The suitcase under my bed is filled with old clothes.

_____ 2. A student ahead of Rodney announce today's lunch choices.

_____ 3. Celebrations during the holiday includes caroling, exchanging gifts, and sharing meals with friends.

_____ 4. The trinket inside the box is a silver locket.

_____ 5. The building opposite this one contain a superb library.

_____ 6. A program about new technology airs on television tonight.

_____ 7. The message throughout all the speeches was to take responsibility for one's actions.

_____ 8. Letters to the editor appear daily in nearly every newspaper.

_____ 9. A bill regarding hazardous wastes sit in a committee.

_____ 10. Weeds near the lake ruins the view.

_____ 11. The crowd outside these two movie theaters grows larger every evening.

_____ 12. A speech for the bride and groom come from the best man.

_____ 13. The wait, pending the conclusion of both investigations, feels endless.

_____ 14. The locks on this door are easy to operate.

_____ 15. A traffic light in front of steady streams of traffic keep the movement of vehicles under control.

_____ 16. The sidewalk around these parks need to be replaced.

▶ Exercise 2 **Draw two lines under the verb in parentheses that agrees with the subject.**

Jewels like that sapphire (fills, <u>fill</u>) the store window.

1. Directions to Atlanta (is, are) available at the information desk.

2. Apple pie with vanilla ice cream (appears, appear) to be today's dessert special.

3. Bouquets of white orchids (decorates, decorate) each table.

4. The song after this one always (soothes, soothe) Kelly's nerves.

5. Louis instead of Carl (plays, play) the role of the "ragpicker" during the matinees.

6. Opinions toward the new policy (vary, varies) greatly.

7. A message from Mom (was, were) on the answering machine when I returned home.

8. Each entry within the guidelines (receives, receive) a thorough reading.

9. The closet below the stairs (holds, hold) all of our party supplies.

10. Clothes by Eileen (looks, look) especially attractive at the student design show.

11. Questions as to media availability (is, are) directed to the press secretary.

12. Events after the Civil War (is, are) covered in a separate history course.

13. A sudden light out of the darkness (startles, startle) the explorers.

14. Results, according to this poll, (shows, show) the incumbent with a comfortable lead.

15. The members across the aisle (believes, believe) a different approach would work better.

16. Players like Frank (practices, practice) long hours and achieve great success.

17. Issues concerning compatibility (is, are) discussed on page 342.

18. Artists with finesse (follows, follow) their inner muses.

19. Talking during movies (disrupts, disrupt) viewers' pleasure.

20. A treasure at the bottom of the sea (awaits, await) the search party.

▶ Writing Link **Write a few sentences describing your favorite hobby. Use at least two subjects modified by prepositional phrases. Be sure the verbs agree with the subjects.**

_____

_____

_____

_____

_____

_____

Lesson 46
Subject-Verb Agreement and Linking Verbs

In sentences with linking verbs, the verb agrees with the subject, not the predicate nominative. Do not be confused by a predicate nominative that is different in number from the subject. Only the subject affects the number of the linking verb.

The first prize **was** season tickets to the symphony.
Players **become** a team when they learn to work together.

▶ **Exercise 1** **Draw two lines under the verb in parentheses that agrees with the subject.**

The cost of the reception (<u>was</u>, were) thousands of dollars.

1. Crashing cymbals (becomes, become) the climax of the musical composition.

2. Biographies (is, are) Mom's favorite type of reading material.

3. Grandfather's farms (is, are) a quiet retreat for the entire family.

4. The constellation the Big Dipper (is, are) becoming the Big Spatula.

5. The dinner menu (was, were) several tempting entrées and nearly a dozen side dishes, appetizers, and desserts.

6. Our vacation (is, are) four days and three nights at a luxurious resort.

7. The cliffs overlooking the blue sea (seems, seem) a perfect spot to paint.

8. The banner (is, are) several sheets of paper fastened together.

9. Mary's morning journey (was, were) leisurely rambles to and from the antique stores.

10. The highlight of the celebration (remains, remain) the fireworks.

11. New television programs (is, are) the topic of this press conference.

12. The piled coats (was, were) an ideal hiding place for my cat Sophy.

13. These pearls (appears, appear) to be one of Aunt Alicia's heirlooms.

14. Balloon rides (becomes, become) a popular attraction when the weather is clear and dry.

15. Jonathan's correspondence (is, are) two postcards and an unfinished letter.

16. Samantha's agenda (seems, seem) a series of disconnected ideas.

17. Jerome's notes (is, are) a neatly organized narrative.

18. The best part of the play (was, were) the chase scenes.

19. Four of the five songs (becomes, become) a beautiful medley when they are sung in sequence.

20. Three games (remains, remain) a complete set.

Name _____ Class _____ Date _____

▶ **Exercise 2** **Write in the blank the linking verb in parentheses that agrees with the subject of each sentence.**

Tulips _____ *are* _____ the centerpiece of the spring garden. (is, are)

1. Sighs _____ the first signal that Carmen is bored. (is, are)

2. A dark forest _____ actually several pieces of painted cardboard placed at the back of the stage. (was, were)

3. Tony's unusual dream _____ disjointed images when he describes it. (becomes, become)

4. Morning chores _____ a determined effort to finish quickly. (becomes, become)

5. The amusing story _____ more unbelievable coincidences than I have ever heard put into one tale. (is, are)

6. Maria's supposedly astounding revelations _____ merely a repetition of her plan for the wedding. (was, were)

7. The horses _____ a gentle herd roaming the countryside. (seems, seem)

8. This collection _____ the best short stories I have ever read. (remains, remain)

9. The art gallery festival _____ really several separate parties with very little in common. (is, are)

10. Don's restaurant guide _____ listings of the most reasonably priced and most enjoyable eateries in the city. (is, are)

11. The show soon _____ individual acts rather than one entertainment. (becomes, become)

12. Presents placed under the tree _____ a reminder that the holidays were approaching. (was, were)

13. Ideas for improving service _____ a study guide for employees. (becomes, become)

14. Phone calls _____ a great way to keep in touch with friends who live far away. (seems, seem)

15. The birds' songs _____ a cheerful chorus outside my window. (is, are)

16. Their special evening _____ two rounds of miniature golf. (was, were)

17. The detective's first clue _____ the muddy footprints on the thick white carpet. (is, are)

18. Tutoring sessions _____ Tyler's best chance to master trigonometry. (appears, appear)

158 *Grammar and Language Workbook, Grade 12*

Lesson 47

Subject-Verb Agreement in Inverted Sentences

Grammar

An inverted sentence is a sentence in which the subject follows the verb. Some inverted sentences begin with *there* or *here.* Look for the subject after the verb, and be sure it agrees with the verb in number.

Over the mantelpiece **hangs** a **portrait** of Lucinda.
There **reside two** of the kindest persons in the neighborhood.

When an interrogative sentence contains an auxiliary verb, the auxiliary verb usually precedes the subject, and the main verb follows the subject.

Does the play **begin** at eight o'clock?

▶ **Exercise 1** **Place a check (✔) in the blank in front of each sentence in which the subject and verb agree.**

__✔__   Do these cameras have film in them?

_____ 1. Has Jennifer seen the new art exhibit?

_____ 2. Under the couch lie the other shoe.

_____ 3. On the shelf sit several valuable first-edition books.

_____ 4. Here are Kacy's chess set.

_____ 5. Does the parade pass this corner?

_____ 6. Above the horizon shine distant stars.

_____ 7. Across Sherman Avenue are the Martins' house.

_____ 8. There is the two final contestants.

_____ 9. Inside the card were a picture of the entire family.

_____ 10. Over the river stretches a beautiful new bridge.

_____ 11. Do the presents belong on the big table or the smaller one?

_____ 12. Below the surface of the water swims many colorful fish.

_____ 13. Has Loretta baked the cake yet?

_____ 14. Through the forest dance mythical creatures in that story.

_____ 15. Here is your slippers.

_____ 16. Do Charles always arrive late?

_____ 17. Under her pillow was the little girl's favorite book.

_____ **18.** On each table are a lovely floral arrangement.

_____ **19.** There sit two of the laziest dogs in the neighborhood.

_____ **20.** Have the movers loaded everything into the van?

▶ **Exercise 2** **Draw two lines under the verb in parentheses that agrees with the subject.**

Ahead of us (drives, <u>drive</u>) Carlos and Michelle.

1. (Does, Do) the players warm up before the national anthem is sung?

2. Here (is, are) everything you need to make chicken parmigiana.

3. Through the rain (trudges, trudge) the weary travelers.

4. Across the threshold (sweeps, sweep) the royal couple.

5. (Has, Have) the customers seen our newest product?

6. There (lies, lie) Julia's prize rosebush.

7. Over the noise (sounds, sound) the dinner gong.

8. Into the arena (marches, march) the Olympic athletes.

9. (Is, Are) the Rodriguezes coming to the picnic?

10. On top of the refrigerator (sits, sit) the box of doughnuts.

11. From the back of the room (comes, come) a shout of joy.

12. Here (begins, begin) a fascinating story.

13. (Do, Does) the yogurt shop sell fat-free yogurt?

14. Beside the prima ballerina (dances, dance) several members of the chorus.

15. Between the two pillars (is, are) a knob that opens the secret compartment.

16. Under the canopy of stars (ambles, amble) Tina and Tom.

17. Through the window (glows, glow) soft candlelight.

18. There (rests, rest) two sleepy children.

▶ **Writing Link** **Write a question you would like to ask a celebrity. Be sure the verb agrees with its subject.**

_____

_____

_____

_____

Lesson 48
Subject-Verb Agreement with Special Subjects

A collective noun names a group. A collective noun is considered singular when it refers to a group as a whole; it is considered plural when it refers to each member of the group individually.

The **committee sponsors** an essay contest every year. (singular)
The **committee disagree** about how to divide the funds. (plural)

Certain nouns that end in -s, such as *mathematics, measles,* and *mumps,* take singular verbs. Other nouns that end in -s, such as *scissors, pants, binoculars,* and *eyeglasses,* take plural verbs. Many nouns that end in -ics may be singular or plural, depending upon their meaning.

Mathematics **fascinates** Cory. (singular)
Eyeglasses **were prescribed** by Jolene's ophthalmologist. (plural)
Physics **is** my favorite science course. (singular)
The physics of the invention **baffle** Dr. Sorenson. (plural)

When a noun of amount refers to a total that is considered as one unit, it is singular and takes a singular verb. When a noun of amount refers to a number of individual units, it is plural and takes a plural verb.

One hundred fifty dollars **seems** like a lot to pay for one dress. (singular)
One hundred fifty dollars **are** packed into that jar. (plural)

A title is always singular, even if a noun within the title is plural.

Wuthering Heights **is** the subject of Corinne's book report.

▶ **Exercise 1** **Draw two lines under the verb in parentheses that agrees with the subject.**

Ten days (has, <u>have</u>) passed since the portraits were taken.

1. The band (plays, play) each Friday night, beginning at seven o'clock.

2. "Creating Images" (is, are) the title of Janice's essay.

3. Believe it or not, these pants (was, were) quite fashionable twenty years ago.

4. Politics (makes, make) some persons do unusual things.

5. The jury (returns, return) with a verdict this afternoon.

6. Student Council (elects, elect) officers a week from Tuesday.

7. Sixty cents (lies, lie) on the sidewalk outside the ice cream shop.

8. Five hundred miles (separates, separate) the college from Doreen's hometown.

9. Robotics (continues, continue) to be an interesting field of study.

10. Our school choir (tours, tour) the West Coast in the spring.

11. Scissors (works, work) best for cutting hair.

12. *Little Women* (has, have) been made into a movie several times.

13. Opera glasses (makes, make) it easier to see performers when one is sitting in the balcony.

14. *The Simpsons* (was, were) my little brother's favorite television program.

15. The board of directors (decides, decide) how much of a dividend to offer stockholders.

16. One thousand dollars (is, are) the reward for finding Heidi's lost dog.

17. Mumps (seems, seem) mild compared to chicken pox.

18. Aeronautics (involves, involve) airplanes and how they operate.

19. The soccer team (hopes, hope) to win the division championship this year.

20. Three hours (was, were) devoted to practicing piano.

▶ **Exercise 2** **Write in the blank the verb in parentheses that agrees with the subject of each sentence.**

Binoculars _____*appear*_____ to be the only equipment Jason forgot to bring. (appears, appear)

1. The Garden Club _____ a seed sale to raise money. (holds, hold)

2. Geometrics _____ popular prints for new clothes. (is, are)

3. Fifteen dollars _____ the price of a full course meal at that restaurant.
(remains, remain)

4. *Cats* _____ a musical that often tours the country. (is, are)

5. Four years of high school _____ a diploma. (merits, merit)

6. The population _____ steadily each year. (grows, grow)

7. Congress _____ new legislation during each session. (enacts, enact)

8. *The Mysteries of Udolpho* _____ a Gothic novel written by Ann Radcliffe. (is, are)

9. Five miles _____ the distance indicated by the sign, but it seems as if we have
driven farther than that. (was, were)

10. Sunglasses with red frames _____ in the sand. (lies, lie)

11. Statistics _____ certain trends, but they can be interpreted in different ways.
(demonstrates, demonstrate)

12. A group _____ to support the school levy. (assembles, assemble)

13. Seven dollars _____ left on the table to cover the check. (was, were)

14. Phonetics, the sounds persons make to form words, _____ the science of speech. (is, are)

Lesson 49
Agreement with Compound Subjects

A sentence with a compound subject (more than one subject) may require either a singular or a plural verb. If the compound is joined by *and* or *both . . . and,* the verb required is usually plural. However, some compound subjects have two parts that make up one unit. These take a singular verb.

Singular: **Peanut butter and jelly is** all my little brother will eat for lunch.
Plural: **Grease and dirt cover** everything in the small workshop.

The verb agrees with the subject that is closer in a compound subject joined by *or, nor, either . . . or,* or *neither . . . nor.*

Singular: Neither crumpets nor **tea was** served at the tea party.
Plural: Larry or the **twins made** that mess.

Any compound subject preceded by *many a, every,* or *each* takes a singular verb.

Many a chick and a gosling **has been raised** on this farm.

▶ **Exercise 1 Underline the compound subject. Choose the verb in parentheses that agrees with the subject and write it in the blank.**

Many a loudmouth and self-styled critic _____ has voiced _____ unwanted opinions.

(has voiced, have voiced)

1. Both Mrs. Albert and Mr. Ling _____ exams on Friday. (is giving, are giving)

2. Neither Jay nor Adrean _____ the leftovers. (wants, want)

3. Ham and beans _____ well with cornbread. (goes, go)

4. The anvil and the hammer _____ neglected in the old horse barn. (sits, sit)

5. Neither Alex nor Corey _____ to liking Sugary Crispies. (admits, admit)

6. Either wheat germ or sesame seeds _____ a good topping for that. (makes, make)

7. Every hill and mountain in this region _____ home to Steenie. (is, are)

8. Both Stu and Ralph _____ constantly. (whistles, whistle)

9. Soup and salad _____ on the lunch menu today. (is, are)

10. Many a tourist and traveler _____ the Statue of Liberty. (has climbed, have climbed)

11. Neither the basin nor the pitcher _____ in the scuffle. (was broken, were broken)

Grammar

12. Neither Francis nor Evelyn _____ to go with us. (chooses, choose)

13. Both Mom and I _____ our dog, but he's nowhere in sight. (has called, have called)

14. Neither the brakes nor the starter _____. (has been fixed, have been fixed)

15. Each muscle and tendon in my entire body _____. (aches, ache)

16. Included in the invitation _____ neither my brother nor my cousin. (was, were)

17. "Every man, woman, and child _____ a new Acme Video Toy in his or her living room." (needs, need)

18. All over England, fish and chips _____ practically a staple for people on the go. (is, are)

19. _____ either Lila or Lilith going to the Twins Convention? (Is, Are)

20. A challenge and an opportunity _____ just the right words for our current dilemma. (is, are)

21. Each judge and contestant _____ for the pageant weeks in advance. (has been preparing, have been preparing)

22. Neither the spaniel nor the Chihuahua _____, but our Doberman is rather hard to control. (bites, bite)

23. Not every teenage male and female _____ talking on the phone, but some keep the lines pretty busy. (likes, like)

24. Neither rain nor snow nor sleet _____ my dad's golfing schedule. (affects, affect)

25. Every used car and truck on the lot _____ discounted one hundred dollars. (is, are)

26. Neither frogs nor ducks _____ in this pond. (swims, swim)

27. Brick and mortar _____ most of the houses in this neighborhood. (decorates, decorate)

28. Neither taxis nor buses _____ after midnight in my hometown. (runs, run)

29. Each speaker and guest _____ a name badge. (has, have)

30. The yellow sweater or the green shawl _____ fine with your new outfit. (looks, look)

Lesson 50
Intervening Expressions

Certain expressions seem to create a compound subject but do not. *Accompanied by, as well as, in addition to, plus,* and *together with* are expressions that introduce phrases that tell about the subject. However, the subject remains singular and takes a singular verb.

Grammar

▶ **Exercise 1 Draw a line under each simple subject. Then write the form of the verb in parentheses that agrees with the subject. Use the present tense of the verb.**

The <u>sky</u>, as well as the cumulus clouds riding across it, _____looks_____ beautiful today. (*look*)

1. Whole milk, as well as sugar and eggs, _____ into the making of ice cream. (*go*)

2. Mike, accompanied by his two sons, _____ soon for the old car show. (*leave*)

3. The attorney, along with the judge, _____ of the jury's verdict. (*approve*)

4. The pianist, accompanied by the violinist, _____ a lovely waltz. (*play*)

5. Seasoned hamburger, plus pasta, _____ delicious. (*taste*)

6. Being prompt to work, together with a neat appearance, _____ the boss's attention. (*get*)

7. Diane, along with her poodle, _____ every day in the park at noon. (*walk*)

8. The farmer, aided by his son, _____ the fields in the spring. (*plow*)

9. The television, as well as the radio, _____ news about the big fire. (*broadcast*)

10. The Belgian horse team, plus the faithful dog, _____ a fine addition to the parade. (*make*)

11. The old car, together with the big wagon, _____ a new coat of paint. (*need*)

12. Eric, in addition to his cousin, _____ his friends to the car races. (*take*)

13. Today the hairdresser, plus the elderly barber, _____ the hair style competition. (*judge*)

14. The swing on the porch, as well as the old rocker, _____ in the wind. (*squeak*)

15. Today Mr. Smith, in addition to Mr. Tanaka, _____ to the golf club with my father. (*ride*)

16. The House of Fashion, as well as Ted's Olde Tailor Shop, _____ our neighborhood with evening wear for prom night. (*supply*)

17. Jewelweed, as well as plantain, _____ to cure poison ivy. (*help*)

18. The high chair, together with the baby crib, _____ empty. (*remain*)

19. German, as well as French, _____ taught at our high school. (*be*)

20. Roast duck, plus turkey, _____ as the main course at the honors banquet. (*serve*)

21. A pet sheep, as well as a calf, _____ Dan's entry at the fair. (*be*)

22. The dictionary, plus the encyclopedia, _____ in furthering education at home. (*aid*)

23. Cherry gelatin, plus fruit cocktail, _____ in a delicious dessert. (*result*)

24. The lion, as well as the family house cat, _____ a member of the feline species. (*be*)

25. My wristwatch, together with the town clock, _____ exactly on time. (*run*)

26. Cocoa, in addition to chocolate chips, _____ a very rich fudge. (*make*)

27. A pink sweater, accompanied by a cap and booties, _____ Grandmother's gift. (*be*)

28. A deer, in addition to several rabbits, _____ Dan's contribution. (*be*)

29. Apple pie, plus vanilla ice cream, _____ a delicious but high-calorie dessert. (*constitute*)

30. The magazine, as well as the big newsletter, _____ short stories and interesting recipes. (*publish*)

31. A no-trespassing sign, accompanied by a no-hunting sign, _____ against the fence. (*lean*)

32. Our new principal, as well as my teacher, _____ from Ontario. (*come*)

33. A seashell, together with many polished stones, _____ my souvenir of my vacation. (*be*)

34. Our neighbor Mrs. Gonzales, along with her two grown children, _____ to vacation in Spain this year. (*plan*)

35. Sam, together with his English setter, _____ for raccoons in the woods. (*search*)

36. An Amish farmer, along with his horses, _____ many fertile acres. (*farm*)

37. The captain, plus his alert crew, _____ at attention for the admiral. (*stand*)

38. Washing clothes, as well as drying them, _____ much harder in the past without electric appliances. (*be*)

Lesson 51
Indefinite Pronouns as Subjects

Many subjects are indefinite pronouns. A verb must agree with an indefinite pronoun used as a subject.

Singular:	**Everyone** in the band **knows** that old melody.
Singular:	**Anybody realizes** the truth in a case like this one.
Plural:	**Many recognize** the usefulness of such a course of action.
Plural:	**Few admit** such an embarrassing mistake.

Some pronouns can be either singular or plural, depending on the nouns to which they refer.

Singular:	**All** of the cake **tastes** good, Michelle.
Plural:	**All** of these cars **are** expensive.

Indefinite pronouns fall into three groups.

Always Singular:	each	everyone	nobody	anything
	either	everybody	nothing	someone
	neither	everything	anyone	somebody
	one	no one	anybody	something
Always Plural:	several	few	both	many
Singular or Plural:	some	all	most	none

▶ **Exercise 1** Draw one line under the indefinite pronoun subject. Draw two lines under the correct form of the verb.

Nothing (stands, stand) in the way of Carla when she puts her mind to a problem.

1. Something (makes, make) that sound during high winds.

2. Nobody (likes, like) outrageous allegations such as these.

3. One (needs, need) to remember all the good times we had in school.

4. Either (seems, seem) an equally good choice in such circumstances as we face now.

5. Someone (tells, tell) him these silly things, and he believes every word without question.

6. On a day like this one, anything (exasperates, exasperate) me completely.

7. Around our neighborhood, no one (says, say) anything bad about public transportation.

8. As usual, Catriona, everything (reads, reading) wonderfully in your story.

9. Several (is, are) ready for the exhibition next week.

10. Most of the students (travels, travel) to the singing workshop this afternoon.

11. Each of the boys on the team (receives, receive) a letter for participation.

12. Few of the soldiers (talks, talk) about that particularly dangerous mission.

13. Some of the kids (loves, love) to swing under the old chestnut tree.

14. Neither really (remembers, remember) what happened that night.

15. Both of the stories (appears, appear) equally true.

16. Now, somebody surely (reads, reading) my column in the student newspaper.

17. Everyone attending the debate (understands, understand) why I said what I did.

18. Hardly anyone (disturbs, disturb) her while she is reading her favorite author.

19. All of the ones here (belongs, belong) to my Great-aunt Nancy.

20. Many of the individuals in our club (feels, feel) the same about it as I do.

21. Nobody (cares, care) for Sally's unique contributions to our class party.

22. Something inside me (says, say) that I shouldn't try a stunt like that.

23. Each of the boxes (contains, contain) a really interesting surprise.

24. Nothing about snakes (attracts, attract) her interest in any way whatsoever.

25. Either of the boys (is, are) good enough for the team.

26. Some of my friends (wears, wear) their hearts on their sleeves.

27. Many of Abigail's friends (hopes, hope) she will come to the party.

28. Someone surely (wants, want) an old bike like yours, Philip.

29. Everyone (says, say) the fireworks were great this year.

30. None of the horses (remains, remain) in the farmer's paddock.

31. Some of the students (cleans, clean) up after the graduation.

32. Everything (conspires, conspire) to put Ernesto off his timing for the big relay race today.

33. Neither of them (cares, care) about a movie like that.

34. One of the generals in the junta (speaks, speak) about justice and a return to democracy in his nation.

35. All of the ice cream (melts, melt) while we sit around and argue.

36. Few of the researchers (appreciates, appreciate) what their efforts mean for the future of our town.

37. Both of the tenants (wishes, wish) they had never begun the repainting job at all.

38. Most (agrees, agree) on the principle, "A sound mind in a sound body."

Lesson 52
Agreement in Adjective Clauses

Grammar

When the subject of an adjective clause is a relative pronoun, the verb in the clause must agree with the antecedent of the relative pronoun.

Patience is one of the *requirements* that *make* a good leader.

In the preceding example the antecedent of *that* is *requirements,* not *one,* because *several* requirements—not just patience—make a good leader. Since *requirements* is plural, *that* is considered to be plural, and the verb in the adjective clause, *make,* must also be plural.

Patience happens to be the only one of the leadership talents that *is* natural to me.

In this example the antecedent of *that* is *one,* not *talents,* because the speaker has only one of the talents of a good leader, *patience.* Since *one* is singular, the verb in the adjective clause, *is,* must be singular.

▶ **Exercise 1** **Draw one line under the antecedent of each relative pronoun. Draw two lines under the correct form of the verb.**

Sally is the only one of our runners who (holds, hold) that distance record at our school.

1. Brad appears to be the only one of the storytellers who (relates, relate) that particular tale.

2. Carey is one of the actors who (is, are) participating in our production.

3. My dog will have to be one of the participants that (is, are) attending canine obedience school next month.

4. The name of that constellation is the only one of the northern star group's names that (escapes, escape) me at the moment.

5. Rita remains one of my friends who (stands, stand) by me in this upheaval.

6. My sister seems the only one in my family who (enjoys, enjoy) tennis at all.

7. This pie tastes like one of the store pies that (bakes, bake) so easily.

8. The *Fokker D VII* was the only one of World War I's many airplanes that (was designed, were designed) with three main wings.

9. Our senior class is one of the few regional senior classes that (is, are) going to that amusement park.

10. Billy Ray is one of my relatives who (likes, like) that model of sports car.

11. A shark is the only one of the sea's creatures that (scares, scare) me at all.

12. Jules Verne is one of the few science fiction writers of the nineteenth century who (is, are) still read.

13. That old elm tree is the only one of all the old trees that still (stands, stand) here.

14. This old sailboat that Sandy and I used is the only one of these many sailboats that (makes, make) me nostalgic for old times.

15. That point is the only new insight of all the ideas that (argues, argue) for your conclusion.

16. That is one of the paintings hanging in this gallery that (impresses, impress) me.

17. Alas, your apology is one of the many things that (indicates, indicate) your sincerity.

18. The old cowboy actor remains the only one of all the western genre actors in that studio who still (cares, care) about the preservation of the West.

19. That beautiful roan horse is one of the horses stabled here that (recognizes, recognize) me when I come up to the fence.

20. John F. Kennedy is the only one of our twentieth-century presidents who (was wounded, were wounded) in World War II.

▶ Exercise 2 **Draw a line under the antecedent of the relative pronoun, and cross out the verb in the adjective clause if it is not correct.**

The movies that was premiered yesterday lacked excitement.

1. The plays that start this week seem pretty interesting, I would say.

2. The Carsons, who lives on Maple Street, are having a graduation party for Billy.

3. Geologists who work for the U.S. Geological Survey are involved in many fascinating subjects.

4. The rains that falls today should really restore the grass's color.

5. Hawn is the only one of the students who do extra credit work on a regular basis.

6. The cats that wait at the door know they will get milk.

7. Those boxes that is filled with cans need to be taken to the recycling center.

8. Why do you keep these old notebooks that clutter up our room?

9. Do you have one of those pocket dictionaries that places a pronouncing guide after each word?

10. Haiku is one of the traditional Japanese verse forms that is popular today.

☑️ Unit 7 **Review**

▶ **Exercise 1** Underline the subject of each sentence. Then choose the verb in parentheses that agrees with the subject and write it in the blank.

Paula _____runs_____ every day after school. (runs, run)

1. Ben and Consuelo often _____ duets. (sings, sing)

2. His fit of sneezing _____ the class. (is disrupting, are disrupting)

3. The job _____ up a lot of his spare time. (takes, take)

4. Two hundred boxes of cards _____ by the club. (was sold, were sold)

5. His frequent fevers _____ a worry to his parents. (was, were)

6. Gathering clouds _____ a storm. (foretells, foretell)

7. Her pets _____ a great joy to her. (is, are)

8. Final exams _____ the last hurdle before graduation. (is, are)

9. Down the mountain _____ the skiers. (speeds, speed)

10. In her pocket _____ several acorns. (was, were)

11. Two dollars _____ not a big tip for this meal. (is, are)

12. The group _____ not _____ on which movie to see. (does agree, do agree)

13. Every student _____ to study. (needs, need)

14. Both Eliza and George _____ to cook. (loves, love)

15. The rock, as well as the waves, _____ the ship. (threatens, threaten)

16. Ireland, besides England, _____ many ancient ruins. (has, have)

17. Some of my brothers _____ sheep. (raises, raise)

18. One of the climbers _____ reached the top. (has, have)

19. Each of the actors _____ a bow. (takes, take)

20. A few of the vacationers _____ to go home. (wants, want)

Grammar

Cumulative Review: Units 1–7

▶ **Exercise 1** Identify the part of speech *(POS)* and the use in the sentence *(USE)* of the italicized word or words. Be specific.

The heavy-weight *champion* won by decision.

POS: __noun_____ USE: __subject of sentence_____

1. We drove *to* Indianapolis to see the Indy 500.

   POS: _____ USE: _____

2. Rayna left *flowers* on her neighbor's front porch.

   POS: _____ USE: _____

3. The mystery held *them* in suspense to the last minutes of the program.

   POS: _____ USE: _____

4. Steve eagerly dove into the *pool* and did not emerge until he had swum half its length.

   POS: _____ USE: _____

5. Is the news good, or have you heard *yet?*

   POS: _____ USE: _____

6. *Well,* I never expected to see you here!

   POS: _____ USE: _____

7. Let's take a *long* drive through the country this afternoon.

   POS: _____ USE: _____

8. Lisel can never decide whether to order a soda *or* iced tea.

   POS: _____ USE: _____

9. *Dr. Harvy* and Judge Garrison play handball on Saturdays.

   POS: _____ USE: _____

10. Did you see Buckingham Palace *when you were in London?*

    POS: _____ USE: _____

11. *Oh,* I think I've got it now.

    POS: _____ USE: _____

12. Whoa! How do I get this horse *to stop?*

    POS: _____ USE: _____

13. The air balloon rose upward, *and* the crowd waved good-bye to its passengers.

    POS: _____ USE: _____

14. Connie often shops *at the local mall,* but she prefers yard sales.

    POS: _____ USE: _____

15. The *gem-colored* bubbles floated across the sky.

    POS: _____ USE: _____

16. Mike wants to play *the saxophone,* so he signed up for band class.

    POS: _____ USE: _____

17. We enjoyed *working* on Grandfather's farm.

    POS: _____ USE: _____

18. *Singing* is not one of my natural gifts, but I enjoy it anyway.

    POS: _____ USE: _____

▶ Exercise 2 **Complete each sentence with the indicative, imperative, or subjunctive form of the verb in parentheses.**

If I _____ were _____ a believer in luck, I would call that accident a piece of bad luck. (subjunctive of *be*)

1. Gary wishes he _____ going to Arkansas for the holidays. (subjunctive of *be*)

2. The sail _____ tautly in the freshening breeze. (indicative of *billow*)

3. _____ the long wall for the new couch, please. (imperative of *measure*)

4. It is vital that she _____ responsibility for the project. (subjunctive of *take*)

5. _____ some of this cold blueberry soup, Lenora. (imperative of *try*)

6. I suggest he _____ his cost estimates and resubmit them. (subjunctive of *revise*)

7. Your sister did the dishes last night, John; please _____ them tonight. (imperative of *do.*)

8. Elisabeth _____ on the work of the United Nations. (indicative of *lecture*)

9. We recommend that she _____ her plan to emigrate. (subjunctive of *reconsider*)

10. To relax after a hard day, Leah _____ her dog. (indicative of *brush*)

▶ **Exercise 3** **Underline each prepositional phrase, and circle its object.**

After the (movie) we went to (Yogi's) for (pizza.)

1. The biologist lived off the land and spent most of his life among the habitats of nature.

2. Abraham Lincoln's sole surviving son Robert became a government official and lawyer for the big industrial tycoons of the late nineteenth century.

3. If they were not so late, we ourselves would have been on time.

4. She does volunteer work for her company.

5. After we stocked all of the shelves, we threw the empty boxes into the dumpster behind the store.

6. Ride straight between the hills and down the valley.

7. The computer in the lab was purchased from the company that did our research.

8. Mr. Fischer will not retire until the end of the school year.

9. Please put the tennis balls beneath the rackets inside the storage cabinet.

10. We waited until the time when he arrived at our meeting place outside the science museum.

11. The article is a guide for people on a tight budget.

12. I walked through the crowded toy store with my little brother in tow.

13. Thousands of tourists attend the Smallwood Crafts Festival each year.

14. Dr. Como retired from his job at the hospital and is now at a mission in Argentina.

15. The recently relocated company provides jobs for several hundred people.

16. Looking at its long-term goals, I believe our company is headed in the right direction.

17. On the long flight home, Gaylene sat next to her state senator.

18. Yesterday, various small birds were singing near the cherry tree.

Unit 8: Using Pronouns Correctly

Lesson 53

Case of Personal Pronouns

Personal pronouns are pronouns used to refer to persons or things. They have three **cases**, or forms, called *nominative*, *objective*, and *possessive*. Each case is determined by how the pronoun functions in a sentence—as a subject, a complement, or an object of a preposition.

CASE	SINGULAR	PLURAL	FUNCTION IN SENTENCE
Nominative	I, you, she, he, it	we, you, they	subject or predicate nominative
Objective	me, you, her, him, it	us, you, them	direct object, indirect object, or object of preposition
Possessive	my, mine, your, yours, her, hers, his, its	our, ours, your, yours, their, theirs	replacement for possessive noun(s)

For a subject or a compound subject, use a personal pronoun in the nominative case

She and **I** competed for first prize.

For a personal pronoun in a compound object, use the objective case

They awarded the band and **him** a music trophy.
Between **you** and **her,** I would pick you.

After a form of the linking verb *be*, use the nominative case of a personal pronoun.

The first one to call in the fire alarm was **she.**
The one who smelled smoke was **he.**

Do not use an apostrophe when spelling possessive pronouns

Is this car **theirs?**
I thought it was **yours.**

The form *it's* is a contraction of *it is.* Do not confuse *it's* with the possessive pronoun *its.*

It's going to snow tonight; I can feel it.
Winter always saves **its** worst for late March.

Before a gerund (an *-ing* form used as a noun), use a possessive pronoun.

Your planning the party was a wonderful gift.
I hope you'll excuse **my** coming late.

▶ **Exercise 1 Draw a line under the correct personal pronoun in parentheses.**

The history of (<u>our</u>, ours) sciences is very old.

1. The history of science is the story of men and women and (their, they) discoveries.

2. Early people who wanted (them, their) lives to go well paid tribute to the forces of nature.

3. (They, Them) made up stories about these forces to explain the world and (it's, its) wonders.

4. Today (we, us) call these stories myths and enjoy reading (they, them).

5. Eventually, in Greece, some people started observing the way (they, their) world worked.

6. (They, Their) observations led to discoveries about the physical laws of (our, ours) universe.

7. Democritus said all matter was made of basic particles, or atoms; the founder of the atomic theory was (he, him).

8. Pythagoras theorized that Earth was round; this contradicted what people thought and it confused (they, them).

9. Archimedes discovered the laws of the lever and the pulley; (they, them) make (you, your) life much easier today.

10. Eratosthenes did calculations with distances on Earth to calculate (it's, its) circumference.

11. The Greek physician Galen developed medical theories; (he, him) encouraged the knowledge of (our, ours) anatomy.

12. During the Dark Ages, Arab philosophers kept science alive, and we owe to (they, them) much of our astronomical knowledge.

13. When Nicolaus Copernicus asserted that all planets orbit the sun, the Earth-centered scientific philosophy of (our, ours) ancestors ended.

14. Galileo used a telescope to study the moon and Venus; it was (he, him) who first saw the four large moons of Jupiter.

15. Johannes Kepler discovered that orbits are not circular; rather, (they, them) are elliptical.

16. Isaac Newton found that visible light is made up of separate bands and that (they, their) different colors make up the spectrum.

17. Newton worked out the laws of gravity, the force that keeps (you, your), (me, mine), and all of (we, us) tied to Earth.

18. Newton also invented calculus; some of (we, us) wish he had invented something else!

Lesson 54
Pronouns with and as Appositives; After *Than* and *As*

An appositive is a noun or pronoun that is placed next to another noun or pronoun in order to identify or give additional information about it.

Use the nominative case for a pronoun that is in apposition to a subject or a predicate nominative.

The team captains, **Maria** and **I,** will schedule practice. (*Captains* is the subject.)
The shortstops were two sisters, **Cora** and **she.** (*Sisters* is the predicate nominative.)

Use the objective case for a pronoun that is in apposition to a direct object, an indirect object, or an object of a preposition.

The judge sentenced the offenders, the **thief** and **him.** (*Offenders* is a direct object.)
We gave the cats, **Rocky** and **her,** some tidbits. (*Cats* is the indirect object.)
The senator spoke to both opponents, **him** and **me.** (*Opponents* is the object of the preposition *to.*)

When a pronoun is followed by an appositive, choose the case of the pronoun that would be correct if the appositive were omitted.

We climbers will beat you to the top of the mountain. (*We* is correct because *we* is the subject of the sentence.)
Don't be so arrogant to **us hikers.** (*Us* is correct because *us* is the object of the preposition *to.*)

In elliptical adverb clauses using *than* and *as,* choose the case of the pronoun that you would use if the missing words were fully expressed.

I am always awake earlier than **she.** (Read: I am always awake earlier than she *is awake.*)
Your words hurt her as much as **me.** (Read: Your words hurt her as much as *they hurt* me.)

▶ **Exercise 1** **Identify the case of the pronoun or pronouns in italics by writing *nom.* (nominative) or *obj.* (objective).**

_____obj._____   Tom told the boys, Mack and *him,* the bad news.

_____ **1.** *He,* a world-traveled explorer, broke his leg in the airport.

_____ **2.** I hoped to finish as soon as *they,* but I'm too slow.

_____ **3.** Neither candidate, Marco or *she,* is particularly well liked.

_____ **4.** I'd like you to meet the reporters, Sal and *her.*

_____ **5.** The three lab assistants, Carl, Sissy, and *she,* compete for the best equipment.

_____ **6.** I can usually exercise more easily than *they.*

_____ **7.** I think you're more easily hurt than *I.*

_____ 8. The two social workers, Alicia and *he,* are very good with children.

_____ 9. The goal of this video game entirely escapes both players, Mala and *her.*

_____ 10. We are sending get-well cards to both accident victims, Zina and *him.*

_____ 11. The performance by the rock band almost deafened me as well as *her.*

_____ 12. We were anxious to meet our new neighbors, Paul and *him.*

_____ 13. I understand you want to talk to the witnesses, Nora and *me.*

_____ 14. Our best computer students, David and *they,* will represent us in the competition.

_____ 15. *She* and *I,* the two co-chairs, will run the fund raiser for the food bank.

▶ **Exercise 2** **Underline the correct pronoun. Identify the case by writing *nom.* for the nominative case or *obj.* for the objective case. Some sentences may have more than one pronoun to identify.**

___nom., obj.___ Your student council candidate, (I, me), will debate my opponent, (he, him).

_____ 1. The police officers, Sam and (he, him), observed (they, them) leaving the scene.

_____ 2. The acrobats, Leroy and (she, her), were both in top shape.

_____ 3. The review praised the three supporting characters, Melody, Hank, and (I, me).

_____ 4. The best spellers, Binte and (he, him), both made the finals.

_____ 5. The two astronomers, Mr. Simpson and (she, her), explained supernovas to (we, us).

_____ 6. The last runners to finish the marathon, Hussein, Jack, and (they, them), crossed the line after dark.

_____ 7. We raised funds to help those whose homes had burned, the Parkers and (they, them).

_____ 8. (We, Us) late risers sent a message to our noisy families, "Don't wake (we, us) sleepers!"

_____ 9. The two tallest, (she, her) and (I, me), always end up sitting in the back.

_____ 10. Kavi and Imamu are better runners than (they, them).

_____ 11. Everyone seemed more concerned about the weather than (I, me).

_____ 12. Your gift moved Mother as much as (I, me).

_____ 13. Sami washes her brushes more often than (he, him).

_____ 14. The sun wakes up Emily later than (I, me).

_____ 15. The babysitter, (she, her), told the outrageous story to (they, them).

Lesson 55
Reflexive and Intensive Pronouns

Observe the following rules when using reflexive and intensive pronouns: Use *himself* and *themselves* instead of the incorrect forms *hisself* and *theirselves*.

Julio fixed the VCR **himself**.
The dogs dug under the fence **themselves**.

When a personal pronoun refers to the subject of a sentence, always use a reflexive pronoun.

Incorrect:	Marjorie treated **her** to an ice cream cone. (her refers to Marjorie)
Correct:	Marjorie treated **herself** to an ice cream cone.
Incorrect:	The baby saw **him** in the mirror. (him refers to the baby)
Correct:	They baby saw **himself** in the mirror.

Avoid the unnecessary use of reflexive pronouns. A reflexive pronoun refers to the subject; it does not *take the place* of the subject.

Incorrect:	Angie and **myself** are science lab partners.
Correct:	Angie and **I** are science lab partners.
Incorrect:	Mae and **yourself** will be team captains.
Correct:	Mae and **you** will be team captains.

▶ **Exercise 1 Underline the correct pronoun in parentheses. Assume that a third-person pronoun refers to a person, place, or thing already in the sentence.**

The cat gave (it, <u>itself</u>) a bath.

1. Harley, would you divide the pie between (him, himself) and me?

2. We can give (us, ourselves) the test at home.

3. Frank and (you, yourself) are going to be late for the big concert.

4. He told (hisself, himself) it didn't matter that he lost the track event.

5. Mom taught (her, herself) algebra from a book when she was studying at home.

6. The puppies inched (theirselves, themselves) up onto the couch.

7. She taught (her, herself) to breathe deeply when she was afraid.

8. He set the clock to wake (hisself, himself) early on the day of the field trip.

9. They laughed (theirselves, themselves) silly over the mistake that I made.

10. Megan removed (her, herself) from the contest yesterday.

11. I saw the squirrels helping (them, themselves) to the birds' feed again.

12. Sam asked (him, himself) why he had done such a silly thing!

Grammar

13. Angela can draw (her, herself) a reasonable picture of a horse.

14. Carol and Chiyo entered (they, themselves) in the swim meet.

15. The Parkers and (you, yourself) will never make it to the movie premiere on time.

16. Homer wanted to walk home by (hisself, himself) after the baseball game.

17. You can see (you, yourself) in the lake's surface.

18. The bear took (it, itself) down the path into the deep, shadowy woods.

19. Jackson finally talked (hisself, himself) into going to the dance.

20. I bought (me, myself) a second-hand suit at the bargain store this morning.

21. Iku and (you, yourself) should see this great foreign film!

22. Raz introduced (hisself, himself) to his new boss.

23. Angela read to (her, herself) until she fell asleep on the couch.

24. Have (you, yourself) and Bob finished your homework?

25. The dogs played among (theirselves, themselves) under the shade trees in the park.

26. The new neighbors and (I, myself) have not met.

27. Makila made (him, himself) a new pair of boots.

28. You mean Tracy and (you, yourself) didn't finish the big history test?

29. Mamie found (her, herself) in a strange part of the building.

30. You need to give (you, yourself) some time to recover from your accident, Akira.

31. James laughed at (hisself, himself) for falling for the joke that Howard played on him.

32. The team members huddled among (theirselves, themselves).

33. Sandi painted (her, herself) a T-shirt with a rain forest background.

34. I told (me, myself) to stop being so self-righteous about everything that is going on.

35. The audience keeps telling (it, itself) the scary film is only a movie!

36. He (hisself, himself) knows how it feels to be left out of any festive gathering.

37. The mother of the boy called (him, himself) in for dinner.

38. The bat hung (it, itself) upside down from the cave roof.

39. The skiers blamed (theirselves, themselves) for the avalanche that destroyed the beautiful valley.

40. The teacher called on (me, myself) to read the long poem aloud.

Grammar

Lesson 56
Who and *Whom* in Questions and Subordinate Clauses

In questions, use *who* for subjects and *whom* for direct and indirect objects and objects of a preposition.

Who came late? (*Who* is the subject of the verb *came*.)
Whom did you drive to the party? (*Whom* is the direct object of the verb *did drive*.)

When a question includes an interrupting expression, such as *did you say* or *do you think*, leave out the expression and say the sentence to determine whether to use *who* or *whom*.

Who do you think took the jewels? (Say: *Who took the jewels?* to determine that *who* is the subject of the verb *took*.)

Use the nominative pronouns *who* and *whoever* for subjects and predicate nominatives in subordinate clauses.

The driver knows **who** hit him. (*Who* is the subject of the noun clause *who hit him*.)
The witnesses identified **who** the speeder was. (*Who* is the predicate nominative of the noun clause *who the speeder was*.)
The troopers will track **whoever** caused the crash. (*Whoever* is the subject of the noun clause *whoever caused the crash*.)

Use the objective pronouns *whom* and *whomever* for direct and indirect objects and objects of a preposition in subordinate clauses.

I asked **whom** she had chosen as lab partner. (*Whom* is the direct object of the verb *had chosen*.)
He is someone with **whom** I have nothing in common. (*Whom* is the object of the preposition *with*.)
I will work with **whomever** you send from the office. (*Whomever* is the direct object of the verb *send*.)

▶ **Exercise 1** **To complete each sentence, underline the correct pronoun from the pair in parentheses.**

I wonder (who, whom) has not heard of Frederick Douglass.

1. Frederick Douglass, (who, whom) was one of the greatest abolitionists in America, was born an enslaved person.

2. (Whoever, Whomever) held an enslaved person had absolute control of that person's life.

3. Frederick was one of twelve children, many of (who, whom) worked in the plantation owner's fields.

4. Frederick's mother, (who, whom) toiled long hours, sent him to live with his Grandmother Bailey.

5. As a child, Frederick often heard about Old Master, a mysterious person (who, whom) seemed to be feared by all the other enslaved persons.

Grammar (sidebar)

6. One day Grandmother Bailey took Frederick, (who, whom) was only six, on a long walk.

7. His grandmother, to (who, whom) Frederick clung, eventually led him to a large yard full of children.

8. Frederick was confused because he did not know (who, whom) many of these children were.

9. When his grandmother left, Frederick understood that he would stay with the others, all of (who, whom) were to be trained to work for Old Master.

10. Later Frederick was sent to another family member, (who, whom) lived in Baltimore.

11. It was this incident that taught Frederick that slaveholders could assign an enslaved person to work for (whoever, whomever) they chose.

12. It was also his new mistress, Sophia Auld, to (who, whom) Frederick owed his eventual literacy.

13. He listened to her read from the Bible and wondered (who, whom) might teach him to read.

14. Sophia Auld taught Frederick to read and then told her husband, (who, whom) was furious.

15. An enslaved person (who, whom) knows how to read will soon challenge his slavery, her husband told her.

16. However, Frederick continued to seek out (whoever, whomever) would help him become a better reader.

17. With pieces of bread, he paid white children (who, whom) he met on his errands to teach him more.

18. He began reading the literature of abolitionists, (who, whom) believed that slavery was wrong and that enslaved persons should be freed.

19. Frederick dreamed of freedom, inspired by the examples of African Americans in Baltimore, many of (who, whom) were free people themselves.

20. Frederick Douglass, (who, whom) equated reading with freedom, eventually escaped from slavery.

21. After Frederick escaped, he took the name Douglass, (who, whom) was a character in a book by Sir Walter Scott.

22. He began to attend the meetings of abolitionists, many of (who, whom) were white.

23. William Lloyd Garrison, (who, whom) edited the abolitionist paper *Liberator,* hired Douglass to speak at anti-slavery meetings.

24. Garrison was a white person for (who, whom) Douglass had a great deal of respect.

25. Douglass's friends worried about him when he spoke, because he was still an escaped enslaved person for (who, whom) bounty hunters searched.

26. (Whoever, Whomever) spoke against slavery, whether white or black, was often in danger.

27. Elijah Lovejoy, (who, whom) wrote against slavery for his newspaper, was killed and his newspaper office burned.

28. No one had to ask (who, whom) he had offended with his ideas.

Lesson 57
Agreement in Number and Gender and with Collective Nouns

An **antecedent** is the word or group of words to which a pronoun refers or replaces. All pronouns must agree with their antecedents.

A pronoun must agree with its antecedent in number (singular or plural) and gender (masculine, feminine, or neuter).

Consuela won **her** fifth spelling bee last week. (*Her* is a singular feminine pronoun that agrees with the antecedent *Consuela.*)
Jacob took **his** grandfather to the doctor. (*His* is a singular masculine pronoun that agrees with the antecedent *Jacob.*)
Carrie and **Emilio** studied for **their** science quiz together. (*Their* is a plural neuter pronoun that agrees with the compound subject *Carrie* and *Emilio.*)
The **opossum,** carrying **its** seven babies, scooted under the woodpile. (*Its* is a singular neuter pronoun that agrees with the antecedent *opossum.*)

Historically, the masculine pronoun has been used for all cases in which the gender of the antecedent is unknown.

Each **student** must take the test in **his** homeroom.

Today, there are several choices for avoiding the exclusive use of the masculine pronoun.

Each **student** must take the test in **his** or **her** homeroom.
Students must take the test in **their** homerooms.
Students must take the test in homeroom.

When the antecedent of a pronoun is a collective noun, the pronoun depends on whether the collective noun is meant to be singular or plural.

The **team** set in motion **its** last play of the game. (The collective noun *team* conveys the singular sense of one unit, requiring the use of the singular pronoun *its.*)
The **team** collected **their** uniforms and gear and headed for the bus. (The collective noun *team* conveys the plural sense of several persons performing separate acts, requiring the use of the plural pronoun *their.*)

▶ **Exercise 1 Draw a line under each personal pronoun and draw a circle around its antecedent.**

My (parents) have their original copy of *Kidnapped*.

1. Robert Louis Stevenson, the Scottish author, is best known for his adventure novels.

2. Stevenson always suffered from poor health; in spite of this, he lived a life notable for its adventure.

3. His father hoped Robert would become an engineer, but the lad found the occupation

    too strenuous.

Grammar

4. As a young man, Stevenson studied law but never took up its practice.

5. Stevenson started traveling to improve his health and soon began writing novels that would leave their impression on millions of readers.

6. In France Stevenson met Fanny Osbourne, who devoted much of her life to seeking a cure for his tuberculosis.

7. *Treasure Island,* published by Stevenson in 1883, secured his fame immediately.

8. *A Child's Garden of Verses* (1885) has given many children their habit of reading poetry.

9. A prolific writer, Stevenson soon completed two other popular novels; their popularity brought the Scot even more fame.

10. Still trying to better his health, Stevenson and Fanny traveled to the South Pacific, where they lived for the rest of his life.

▶ Exercise 2 **Complete each sentence by writing a personal pronoun that agrees with the antecedent. Draw a line under the antecedent.**

The Brontë family is respected for _____its_____ place in English literature.

1. The Brontë sisters are known for _____ literary works.

2. Patrick Brontë was born in Ireland but worked as a parish curate in Haworth, England, during all of _____ adult life.

3. The six Brontë children were badly affected when _____ mother died.

4. Their father tried to find someone to care for _____ children.

5. Four of the girls were sent away to a school not known for _____ healthy atmosphere.

6. Charlotte always believed that the school helped end _____ older sisters' lives at an early age.

7. Charlotte, Emily, and Anne, who survived, read voraciously and created fantasy kingdoms in _____ home in Haworth, England.

8. Their brother, frustrated in _____ ambitions to achieve success as a painter or a writer, soon fell ill.

9. Charlotte tried to establish a school but was disappointed by _____ failure.

10. The girls published poems under pseudonyms, for they did not want readers to know _____ identities.

Lesson 58
Agreement in Person

A pronoun must agree in person with its antecedent.

Do not use the second-person pronoun *you* to refer to an antecedent in the third person. Use a suitable third-person pronoun.

Incorrect: The Harpers went to the museum, where **you** saw the fossilized skeletons of several dinosaurs.

Correct: The Harpers went to the museum, where **they** saw the fossilized skeletons of several dinosaurs.

When a pronoun has another pronoun as its antecedent, be sure the two pronouns agree in person. Do not shift from *they* to *you, I,* to *you,* or *one* to *you.*

Incorrect: **They** swam to the far shore, where **you** could find shells.
Correct: **They** swam to the far shore, where **they** could find shells.
Incorrect: I hate it when **you** get up early and it's cold.
Correct: I hate it when **I** get up early and it's cold.
Incorrect: If **one** is very observant, **you** might see a salamander.
Correct: If **one** is very observant, **one** might see a salamander.

▶ **Exercise 1 Circle the *you* in each sentence. Then write a third-person pronoun to complete the sentence correctly.**

__they__ They tried to reach the plateau, where (you) could rest.

_____ 1. Kari dries her hair in the sun, even though you could use a hair dryer.

_____ 2. Uncle Fen likes to paint the kinds of pictures that you can sell.

_____ 3. They tried to study, but there was too much noise around you.

_____ 4. The children like to sleep in the room where you can see the sun rise.

_____ 5. When one first comes upon the scene, you might gasp in surprise.

_____ 6. The children watched the kite rise up and up until you couldn't see it anymore.

_____ 7. When one first steps into that stream, you should be prepared to scream from the cold.

_____ 8. The class members left their coats in the room where you also store the extra books.

_____ 9. According to the manual, one must unplug any electrical cord before you can make any repairs.

_____ 10. Our dogs are so rambunctious that they exhaust you!

_____ 11. We went to a new deli where you can get real lox and bagels.

_____ 12. Carlos took the higher path where you could see the deer.

Grammar

_____ 13. The Larsons love mornings when you can see the sunrise.

_____ 14. Often, if one is up early, you can see the first-quarter moon.

_____ 15. Cory and Tania swung so high on the swings that you almost fell off.

_____ 16. My dog acts like such a comic that you can't help but laugh.

_____ 17. She climbed to the observation deck where you can see for miles.

_____ 18. My aunt and uncle took courses at the New University, where you pay very little tuition.

_____ 19. We ran onto the frozen pond, which was so slippery that you slid all over the place.

_____ 20. Ralph took his parents to the Italian restaurant, where you could order any pasta dish imaginable.

_____ 21. The lions crept along in the high grass, which is what you do in stalking prey.

_____ 22. I have a cat who watches birds on television, and you often wonder if he knows they are not really in the room.

_____ 23. The boys didn't want to sit in the first row where you can't see the screen.

_____ 24. After one has eaten too much, you may feel unwell.

_____ 25. At the fair, Jack may take first place in the shot put, an event in which you must hurl an iron ball as far as possible.

_____ 26. We played musical chairs, that game in which you compete for a seat.

_____ 27. One should always do what you can.

_____ 28. The fans crowded around the rock star so that you could get a better look at him.

_____ 29. Is he sitting where you can see the screen?

_____ 30. Susan programmed the VCR so you could see the science program.

_____ 31. My after-school job makes me so tired that you fall asleep in the early evening.

_____ 32. The salmon struggled to jump upstream, where you would reach quiet pools.

_____ 33. She took her backpack on a long hike so that you could get away from the city noise.

_____ 34. If students have not studied for a test, you are always glad if it is postponed.

_____ 35. I put my gloves in a sensible place—and that always turns out to be a place you can't remember

_____ 36. They love to enter races in which you usually finish ahead of the crowd.

Lesson 59
Agreement with Indefinite Pronoun Antecedents

Use a **singular personal pronoun** when the antecedent is a singular indefinite pronoun, and use a **plural personal pronoun** when the antecedent is a plural indefinite pronoun.

Each of the girls on the team has **her** own shin pads.
Both of the dogs lost **their** collars.

Note in the first sentence, with the prepositional phrase *of the girls,* that even though the object of the preposition *of* is plural, *girls,* you use the personal pronoun that agrees with the indefinite pronoun *each.*

Traditionally, the indefinite antecedent has taken a masculine pronoun. Today, you may use a variety of forms.

Each has **his** report.   **Each** has **his** or **her** report.
Each has **her** report.   **All** have **their** reports.

SINGULAR INDEFINITE PRONOUNS

anybody	anyone	anything	each	either	everybody
everyone	everything	much	neither	nobody	no one
nothing	one	other	somebody	someone	something

PLURAL INDEFINITE PRONOUNS

several	both	few	many

SINGULAR OR PLURAL INDEFINITE PRONOUNS

some	all	any	most	none

▶ **Exercise 1** Underline the antecedent in each sentence. In the blank, write a personal pronoun that agrees with the antecedent. In some cases, you may write more than one pronoun.

<u>Each</u> one must bring ____<u>his or her</u>____ own art materials.

1. Few of the gardeners abandon _____ gardens in the summer.

2. Everyone will be required to turn in _____ science report next week.

3. Many of the videos were not in _____ correct jackets.

4. Each of the sopranos has learned _____ part for the oratorio.

5. If anyone has a different idea, I'd like to hear _____ express it.

6. One of the photos has _____ own separate cellophane cover.

7. Each of the fathers took _____ daughter to the banquet.

8. Neither of the women gave _____ testimony at the trial.

9. No one at the game wanted _____ team to lose.

10. Suddenly, all of the computers flashed error messages on _____ screens.

11. Both of the brothers took _____ astronomy lessons seriously.

12. Either of the sisters can recite _____ original poem.

13. Somebody has left _____ history project in the art room.

14. Everything in the museum had _____ name correctly labeled.

15. Both of the semifinalists brought _____ supporters to the tournament.

16. Everybody wants to show _____ courage in a crisis.

17. Does anyone know the combination to _____ lock?

18. Many of the travelers lost _____ luggage in the crash.

19. A few of the books are harder to read than _____ covers would suggest.

20. Several took _____ tests later than the other students.

21. Nobody in the room wants to give _____ opinion.

22. One of the flowers has dropped _____ petals.

23. Many of our friends have painted _____ homes recently.

24. Each of the brothers has _____ own area of expertise.

25. More of their relatives came to _____ family reunion this year.

26. Several of the birds ate _____ fill at the feeder.

27. Everyone must declare _____ major by junior year.

28. One of the sisters rode _____ bicycle to school every day.

29. Each of the garden tools has _____ own place in the garage.

30. Does anyone know the exact time of _____ birth?

31. Few of the tributaries have had _____ water quality improved recently.

32. Several of the skiers broke _____ legs on the slopes.

33. One of the cars had _____ tires stolen.

34. Both of the actors got _____ awards on the same night.

35. Everything in nature has _____ own place.

36. Has anyone lost _____ ring?

37. Another of those storms has left _____ mark on our region.

38. Someone has left _____ band instrument on the bus.

Lesson 60
Clear Pronoun Reference

Clearly state the antecedent of a pronoun. A pronoun should not be able to refer to more than one antecedent.

Never use the pronouns *this*, *that*, *which*, and *it* without a clearly stated antecedent. Each time you use these pronouns, be sure you express, in a word or two, the object or idea that you wish these words to stand for.

Vague: The audience members kept screaming at the monster, but **that** didn't keep me from enjoying the film.

Clear: The audience members kept screaming at the monster, but **their response** didn't keep me from enjoying the film.

Vague: The computers were all being used, **which** always happens when I have an assignment.

Clear: I couldn't do my assignment on the computers, **which** were all in use at the time.

Vague: My sisters have learned a lot by playing in the school orchestra, so I have also chosen **it** as my extracurricular activity.

Clear: My sisters have learned a lot by playing in the school orchestra, so I have also chosen **music** as my extracurricular activity.

If a pronoun seems to refer to more than one antecedent, reword the sentence to make the antecedent clear, or eliminate the pronoun.

Unclear Antecedent: When you put the car in the garage, don't forget to lock **it**.
Clear Antecedent: Lock the car after you put **it** in the garage.
No Pronoun: Park in the garage and lock the **car**.

Do not use *you* and *they* as indefinite pronouns. Name the person or group to which you are referring.

Indefinite: At the council meeting, **you** must ask to be recognized.
Clear: At the council meeting, **members** must ask to be recognized.
Indefinite: In the orchestra, **they** must practice scales.
Clear: In the orchestra, **players** must practice scales.

▶ **Exercise 1** Draw a line under each use of *it, you,* and *they*. At the end of each sentence, write a word or phrase to replace the underlined word.

In a book about whales, <u>they</u> described whale songs. <u>the authors</u>

1. In the championship game, they had to end the contest early because of threatening weather.

_____

2. Since my father enjoyed his birthday party so much, I was glad I had not forgotten it.

_____

3. When the freeway is slippery, you are supposed to be smart enough to slow down. _____

4. As members of the cast, they had to get up at 4:00 A.M. and go to the film studio.

_____

5. Do they know how birds fly such a long way during migration? _____

6. After the football game, they returned to the field to get their awards. _____

7. After the children were rescued from the raging creek, the reporters announced it on the news.

_____

8. In the desert you must be sure to carry plenty of water. _____

9. When you pack your clothing in your luggage, don't forget to label it. _____

10. I loved diving in the huge Pacific waves last summer, so I hope we'll visit it again this year.

_____

▶ **Exercise 2** **Rewrite each sentence to remove the italicized *this, that, which,* or *it,* or give the pronouns a clear antecedent.**

I love science, *which* began in grade school. ___My love for science began in grade school___

_____

1. I was not happy after the house was painted, but *it* was the best the painter could do. _____

_____

2. Perhaps the mail will bring my acceptance, *which* will be here by late afternoon. _____

_____

3. Take a break, *which* will be about ten minutes. _____

4. The video store features adventure films, *which* is the place to go. _____

_____

5. Jake and Angie do not get along, and *that* is a problem because they are sister and brother.

_____

6. The pies have already cooled, *which* is surprising. _____

_____

7. The school is for boys only, and *that* is why Mark wants to go there. _____

_____

8. The storm started before the roof was shingled, and *that* meant the plywood got soaked.

_____

☑ Unit 8 **Review**

▶ **Exercise 1** **Choose the correct pronoun from each pair in parentheses and draw a line under it.**

Randy and Butch took (his, <u>their</u>) parents out to dinner.

1. (We, Us) finalists decided to donate our winnings to a homeless center.

2. (Who, Whom) do you think the voters will choose for attorney general?

3. Each of the squirrels buried (its, their) acorns separately.

4. The filmmaker and (they, them) gave an interview to (he, him).

5. The coaches, Mr. Taylor and (he, him), huddled with the captains, Marsha and (she, her).

6. My cousin Alex has always been more athletic than (I, me).

7. We speculated about (who, whom) had robbed the bank.

8. The major wanted to train the horses (hisself, himself), Colonel.

9. Just between you and (I, me), the lap times are bad!

10. We took some sandwiches to Jack and (he, him).

11. There is no scientist for (who, whom) I have greater respect.

12. Angie taught (her, herself) to speak French.

13. Does your news surprise (him, he) as much as (I, me)?

14. I need to hire (whoever, whomever) knows the most about computers.

15. Don't look at (we, us) freshmen as though (we, us) were some kind of lower life form!

16. (He, Himself) and Kara have argued over this subject for years.

17. How surprised we were when the last person to come to the party was (she, her).

18. The birds (theirselves, themselves) decide which trees to use as nests.

19. The mayor met with both groups of protestors, (they, them) and (we, us).

20. (Their, They) taking an interest in my future really encouraged me to try harder.

21. Liam told (him, himself) that he should not give up so easily.

22. I want to hear the story from (whoever, whomever) saw the action.

23. Jane reminded (her, herself) that the problem (she, her) had could be overcome.

24. The man with the gray beard, (who, whom) lives on the hill, told (I, me) a wonderful story.

Cumulative Review: Units 1–8

▶ **Exercise 1** **Draw a line under each prepositional phrase. There may be more than one prepositional phrase in a sentence.**

He put the tools <u>inside the garage</u> <u>near the firewood</u>.

1. They ran along the end of the cliff.

2. The soldier rushed into headquarters with an urgent message.

3. The baby peered at the mobile above her bed.

4. The detective looked suspiciously at the suspect.

5. The magma inside the earth forced its way to the surface.

6. The cat crouched in the weeds, his eye on a bird.

7. The squirrel scrambled up the tree and onto the phone wires, where it ran across our yard chattering at our dog.

8. We went to the pool after the test.

9. The soldiers stood at attention beside the flagpole.

10. Jake whispered to Kei while the teacher talked to the class.

11. All kinds of invertebrates are found in the stream.

12. Before you leave, let me get a schedule for your mother.

13. Everyone came to the party late, except Yuji.

14. As we flew beyond the city, we could see the canyons beneath the plane.

15. Leave your muddy boots outside the house when you come back from your hike.

16. The farmer leaned against the fencepost, her eyes on the approaching storm.

17. Our films will be shown in the festival.

18. The dog sat beside the baby, under the awning, beyond the pool.

19. Against the wind, the fleeing residents struggled, dragging their belongings behind them.

20. Get your feet off the chair, and wipe the mud from the cushion!

▶ **Exercise 2** **Draw a line under the correct form of the verb in parentheses.**

Several of the skiers (gives, <u>give</u>) lessons to disabled people.

1. Be careful. The rungs of that ladder (bends, bend)!

2. Where do you suppose the keys to this lock (is, are)?

3. I don't know what the comic and the singer (thinks, think) they're going to do for an encore.

4. We (was, were) sure the storm would lift our roof off and blow it away!

5. This film (appears, appear) to be one of those that (interests, interest) you.

6. One of the new lambs (looks, look) black.

7. They (expects, expect) heavy flooding where the tributary (meets, meet) the main river.

8. The band and the majorettes (performs, perform) at halftime.

9. (Does, Do) my pants and vest match this hat?

10. (Does, Do) either your brother or your sister like hockey?

11. The daffodils and the tulips (blooms, bloom) beautifully.

12. This pair of boots, covered with river mud, (looks, look) like yours.

13. The footprints down by the stream (seems, seem) too large for a raccoon.

14. These kinds of tape recorders (operates, operate) with difficulty.

15. Ahmed and Dalila (competes, compete) against each other.

16. One of the math teachers also (coaches, coach) the girls' volleyball team.

17. The bus with the band members and instruments (follows, follow) the team bus.

18. The papers on the table (was, were) the ones I thought I had lost.

19. The rules at the recreation center (requires, require) all swimmers to shower before entering the pool.

20. Each of the class presidents (heads, head) a fund-raiser for disabled children.

▶ **Exercise 3** **Draw a line under the subordinate clause and write whether it is an adjective clause (adj.), an adverb clause (adv.), or a noun clause (N). Some sentences might have more than one subordinate clause.**

_____adj._____ The captain, who had survived the wreck, could not explain the disaster.

_____ 1. The little girl who answered the door said very little.

_____ 2. After the rain, the robin sang in the treetop while we stood and listened.

_____ 3. What the prince suggested surprised the prime minister.

_____ 4. You should try shopping in the big mall when you visit our town.

_____ 5. If the rain continues, we will have to cancel the picnic.

_____ 6. The poem for which she is known laments the death of her husband.

_____ 7. Lucy carries her diary with her wherever she goes.

_____ 8. The poor count loved one who would not have him.

Grammar

_____ **9.** The raccoon eats whatever it can find.

_____ **10.** Because snow fell last night, John got up early and went for a walk in the woods.

_____ **11.** Since the wild geese flew overhead, Ron has been very melancholy.

_____ **12.** November 22, 1963, was when an assassin killed President Kennedy in Dallas.

_____ **13.** The problem that we would not deal with has now grown too large to handle.

_____ **14.** The cardinal sings beautifully as it sits on that high branch.

_____ **15.** What our children need depends on many factors.

_____ **16.** We need to practice hard so that we can beat Central.

_____ **17.** Great-aunt Samantha, whose old Gothic house fascinated me, left me something in her will.

_____ **18.** The young detective, who worked diligently, discovered what had eluded the chief inspector.

_____ **19.** The long day wanes as if the sun has become tired of shining.

_____ **20.** The baroness, who believed her husband was dead, cried with joy when he opened her chamber door.

▶ Exercise 4 **Draw a line under the correct word in parentheses.**

Do you know (who, whom) won the short story contest?

1. Every one of the boys brought (his, their) own equipment.

2. They peered over the edge of the cliff, where (you can, they could) often see bluebirds.

3. Not everyone can risk (his or her, their) life to save someone in mortal danger.

4. Mr. Toki and his sons spent part of (his, their) day on a treasure hunt.

5. Even if one dislikes snakes, (you have, one has) to admit that snakes are fascinating creatures.

6. Yoko and (I, myself) disagree on everything except soccer.

7. A few of the speakers are unhappy with (they, their) choice of subjects.

8. The team sat quietly after (its, their) devastating loss.

9. (Who, Whom) was that stranger in the tan suit?

10. If one studies hard enough, (you, one) can sometimes get into college early.

11. The detective wondered (who, whom) Randolph had called before he disappeared.

12. Whenever you discover (who, whom) wrote that, tell me.

Unit 9: Using Modifiers Correctly

Lesson 61
Modifiers: Three Degrees of Comparison

Grammar

Most adjectives and adverbs have three degrees of comparison: the positive, the comparative, and the superlative.

The positive form of a modifier cannot be used to make a comparison. (This is the form that appears as the entry word in a dictionary.) The comparative form shows two things being compared. The superlative form shows three or more things being compared.

POSITIVE: The chicken enchiladas are **spicy.** (adjective)
               Maple trees grow **slowly.** (adverb)
COMPARATIVE: The chicken enchiladas are **spicier** than the cheese ones. (adjective)
               Maple trees grow **more slowly** than poplars. (adverb)
SUPERLATIVE: The chicken enchiladas are the **spiciest** dish on the menu. (adjective)
               Of these three trees, the maple grows **most slowly.** (adverb)

Most one- and two-syllable modifiers add *-er* to form the comparative and *-est* to form the superlative. (The addition of *-er* or *-est* sometimes makes a spelling change necessary.)

The room is **gloomier** on overcast days. (The *y* in gloomy changes to an *i.*)

Use *more* and *most* (or *less* and *least*) to form the comparative and superlative forms if a modifier has three or more syllables, if an adverb ends in *-ly,* or if *-er* or *-est* sounds awkward.

Eric took the **least difficult** route down the mountain.
He steered **more cautiously** as the road grew steeper.
Irina was the **most nervous** of the three. (not *nervousest*)

▶ **Exercise 1 Write in the blank the correct form of the modifier in parentheses.**

Pesticides are much _____ costlier _____, in environmental terms, than people once realized. (*costly*)

1. Biologist Rachel Carson was one of the first people to realize that pesticides were altering the

   environment _____ than living things could adapt. (*fast*)

2. Carson's book *Silent Spring* is widely regarded as one of the _____ books of

   the past half-century. (*influential*)

3. Her _____ book, *The Sea Around Us,* had already established Carson as an

   important writer. (*early*)

4. *Silent Spring* took four and a half years to write, much _____ than Carson had

   anticipated. (*long*)

5. In the 1960s, when *Silent Spring* was published, many people believed that pesticides were

   _____ than the insects they were meant to kill. (*safe*)

6. After all, insects carried some of the world's _____ diseases. (*deadly*)

7. *Silent Spring* climbed the best-seller lists even _____ than *The Sea Around Us* had. (*quickly*)

8. The chemicals Carson wrote about in *Silent Spring* were some of the _____ the planet had ever seen. (*toxic*)

9. Birds appeared to be _____ to the effects of pesticides than other animals. (*sensitive*)

10. The rate at which fish and birds died after their habitats had been sprayed was

    _____ than anything Carson had witnessed before. (*rapid*)

11. Chemical pesticides are still widely used today, but in much _____ quantities. (*small*)

12. The _____ of these chemicals, DDT, has been banned in the United States. (*powerful*)

13. A number of other countries, however, have _____ regulations than the United States does. (*weak*)

14. Synthetic pesticides remain in the environment much _____ than was once believed. (*long*)

15. Their _____ impact could be on water quality. (*great*)

16. Some pesticides are known to cause cancer in amounts much _____ than originally thought. (*small*)

17. Since the publication of *Silent Spring*, _____ methods of pest control have been developed. (*safe*)

18. Beneficial insects such as ladybugs are used _____ than before. (*often*)

19. Rachel Carson probably had a _____ influence on the modern environmental movement than any other single person. (*great*)

20. Thanks to pioneers such as Rachel Carson, concerned citizens worldwide are taking a

    _____ stance on environmental issues. (*tough*)

Lesson 62
Modifiers: Irregular Comparisons

A few modifiers form the comparative and superlative degrees irregularly.

MODIFIERS WITH IRREGULAR FORMS OF COMPARISON

POSITIVE	COMPARATIVE	SUPERLATIVE
good	better	best
well	better	best
bad	worse	worst
badly	worse	worst
far (distance)	farther	farthest
far (degree, time)	further	furthest
little (amount)	less	least
many	more	most
much	more	most

▶ **Exercise 1** **Write in the blank the correct form of the modifier in parentheses.**

Corva played _____ worse _____ on Sunday than she had on Saturday. (*badly*)

1. Of my three sisters, Rita lives the _____ away. (*far*)

2. Groceries seem to cost _____ every week. (*much*)

3. Colleen described the _____ blizzard she'd ever driven through. (*bad*)

4. The birds ate _____ food than we expected. (*little*)

5. This article delves _____ into the subject than I realized. (*far*)

6. Seán had _____ job skills than any other applicant. (*many*)

7. He played the sonata _____ the first time than the second time. (*well*)

8. Laura signed up _____ walkathon sponsors than anyone else in the class. (*many*)

9. This road is in _____ condition than it was last year. (*good*)

10. The corn is in the _____ field from the house. (*far*)

11. Beth had collected the _____ tip money of anyone working Saturday night. (*little*)

12. The _____ back George could remember was kindergarten. (*far*)

13. Claudio's car was parked _____ away than I remembered. (*far*)

14. Nancy's broken finger hurt _____ than she had expected it to. (*bad*)

15. The second draft of Jim's paper was _____ than the first. (*good*)

16. Of the three new landscape plants, the lilac survived the winter in _____

    condition. (*good*)

17. Perry hit the ball _____ of all. (*badly*)

18. Which test question gave you _____ amount of trouble? (*little*)

19. Melanie believed that _____ research would be required. (*far*)

20. She chose the path of _____ resistance. (*little*)

21. Please devote _____ amount of time possible to this task. (*little*)

22. These heavier upholstery fabrics are _____ choices than the linen. (*good*)

23. Is Mercury or Venus _____ from Earth? (*far*)

24. Sadao likes this design _____ of all. (*much*)

25. I like broccoli, but I like asparagus _____. (*well*)

26. The _____ away I got, the fainter the smell grew. (*far*)

27. My singing is _____ than my guitar playing. (*good*)

28. She asked for _____ time to complete the project. (*much*)

29. This was _____ interesting of the three books I bought. (*little*)

30. Midori drives _____ to work each day than I do. (*far*)

31. Kareem's SAT score was _____ than his brother's. (*good*)

32. My cold seems _____ today than yesterday. (*bad*)

33. I don't want to discuss the matter any _____. (*far*)

34. The _____ meal of my life was last Thanksgiving. (*good*)

35. Fifty miles was the _____ she had ridden her bike in a single day. (*far*)

36. That was the _____ tennis match of my life! (*bad*)

37. Peter passed the ball _____ than any other player. (*well*)

38. You have _____ patience with him than I do. (*much*)

39. Ivy is one of the _____ plant choices for this location. (*good*)

40. The creative writing class is _____ popular than the watercolor class. (*much*)

41. This cookbook has one of the _____ indexes I've ever seen. (*good*)

42. He was _____ cautious than he should have been. (*little*)

43. When I'm on stage, how I look is the _____ thing from my mind. (*far*)

44. The Cubs played their _____ game of the season. (*bad*)

Grammar

Lesson 63
Modifiers: Double and Incomplete Comparisons

Do not make a **double comparison** by using *-er* or *-est* with the words *more, most, less,* or *least.*

INCORRECT:	There must be a **more easier** way to solve this problem.
CORRECT:	There must be an **easier** way to solve this problem.
INCORRECT:	The black and white kitten is the **most friendliest** one.
CORRECT:	The black and white kitten is the **friendliest** one.

Do not make an **incomplete comparison** by omitting *other* or *else* when you compare one member of a group with another.

UNCLEAR:	The Labrador retriever is larger than any dog in the kennel.
CLEAR:	The Labrador retriever is larger than any **other** dog in the kennel.
UNCLEAR:	There are more bats here than anywhere in the state.
CLEAR:	There are more bats here than anywhere **else** in the state.

▶ **Exercise 1 Underline any double or incomplete comparisons.**

The first poem is shorter <u>than any poem</u> in the entire book.

1. The green paint is more bolder than the yellow.

2. Amber is the most friendliest person in the group.

3. The tree shading the front porch is older than any tree in the yard.

4. Emily had never seen stars more brighter than on that night.

5. The red convertible is shinier than any in the parking lot.

6. The Rockies are more higher than the Appalachians.

7. Mrs. Jiminez, a soprano, is taller than anyone in the choir.

8. There must be a more simpler route.

9. The kitchen is larger than any room in the house.

10. Joel wore the most weirdest costume of all.

11. Which of these three pears is most ripest?

12. The bookstore is open later than any shop in the plaza.

13. Chris's bowling ball is the most heaviest of all.

14. Jamal's winning entry was more detailed than any painting in the show.

15. The dining room is the most draftiest in the house.

16. The suitcase on the bottom is larger than any in the trunk.

17. *Gandhi* is longer than any movie we have watched.

18. In winter, chickadees are the most commonest birds at our feeder.

19. She walked farther on Saturday than on any day of the week.

20. Melanie was taller than any woman in her family.

▶ Exercise 2 **Circle any double or incomplete comparisons. Write *DC* in the blank for each double comparison and *IC* for each incomplete comparison. Write *C* if the sentence is correct.**

_____IC_____ In terms of area, Alaska is larger (than any state) in the United States.

_____ 1. In terms of population, however, it is the second most smallest.

_____ 2. Only Wyoming has fewer people than Alaska.

_____ 3. Alaska's most largest city is Anchorage.

_____ 4. Perhaps more than any state, Alaska is blessed with natural beauty.

_____ 5. Eight national parks protect Alaska's most loveliest areas.

_____ 6. The most highest point in the state is Mt. McKinley.

_____ 7. Also known as *Denali*, it is higher than any mountain in North America.

_____ 8. Alaska's most earliest inhabitants were Inuit and other native peoples.

_____ 9. The first white settlers arrived later than the native peoples.

_____ 10. In 1880, fewer than 1 percent of Alaska's residents were non-native.

_____ 11. Native Americans are no longer Alaska's most largest ethnic group.

_____ 12. Alaskans of non-native descent make up a much more larger percentage of the population.

_____ 13. Alaska is richer in natural resources than any state.

_____ 14. Its fishing industry is larger than any state's.

_____ 15. Due to harsh conditions, however, there is less farming than fishing.

_____ 16. Alaska has a shorter growing season than any state.

_____ 17. Lumber is of more greater importance than farming.

_____ 18. Oil has a greater influence on Alaska's economy than any industry.

_____ 19. The most biggest economic boom followed the first oil discoveries in 1968.

_____ 20. Huge off-shore oil deposits were discovered over a decade later than the first oil discoveries.

Lesson 64
Using *Good* or *Well*; *Bad* or *Badly*

Always use *good* as an adjective. *Well* may be used as an adverb of manner telling how ably something is done or as an adjective meaning "in good health."

Rock collecting is a **good** hobby for young children. (adjective)
That suit looks **good** on you. (adjective after a linking verb)
Cody performed his many duties **well**. (adverb of manner)
Andrew does not appear **well** this morning. (adjective meaning "in good health")

Always use *bad* as an adjective. Therefore, *bad* is used after a linking verb. Use *badly* as an adverb. *Badly* almost always follows an action verb.

Eating lunch first was a **bad** idea. (adjective)
The potatoes smelled **bad**. (adjective following a linking verb)
I feel **bad** about forgetting his birthday. (adjective following a linking verb)
The entire team played **badly** last night. (adverb following an action verb)

▶ **Exercise 1 Circle the correct form of *good*, *well*, *bad*, or *badly*.**

Because I had practiced, I recited my lines (good, <u>well</u>).

1. Joel felt (bad, badly) about calling his sister insensitive.

2. Michela slept (good, well) after a long day of driving.

3. With three members missing, the small group played (bad, badly).

4. The newspaper needed (bad, badly) to hire a proofreader.

5. Connor did (good, well) his first day on the job.

6. My rose garden is finally starting to look (good, well).

7. Alyssa wanted (bad, badly) to visit the art museum.

8. After hiking uphill all day, my muscles ached (bad, badly).

9. She looked as if she were feeling (good, well).

10. Karl wanted (bad, badly) to find a new roommate.

11. Everyone else's generosity made Sam feel (bad, badly) about his own stinginess.

12. Judy missed the baby shower because she was not feeling (good, well).

13. You don't have to tell me that my hair looks (bad, badly) today.

14. So far, my day has gone (bad, badly).

15. My puppy's obedience training is going very (good, well).

16. Tamara went over the instructions (good, well).

17. She did (good, well) on the advanced placement exam.

18. My mother still plays the piano (good, well).

19. Michael's new car runs (bad, badly) on humid days.

20. I know the melody to that song (good, well).

▶ **Exercise 2** Circle each incorrect use of *good, well, bad,* or *badly*. Write the correct word in the blank. Write *C* if the sentence is correct.

_____ **bad** _____ Kim thought the ground beef smelled (badly.)

_____ **1.** I felt bad about missing my sister's game.

_____ **2.** Carrots don't grow good in this soil.

_____ **3.** We could see quite good from the balcony.

_____ **4.** Arnie looks good in that green shirt.

_____ **5.** Shira felt badly about missing the meeting.

_____ **6.** Considering she hasn't taken voice lessons, she sings good.

_____ **7.** This is a good place to plant lily-of-the-valley.

_____ **8.** Why do you think this model sells so bad?

_____ **9.** She was feeling well enough to go out on Saturday.

_____ **10.** The class responded good to my report.

_____ **11.** She painted well enough to be accepted into the advanced art class.

_____ **12.** The blender worked good when we made yogurt shakes last night.

_____ **13.** His English teacher told him that he wrote well.

_____ **14.** My six-year-old sister doesn't read very good yet.

_____ **15.** Min knew the material good enough to pass the exam.

_____ **16.** I have always spelled bad.

_____ **17.** Ramon wanted bad to take a photography class.

_____ **18.** The farmers' market is stocked good on Saturday mornings.

_____ **19.** I felt badly after he told me the news about his father.

_____ **20.** Marella ran the volunteer organization well.

Lesson 65
Double Negatives

Never use a **double negative** or two negative words in the same clause. Use only one negative word to express a negative idea. The adverbs *barely, hardly,* and *scarcely* are also negative words.

INCORRECT:	I did**n't** buy **no** magazines.
CORRECT:	I did**n't** buy **any** magazines.
CORRECT:	I bought **no** magazines.
INCORRECT:	Kelly **never** did **nothing** to help Fiona.
CORRECT:	Kelly **never** did **anything** to help Fiona.
CORRECT:	Kelly did **nothing** to help Fiona.

▶ **Exercise 1** **Place a check (✔) in front of the sentences in which the negative is misused.**

✔____   I don't get no respect.

____ **1.** I don't remember nobody like that.

____ **2.** We will never do it again.

____ **3.** No, her name was not Esmerelda.

____ **4.** Unfortunately, we don't have none.

____ **5.** I didn't buy any of those.

____ **6.** Those pants don't look no good on you.

____ **7.** Wasn't that a blimp that I saw?

____ **8.** There won't be any of that going on here!

____ **9.** The colonel didn't say we couldn't do it.

____ **10.** Doesn't the rain sound loud on the tin roof?

____ **11.** I was not prepared for no test.

____ **12.** Don't you know that mermaids aren't real?

____ **13.** I don't mind tasting no snow.

____ **14.** There wasn't hardly any milk left for the cereal.

____ **15.** Clarissa and Jean Edmond went to the lake.

____ **16.** It's just not possible that I didn't get none!

____ **17.** We didn't have the puppy scarcely a week.

____ **18.** He believes there aren't none to be found.

____ **19.** Didn't the fisherman catch anything today?

Grammar

_____ **20.** We will wait until we can't stand it anymore.

_____ **21.** The stars don't shine none when it's raining.

_____ **22.** I just don't want to talk to you no more.

_____ **23.** Ah, well, there isn't hardly a point to it anymore.

_____ **24.** I don't listen to the radio to get no news!

_____ **25.** We waited for you but you didn't come.

_____ **26.** I'll never give my heart again.

_____ **27.** Sheila won't wait if you're not there on time.

_____ **28.** Karl doesn't think about nobody but himself.

_____ **29.** I never read no book by that author.

_____ **30.** She doesn't study any language but English.

_____ **31.** I can't barely believe that.

_____ **32.** We simply didn't want to hear no music by that group.

_____ **33.** Sandra got no news from Michele.

_____ **34.** Tobacco doesn't do nobody no good.

_____ **35.** There are only a few of us who don't like that movie.

_____ **36.** If you don't know the facts, you shouldn't talk as if you do.

_____ **37.** Lester doesn't do no strenuous exercise.

_____ **38.** Didn't you do any research?

_____ **39.** The cleaning service doesn't do no windows.

_____ **40.** I didn't buy nobody a valentine.

▶ **Exercise 2** Circle the two negative words in each double negative. Write *C* in the blank if the sentence is correct.

_____ I (wasn't) getting (nowhere) with my plan for starting a business.

_____ **1.** Josie never got called by no salespeople at dinnertime.

_____ **2.** She eats chicken and fish, but she doesn't eat no red meat.

_____ **3.** Jake's new truck doesn't have no stereo yet.

_____ **4.** She wasn't accepted by none of her first-choice colleges.

_____ **5.** Mira's salad is the one that doesn't have no tomato in it.

_____ **6.** If I don't get home by six, I won't have time for dinner.

_____ **7.** He didn't want his parents to throw no big graduation party.

_____ **8.** Mr. Alvarez didn't want to bake no cookies on such a hot day.

_____ **9.** Jim hasn't made friends with none of the other counselors.

_____ **10.** Rachel wasn't sure about nothing on the test.

_____ **11.** I locked the door, but I didn't lock no windows.

_____ **12.** Mike didn't want to fix the old car, and neither did I.

_____ **13.** We realized too late that we hadn't packed no can opener.

_____ **14.** Carol's bus didn't come no earlier yesterday.

_____ **15.** You are not permitted to drop no classes after this week.

_____ **16.** Rami didn't like to drink nothing containing caffeine.

_____ **17.** The driver's window doesn't open, and the horn doesn't work.

_____ **18.** Most doctors don't have no weekend office hours.

_____ **19.** Tana never knows what time it is, because she doesn't wear no watch.

_____ **20.** After Rosellen repaired the phone, it wasn't working no better.

▶ **Exercise 3 Circle the word in each sentence for which the word *any* will correct a double negative. Write *C* in the blank if the sentence is correct.**

_____ Very few people can say that they never get (no) headaches.

_____ **1.** Chronic headaches should always be reported to a doctor, to make sure there aren't no serious health problems.

_____ **2.** Many headache sufferers have no knowledge of prevention strategies.

_____ **3.** People usually get tension headaches when they don't have no suitable outlets for stress in their lives.

_____ **4.** There isn't no single best way to avoid tension headaches.

_____ **5.** It would not make no sense for all headache sufferers to use the same stress-reduction techniques.

_____ **6.** Although some stress is purely physical, most is not caused by no injury or illness.

_____ **7.** Rather, emotional stress often leads to muscle tension.

_____ **8.** People who get frequent headaches often cannot find relief from no over-the-counter medications.

Grammar

_____ 9. Practicing a stress-reduction technique doesn't mean a person won't have no more headaches, either.

_____ 10. Biofeedback, yoga, and other relaxation techniques don't provide no guarantees.

_____ 11. However, if one method doesn't appear to be of no help, another can be tried.

_____ 12. Not all headaches are caused by muscle tension.

_____ 13. Migraine headaches don't have no one known cause.

_____ 14. A migraine headache doesn't usually come as no surprise to its victim.

_____ 15. A migraine is often preceded by an "aura" consisting of symptoms such as blurred vision or no tolerance for loud noises.

_____ 16. Migraine sufferers often can't participate in no everyday activities while they have a headache.

_____ 17. Another type of headache, the cluster headache, often appears during sleep.

_____ 18. Cluster headaches are sometimes preceded by the sufferer seeing flashes of bright lights.

_____ 19. Most people take painkillers but don't bother to pinpoint no cause for their headaches.

_____ 20. There simply aren't no easy cures for this common problem.

▶ Writing Link **Write three sentences using a variety of double negative sentences. Then rewrite the sentences with correct, but equally expressive, usage.**

_____

_____

_____

_____

_____

_____

_____

_____

_____

_____

_____

Lesson 66
Misplaced and Dangling Modifiers

Place modifiers as close as possible to the words they modify in order to make the meaning of the sentence clear.

A misplaced modifier modifies the wrong word or seems to modify more than one word in a sentence. To correct a misplaced modifier, move the modifier as close as possible to the word that it modifies.

MISPLACED: I want to buy a computer for my mother with a modem.
CLEAR: I want to buy a computer with a modem for my mother.
MISPLACED: At the picnic we served strawberry mousse to everyone in paper cups.
CLEAR: At the picnic we served strawberry mousse in paper cups to everyone.

A dangling modifier does not logically modify any word in the sentence. To correct a dangling modifier, supply a word that the dangling modifier can logically modify.

DANGLING: Waiting for a ride home, rain started to fall. (Was the rain waiting for a ride home?)
CLEAR: While I was waiting for a ride home, rain started to fall.
DANGLING: Having found the missing boy, the search was called off. (Who found the boy?)
CLEAR: Having found the missing boy, Officer Hadley called off the search.

The word *only* should immediately precede the word or group of words it modifies. If *only* is placed elsewhere, the sentence's meaning may be unclear.

UNCLEAR: Maria only has her German class on Friday. (Does she have her class on any other days?)
CLEAR: Maria has her German class only on Friday.
UNCLEAR: They only went to the movies on weekends. (Did they do anything else?)
CLEAR: They went to the movies only on weekends.

▶ **Exercise 1** Circle each misplaced modifier and draw an arrow to the word it should modify. Write *C* in the blank if the sentence is correct.

_____   I served pizza to the children on paper plates.

_____ 1. Before leaving on Friday, hors d'oeuvres will be available for the workshop

   participants.

_____ 2. Driving all night, the sun was coming up when we arrived.

_____ 3. Before leaving his house, the dentist's office called, and Ricardo rescheduled his

   appointment.

_____ 4. Waiting outside for an hour, the cold wind was all I could think about.

_____ 5. Alone in a strange house, every little noise frightened Jessie.

_____ 6. Studying quietly, my brother's loud music disturbed me.

_____ 7. Bored with sitting in her hotel room, Joanna went shopping.

_____ 8. I discovered a nest mowing the lawn.

_____ 9. Unfamiliar with the game, golf seemed difficult to Pat.

_____ 10. Colleen stir-fried vegetables for her guests in the wok.

_____ 11. Newly married, the apartment seemed just right for Bill and Miriam.

_____ 12. Working in the yard all day, I like to listen to the radio.

_____ 13. With their herds increasing, accidents involving deer are on the rise.

_____ 14. Tossing and turning, thoughts of the next day's trip kept Aisha awake.

_____ 15. Brushing against my legs, I couldn't ignore the hungry cat.

_____ 16. New at the job, the duties seemed easy to Tomas.

_____ 17. Walking past the window, I noticed streaks in the glass.

_____ 18. Not as hot as Florida, I'd rather visit South Carolina.

_____ 19. Driving in the center lane, a patch of ice caused Anna to skid.

_____ 20. Sweeter than orange juice, I prefer apple juice.

_____ 21. Thinking about the day's events, I walked up the stairs.

_____ 22. Don had a review published in the newspaper of his favorite book.

_____ 23. Trying to impress my supervisor, nobody worked harder than I did.

_____ 24. My grandfather cooked a complete holiday dinner for the family with all the trimmings.

_____ 25. Finally nodding off, the alarm clock woke Beth.

_____ 26. Working in the quiet basement, the doorbell startled Eric.

_____ 27. We waited to hear if the baby was a girl or a boy with nervous anticipation.

_____ 28. Hoping for good news, I checked the mailbox every day.

_____ 29. Lunch was provided for everyone in a box.

_____ 30. My mother adopted a cat, lonely after I moved out.

▶ **Exercise 2** Underline each dangling modifier. Circle each misplaced modifier and draw an arrow to the word it should modify. Write *C* in the blank if the sentence is correct.

_____   Walking on the beach, the surf washed over our ankles.

_____ **1.** Watching television, a show came on that Tricia wanted to see.

_____ **2.** While tuning his guitar, a string broke.

_____ **3.** Watching the sun set, the boats sailed across the water.

_____ **4.** Every week while doing laundry, the detergent runs out.

_____ **5.** Wearing her new dress, Linda entered the restaurant.

_____ **6.** After waiting for an hour, Frannie's name was called.

_____ **7.** Writing my term paper, the printer ran out of paper.

_____ **8.** While delivering the new sofa, a muddy footprint was left on the carpet.

_____ **9.** Unable to start his car, a taxi took Jack to the airport.

_____ **10.** Walking across the bridge, the hotel could be seen.

_____ **11.** Shopping in a crowded store, my mother's wallet was stolen.

_____ **12.** My sister missed an entire week of swimming with the chicken pox.

_____ **13.** Filling the birdfeeder, a chickadee appeared.

_____ **14.** I was invited to the impressionist exhibit by Tannie.

_____ **15.** To win basketball games, practice sessions must be attended.

_____ **16.** Unable to attend the out-of-town wedding, I sent a gift.

_____ **17.** Driving in fog, the tail lights of the car in front of Stephen were hard to see.

_____ **18.** After reading this book, a fence will be easy to build.

_____ **19.** Walking across the frozen pond, the ice broke.

_____ **20.** A dog should be treated by a veterinarian if he has worms.

▶ **Exercise 3** Insert a vertical line to indicate where the word *only* should be placed to make each sentence match the meaning in parentheses.

My grandmother works|on Saturday. (She works one day a week.)

1. My grandmother works on Saturday. (She works alone.)

2. My grandmother works on Saturday. (She does nothing else on Saturday.)

3. Ivy grows on this slope. (It grows nowhere else.)

Grammar

4. Ivy grows on this slope. (Nothing else grows there.)

5. Trout swim in that part of the lake. (No other fish swim there.)

6. Trout swim in that part of the lake. (They swim nowhere else in the lake.)

7. Mr. Sato taught driver's education. (He taught one course.)

8. Mr. Sato taught driver's education. (No one else taught it.)

9. Thom did laundry last night. (He did nothing else last night.)

10. Thom did laundry last night. (No one else did laundry.)

11. Terese sang the first verse. (She didn't sing any other verses.)

12. Terese sang the first verse. (No one else sang it.)

13. Jaime reads mystery novels. (No one else reads them.)

14. Jaime reads mystery novels. (He reads no other novels.)

15. Corrine drove the truck. (No one else drove it.)

16. Corrine drove the truck. (She didn't drive other vehicles.)

17. Our group had blue paint. (No other group had blue paint.)

18. Our group had blue paint. (The group had only one color.)

19. Eduardo swam a mile. (No one else did.)

20. Eduardo swam a mile. (He didn't swim any farther.)

▶ **Writing Link** **Write a paragraph about a person you admire. Use three correctly placed modifiers, and use the word *only* at least once.**

_____

_____

_____

_____

_____

_____

_____

_____

_____

_____

_____

_____

Grammar

☑ Unit 9 **Review**

▶ **Exercise 1** Complete each sentence with the comparative or superlative form of the modifier in parentheses.

This is the _____grimiest_____ floor I've ever seen. (*grimy*)

1. Donna had never stayed at a _____ resort. (*luxurious*)

2. Mr. Lampros entered his _____ chili recipe in the contest. (*spicy*)

3. Oscar is the _____ performing dog I've ever seen. (*funny*)

4. Nobody is _____ than Jill about the play being canceled. (*upset*)

5. You should drive _____ in snow. (*slowly*)

6. The last section was the _____ to write. (*difficult*)

7. Gen grew even _____ after climbing eight flights of stairs. (*tired*)

8. This lab test is one of the _____ we can use. (*sensitive*)

9. She was even _____ after her solo than before. (*nervous*)

10. That documentary was _____ than the one I saw yesterday. (*powerful*)

11. Jason's _____ appointment today is with the admissions committee. (*early*)

12. Carol hoped her design would be judged _____. (*original*)

13. Child care was _____ than Tory had anticipated. (*expensive*)

14. Molly will plant a _____ variety of tomatoes this year. (*hardy*)

15. The _____ way to protect your eyes is with safety goggles. (*good*)

16. For at least a month, this knee will be _____ than your other one. (*weak*)

17. Only the _____ athletes will make the team. (*able*)

18. The _____ distance between two points is a straight line. (*short*)

19. I have always been _____ than anyone else in my family. (*clumsy*)

20. Carin was voted _____ by her classmates. (*creative*)

21. The lake is _____ this morning than it was last night. (*calm*)

22. The _____ temperature of the day is in the morning. (*low*)

23. While we were lost, Sabrina had a _____ attitude than anyone else in the car. (*good*)

24. Andrew seems _____ about the project now that Kelsey is involved.

    (*enthusiastic*)

Grammar

Cumulative Review: Units 1–9

▶ **Exercise 1** Underline each subordinate clause. Write *adj.* in the blank for each adjective clause, *adv.* for each adverb clause, and *N* for each noun clause.

_____adj._____ The horse that I saw run so fast lives on this farm.

_____ **1.** I will do it though I would rather not.

_____ **2.** What the king decreed gladdened the hearts of people.

_____ **3.** I met a person whose name is Ashford Carleton Edmond.

_____ **4.** Charlie makes everyone happy wherever he goes.

_____ **5.** The sailing ship that we saw yesterday has anchored in the bay.

_____ **6.** Jamie calculated on his fingers what the answer might be.

_____ **7.** Miguel de Cervantes, who was born in Spain, wrote *Don Quixote*.

_____ **8.** Billy throws knuckleballs better than anyone else in the league can throw them.

_____ **9.** Whatever the weather does tomorrow will not stop our picnic plans.

_____ **10.** Liam told the truth because that is always the best policy.

_____ **11.** The *Hindenberg*, which was a giant passenger airship built in Germany,

crashed in New Jersey in 1937.

_____ **12.** Didn't you know that this necklace belonged to Queen Marie Antoinette?

_____ **13.** If you don't want to do it, just tell me.

_____ **14.** There is the church where my brother was married last Saturday.

_____ **15.** I already told you where I put your books.

_____ **16.** Though I am tired, I will go a bit farther.

_____ **17.** We went there so that I could buy a magazine.

_____ **18.** The storm grew worse after the electricity went off.

_____ **19.** Captain Nemo is the fictional character who commanded the *Nautilus*.

_____ **20.** The detective suspected that the butler really did do it.

_____ **21.** Karl and Shawna didn't like the movie as it had no plot.

_____ **22.** Because he's made up his mind, Clark feels at peace now.

_____ **23.** Carissa practiced her singing in order that she might earn a college scholarship.

_____ **24.** You'll just have to wait until the sun comes out.

▶ **Exercise 2** Write in the blank the tense of the italicized verb or verb phrase. Write *past* for *past*, *past prog.* for past progressive, *past perf.* for past perfect, *pres.* for present, *pres. prog.* for present progressive, and *pres. perf.* for present perfect.

_____past prog._____ Bob and Carol *were singing*.

_____ 1. We *have run* the race.

_____ 2. Thomas *had solved* the problem.

_____ 3. Frank and Mary *had arrived* by eight o'clock.

_____ 4. King Robert the Bruce *liberated* Scotland from foreign rule.

_____ 5. All of us in my family *love* motorcycles.

_____ 6. The plane *has left* already.

_____ 7. I think the old bicycle finally *wore* out.

_____ 8. You *have seen* that television program a million times.

_____ 9. Surely you *had studied* for the final?

_____ 10. Dad says our dog *has reached* his full height.

_____ 11. We *are leaving* on the thirteenth of June.

_____ 12. I *am taking* out the garbage right now.

_____ 13. The field marshal of the war games *has planned* the attack well.

_____ 14. The author *writes* more of her book daily.

_____ 15. Those salespeople *talk* all the time.

_____ 16. The frog *hopped* onto the porch.

_____ 17. The ocean waves *roll* in.

_____ 18. When I finish my report, I will ask Clara if she *has finished* hers.

_____ 19. Susan *was mowing* the yard when we arrived.

_____ 20. I *remember* that actor well.

_____ 21. I *had told* the story by the time the bus showed up.

_____ 22. Ken *stands* forlornly by the window.

_____ 23. What *had happened* in the movie by the time the sheriff appeared in it?

_____ 24. The high wind *whistled* eerily in the old ruins.

_____ 25. I have decided that I *am buying* this CD.

Grammar

▶ **Exercise 3** Write *act.* before each italicized verb in the active voice and *pass.* before each in the passive voice.

_____act._____   I *will wash* my clothes today.

_____   **1.** Deelra *seeks* employment here.

_____   **2.** The window *was broken*.

_____   **3.** The yard *was mowed* by him.

_____   **4.** We *painted* the garage.

_____   **5.** I *am writing* a novel.

_____   **6.** The report *was finished* by Samantha yesterday.

_____   **7.** The buzzing doorbell *was* finally *answered*.

_____   **8.** We *will drive* to the White Mountains this summer.

_____   **9.** The king *was being deposed* by the mob.

_____   **10.** Our victory over Central *will be praised* by the newspapers.

_____   **11.** I *was asked* by the officer to produce my driver's license.

_____   **12.** The usher *asked* me to move to the back row.

▶ **Exercise 4** Write *ind.* if the italicized verb is in the indicative mood, *imp.* if it is in the imperative mood, and *sub.* if it is in the subjunctive mood.

_____imp._____   *Wash* the dishes.

_____   **1.** I wish she *were* here now.

_____   **2.** Deelra *seeks* employment here.

_____   **3.** Bob *will drive* to the state fair.

_____   **4.** If he *were* a dependable person, he would have brought it.

_____   **5.** Sometimes I feel as if I *were* pretty foolish.

_____   **6.** *Get* the car keys, would you?

_____   **7.** The children said they *were* tired.

_____   **8.** It is important that we not *be* late.

_____   **9.** If I *were* she, I would go back to school.

_____   **10.** We asked that she *wait* until we were ready.

_____   **11.** *Were* you *expecting* him to pitch a fastball?

_____   **12.** I must *be* mindful of my duties.

Usage

Unit 10: Usage Glossary

Lesson 67
Usage: *a* to *altogether*

Words that are similar are sometimes confused. Certain other words should be avoided in formal writing and speaking.

a, an Use *a* with words that begin with a consonant or "yew" sound. Use *an* with any vowel sound, including words that begin with a silent *h*.

a hat   **a** euphemism   **a** university   **an** acre   **an** hour

a lot, alot *A lot* should be written as two words or avoided completely.

A lot of these recipes call for eggs.

a while, awhile *A while* is an article and a noun; *awhile* is an adverb.

After dinner I read for **a while**.   Cary is resting **awhile**.

accept, except *Accept* is a verb meaning "receive" or "agree to." *Except* is a preposition meaning "but" or, less commonly, a verb meaning "leave out."

We **accept** your recommendations.   I'll take all **except** the last one.
I feel I must **except** this one item from the list.

adapt, adopt *Adapt* means "adjust" or "change." *Adopt* means "take for one's own."

The cat **adapted** well to the apartment.   Would you like to **adopt** a kitten?

advice, advise *Advice* is a noun meaning "recommendation." *Advise* is a verb meaning "give advice."

I asked my sister's **advice** about college.   She **advised** me not to rush into anything.

▶ **Exercise 1** Underline the word or expression in parentheses that best completes each sentence.

The green book is (a, an) history of modern dance.

1. Before Saturday, I hadn't seen Mariana in (a while, awhile).

2. There seem to be (a lot, alot) of butterflies in this area.

3. Tim didn't want the committee to (accept, except) my proposal.

4. Dave wanted some (advice, advise) on choosing a law school.

5. I would (advice, advise) you to check the air in your spare tire.

6. My uncle has always driven (a, an) European car.

7. Waiting for the bus, I decided to read (a while, awhile).

8. Denise has (a lot, alot) of trouble learning new names.

9. My sister is a vegetarian, so we had to (adapt, adopt) the recipe.

10. The company has (adapted, adopted) a new performance evaluation system.

---

affect, **effect** *Affect* is a verb meaning "influence." *Effect* is a noun meaning "result" or, less commonly, a verb meaning "bring about."

Strenuous exercise can **affect** one's appetite. (verb)
Strenuous exercise can have an **effect** on one's appetite. (noun)
Strenuous exercise sometimes **effects** an appetite loss. (verb)

ain't *Ain't* should not be used in speaking or writing except as part of a quotation.

all ready, **already** *All ready* means "completely ready." *Already* is an adverb meaning "before" or "by this time."

I am **all ready** to leave for the weekend.
I have **already** packed my suitcase.

all right, **alright** *All right* should always be written as two words.

Robin said it was **all right** if I borrowed her car.

all together, **altogether** *All together* means "in a group." *Altogether* is an adverb meaning "completely" or "on the whole."

We were **all together** at the meeting.   Sam was **altogether** surprised.

▶ **Exercise 2 Correct the word or words in italics. If the sentence is correct, write C.**

_____effects_____ Scientists are still debating the long-term *affects* on Earth's climate.

_____ **1.** Kendra is not *all together* certain she wants to join.

_____ **2.** The flowers I sent Crissa did not have the intended *effect*.

_____ **3.** Would it be *alright* if I borrowed your tape player?

_____ **4.** Everyone *accept* Byron had at least a part-time job.

_____ **5.** *Ain't* it a surprise to see Sally playing basketball?

_____ **6.** I don't think the new store hours will *effect* my work schedule.

_____ **7.** The backpack I bought last year still looks *alright*.

_____ **8.** Daniel hoped that the new policy would *effect* an increase in sales.

_____ **9.** Kyle wasn't *all together* sure the movie started at seven.

_____ **10.** By the time we arrived, the game had *all ready* started.

Lesson 68
Usage: *allusion* to *would of*

---

allusion, **illusion** An *allusion* is an "indirect reference." An *illusion* is a "false idea or appearance."

The new play contained **allusions** to popular song lyrics.
This warm weather gives the **illusion** of spring.

anywheres, **everywheres** Write these words without the final *-s: anywhere, everywhere.*

being as, **being that** Use *because* or *since.*

Because we arrived early, we didn't have to wait in line.
My aunt will cook for the party **since** she is a chef.

beside, **besides** *Beside* means "next to." *Besides* means "in addition to."

My dog walked **beside** me.   We saw three swimmers **besides** Theo.

between, **among** *Between* relates or compares two entities. *Among* shows a relationship in which more than two entities are considered as a group.

We built a fence **between** the garage and the parking lot.
Let's plant crocuses **among** the other perennials.

borrow, **lend**, **loan** The verbs *borrow* and *lend* are opposites. *Loan* should be used as a noun.

Jo never **borrows** money.   Will you **lend** me a pen?   James took out a **loan** for his car.

▶ **Exercise 1** **Underline the word or expression in parentheses that best completes each sentence.**

Music lovers can choose (among, between) many different styles.

1. Just about (anywhere, anywheres) one travels, a wide variety of radio stations is available.

2. (Beside, Besides) the usual assortment of stations, a few specialize in jazz.

3. Jazz (borrows, lends, loans) elements from two other American musical styles—blues

    and ragtime.

4. In blues, certain "flattened" notes create the (allusion, illusion) of a human voice.

5. (Being as, Because) these notes sound sad, they are called "blue."

6. Ragtime got its name (being that, because) it has an uneven or "ragged" rhythm.

7. Jazz compositions sometimes contain musical (allusions, illusions) to blues and ragtime.

8. A uniquely American creation, jazz is now known (everywhere, everywheres).

9. Musicians working in other styles often (borrow, lend, loan) jazz techniques.

10. In the eyes of many, jazz greats such as Duke Ellington have earned places of honor

(beside, besides) the great classical composers.

---

bring , take *Bring* means "transport from a distant place to a closer one." *Take* means "transport from a nearby place to a more distant one."

Please **bring** me a souvenir from Lisbon.   I will **take** the dogs with me on vacation.

can , may *Can* signifies ability. *May* signifies permission or means "might."

She **can** skate better than anyone else in her family.   **May** I borrow your pen?

can't hardly , can't scarcely Avoid using *hardly* or *scarcely* with *not* or *-n't*. This construction creates a double negative.

continual , continuous *Continual* means "occurring repeatedly." *Continuous* means "proceeding without interruption."

Continual cold snaps damaged the crop.   We had **continuous** snow all morning.

could of , might of , must of , should of , would of *Have*, not *of*, should follow *could*, *might*, *must*, *should*, and *would*.

▶ **Exercise 2** **Substitute the correct word or expression for the one in parentheses and write it in the blank. Write *C* if the sentence is correct.**

_____must have_____ Edward Kennedy Ellington (must of) known as a child that he was destined for great things.

_____ **1.** Duke's Ellington's parents and teachers (continuously) reinforced a sense of pride in the young boy.

_____ **2.** Ellington (couldn't hardly) remember experiencing racism while he was growing up.

_____ **3.** Washington, D.C., although segregated, (may) have been one of the best places an African American child could grow up in the early 1900s.

_____ **4.** If not for a mishap on the playing field, Duke (might of) chosen a career in baseball.

_____ **5.** An incident in which the young Duke was hit on the head by a bat (could of) changed the course of musical history.

_____ **6.** Soon after the head injury, Duke's mother (brought) him to a piano teacher to introduce him to a less dangerous hobby.

_____ **7.** One (can) hardly believe that he disliked piano lessons as a child.

_____ **8.** It was not until the teenage Ellington heard ragtime that he (took) a real interest in music.

Usage

Lesson 69
Usage: *different from* to *regardless*

---

different from, different than *Different from* is preferred.

This salad is **different from** the one I bought yesterday.

doesn't, don't *Doesn't* is used with *he, she, it,* and all singular nouns. *Don't* is used with *I, you, we, they,* and all plural nouns.

She **doesn't** know my phone number.
Don't you want to come with us?

emigrate, immigrate *Emigrate* means "to leave a country or region." *Immigrate* has the opposite meaning, "to come to a country to live."

Many people **emigrate** from war-torn countries.
Caitlin's cousin will **immigrate** to the United States.

farther, further Use *farther* to refer to physical distance. Use *further* to refer to time or degree.

She rode **farther** than I did.
Further study is needed.

fewer, less Use *fewer* with nouns that can be counted, except when referring to *money*. Use *less* with nouns that cannot be counted.

Serena made **fewer** sales than Whitney, but Whitney took in **less** money.

▶ **Exercise 1** Underline the word in parentheses that best completes each sentence.

Ryan (<u>doesn't</u>, don't) think we need a new telephone.

1. Clayton decided to research the topic (farther, further).

2. Jim's grandfather (emigrated, immigrated) from Poland after the war.

3. Our group collected (fewer, less) aluminum cans than any other.

4. Enzo looks different (from, than) anyone else in his family.

5. Natalie's parents (emigrated, immigrated) here the year her brother was born.

6. Trevor's new job is (farther, further) from home than his old job.

7. (Doesn't, Don't) it seem as if it always rains on Saturday?

8. Carrie ordered (fewer, less) soft drinks this month than last.

9. Derrick's political views are different (from, than) mine.

10. This sandwich has (fewer, less) mayonnaise than the one I usually order.

Usage

good , well *Good* is an adjective. *Well* is an adverb. To describe a person's health or appearance, *well* is used as an adjective.

This is a **good** book.   Andrew sings **well**.   Gretel feels **well**.

had of *Of* should not be used between *had* and a past participle.

If I **had** eaten lunch, I wouldn't be hungry now.

hanged , hung *Hanged* means "put to death by hanging." Use *hung* in all other cases.

Convicted murderers were sometimes **hanged**.
Ethan **hung** his coat in the closet.

in , into *In* means "inside" or "within a place." *Into* indicates movement from outside to within.

The shovel stood **in** the garage.   Max crawled **into** the tent.

irregardless , regardless Always use *regardless*.

Finish the job, **regardless** of how long it takes.

Usage

▶ Exercise 2 **Substitute the correct word or expression for the one in italics, and write it in the blank. Write *C* if the sentence is correct.**

_____well_____ On a limited budget, Laina has decorated her new restaurant *good.*

_____ 1. The furnishings would have cost much more if she *had of* bought them all new.

_____ 2. Instead, Laina searched *into* attics and basements for treasures to recycle.

_____ 3. Her motto is, "If it looks good, use it, *regardless* of where it came from."

_____ 4. On the windows, she *hanged* old wooden shutters she found in her grandmother's garage.

_____ 5. In front of these, she *hung* plants donated by a high school botany class.

_____ 6. At flea markets she collected dozens of secondhand chairs and, *irregardless* of style, painted them all the same dark green.

_____ 7. The tables, no two the same size and shape, look *well* together thanks to matching tablecloths.

_____ 8. On the walls Laina has *hanged* old calendar pictures in inexpensive frames.

_____ 9. Customers who walk *in* the dining room will never guess the origins of its furnishings.

_____ 10. The place simply wouldn't have the same charm if people *had of* thrown all these old things away.

Lesson 70
Usage: *this kind* to *reason is because*

---

this kind, these kinds *This* and *that* are singular. *These* and *those* are plural.

This kind of dog is well behaved around children.
Purchasing **these kinds** of products is less harmful to the rainforest.

lay, lie *Lay* means "to put" or "to place" something. *Lay* always takes a direct object. *Lie* means "to recline" or "to be positioned." *Lie* never takes a direct object.

Please **lay** the towels on the dresser.
Carol decided to **lie** down for a while.

learn, teach *Learn* means "to acquire knowledge." *Teach* means "to give knowledge."

Gina wants to **teach** kindergarten.
I am trying to **learn** this song.

leave, let *Leave* means "to go away." *Let* means "to allow" or "to permit."

Don't **leave** until you have signed the registration form.
Jessica **let** her baby brother open her birthday gifts.

like, as *Like* is a preposition and introduces a prepositional phrase. *As* is a subordinating conjunction and introduces a subordinate clause.

Experiments **like** this one often fail.
As we had hoped, the experiment was a success.

Usage

▶ **Exercise 1** **Underline the word or words in parentheses that best complete each sentence.**

The package was (laying, <u>lying</u>) on the counter.

1. I wish someone could (learn, teach) me to whistle.

2. Please don't (leave, let) that vase fall.

3. (This kind, These kinds) of pizza has white sauce.

4. Travis worked out regularly, (like, as) all athletes should.

5. The black dog (lies, lays) in the shade.

6. Small cars (like, as) this one get good gas mileage.

7. We will have to (leave, let) early to catch the bus.

8. (This kind, These kinds) of flowers will grow in the shade.

9. I completed the project, (like, as) you requested.

10. Please (learn, teach) me that math trick.

Usage

loose , lose   *Loose* is an adjective. *Lose* is a verb.

He tied the rope in a **loose** knot.
Be careful not to **lose** these tickets.

passed , past   *Passed* is the past form and past participle of the verb *pass*. *Past* may be an adjective, a preposition, an adverb, or a noun.

Climbing the hill, we **passed** three trucks.
We drove **past** Yasmin's house.

precede , proceed   *Precede* means "to go or come before." *Proceed* means "to continue" or "to move along."

A short film **preceded** the lecture.
The meeting **proceeded** without us.

raise , rise   *Raise* means "to cause to move upward." *Rise* means "to move upward."

We **raise** the flag each morning.
The flag **rises** slowly.

reason is because   This expression is redundant. Use *because* alone, or use *the reason is that*.

The **reason** I called you **is that** I forgot Taylor's phone number.
I called you **because** I forgot Taylor's phone number.

▶ **Exercise 2**   **Underline the word in parentheses that best completes each sentence.**

Watch out for (<u>loose</u>, lose) gravel.

1. A short film (preceded, proceeded) the luncheon.

2. The reason we took two cars is (because, that) Reggie had to be back early.

3. Let's (precede, proceed) with our original plan.

4. The price of lettuce seems to (raise, rise) every week.

5. My brother accidentally drove right (passed, past) us.

6. Carlotta was afraid she might (loose, lose) her only house key.

7. The ring my grandmother gave me is (loose, lose) on this finger.

8. I hope I (passed, past) the entrance exam.

9. The entire chorus bows when the curtain (raises, rises).

10. The reason we ate dinner late is (because, that) I had to work until seven.

Lesson 71
Usage: *respectfully* to *whom*

respectfully , respectively   *Respectfully* means "with respect." *Respectively* means "in the order named."

George **respectfully** thanked his music teacher for attending his recital.
The drawing and painting classes are offered on Monday and Wednesday **respectively**.

says , said   *Says* is the third-person singular form of the verb *say. Said* is the past tense of *say.*

My brother always **says** he'll help.
Yesterday, he **said** he'd walk the dog.

sit , set   *Sit* means "to place oneself in a sitting position." *Set* usually means "to place" or "to put," and it generally takes an object.

You may **sit** anywhere but on the stairs.
We **set** the dirty dishes on the counter.

than , then   *Than* is a conjunction. *Then* is an adverb.

Jamie is now taller **than** her mother.
She was much shorter **then**.

this here , that there   Avoid using *here* and *there* after *this* and *that*.

Please file **these** folders in **that** cabinet.

who , whom   Use *who* for the subjective case. Use *whom* for the objective case.

Who will greet the guests?
To **whom** should I address the invitation?

▶ **Exercise 1** **Substitute the correct word or words for the one in italics, and write it in the blank. Write *C* if the sentence is correct.**

_____said_____	Andy *says* he'd paint the porch last weekend.
_____	1. *This here* chair is broken.
_____	2. At seven-thirty, Roberto and Toni left for school and work *respectively*.
_____	3. The vet asked me to *sit* the kitten on the table.
_____	4. Camille always *said* she'll clean up when she's finished cooking.
_____	5. Abraham Lincoln slept in *this here* bed.
_____	6. *Who* do you think I should call about the broken window?

_____ 7. Corey's new swimming instructor is none other *then* my best friend.

_____ 8. Yesterday she *says* she couldn't make it to the game because her car broke down.

_____ 9. I think I like the blue sofa better *then* the green one.

_____ 10. My aunt was in the army *then*.

_____ 11. Please *set* here until I call your name.

_____ 12. Turn left down *that there* street.

_____ 13. I work on Saturday morning; *than* I relax in the afternoon.

_____ 14. That dog does nothing but *set* on the porch all day.

_____ 15. The reporter greeted the senator *respectively*.

_____ 16. Did you find out *whom* brought this great pasta salad?

_____ 17. Ice and steam are, *respectively*, a solid and a gas.

_____ 18. The author's new book is longer *then* her first one.

_____ 19. Please *sit* your glass on a coaster.

_____ 20. We lowered our voices *respectively*.

_____ 21. This morning Martina *says* she wants to drive to the lake.

_____ 22. *This here* is yesterday's newspaper.

_____ 23. *Who* did you invite to the party?

_____ 24. *That* is the hospital where I was born.

_____ 25. José looked shorter in person *then* he had on television.

▶ **Writing Link** **Write a brief paragraph about a favorite class or teacher. Use the words from page 225.**

_____

_____

_____

_____

_____

_____

_____

_____

Usage

✓ Unit 10 Review

▶ **Exercise 1** Underline the incorrect word in each sentence. Write the correct word(s) in the blank.

_____preceding_____ More outspoken than any First Lady <u>proceeding</u> her, Eleanor Roosevelt (1884–1962) changed the role of presidential spouse.

_____ 1. Eleanor Roosevelt pursued her political goals even farther than many elected officials.

_____ 2. Irregardless of a cause's popularity, she made her opinions known.

_____ 3. She frequently gave advise to her husband, President Franklin Delano Roosevelt.

_____ 4. She was more passionate about social justice then most Americans.

_____ 5. Beside her behind-the-scenes role in the White House, she left her mark on history in other ways.

_____ 6. Eleanor Roosevelt championed alot of causes, from civil rights for African Americans to full equality for women.

_____ 7. She believed strongly that no group should be treated differently than any other.

_____ 8. She could not except injustice in any guise.

_____ 9. Her opinions had an affect on many laws still in force today.

_____ 10. Thanks largely to Eleanor Roosevelt's efforts, the UN adapted the Declaration of Human Rights in 1948.

_____ 11. Her continuous attempts to right social wrongs did not go unnoticed by the American public.

_____ 12. Opinionated people as Eleanor Roosevelt are often unpopular.

_____ 13. She was certainly more controversial than any First Lady whom came before her.

_____ 14. Even her critics, however, admired the way she spoke her mind and than fought for what she believed in.

_____ 15. In the years since Eleanor Roosevelt's death, her reputation has continued to raise.

Usage

Cumulative Review: Units 1–10

▶ **Exercise 1** **Draw one line under each prepositional phrase and two lines under each participial phrase. Circle each gerund phrase.**

(Weeding gardens) is hard work so, feeling exhausted, we rested on the patio.

1. Carlos, walking briskly, went to the music store to buy a CD with the money he earned.

2. Considered "man's best friend," a dog's loud barking is a sign of loyalty.

3. Hearing about the great holiday sales, the people swarmed stores on Main Street, in the mall, and throughout the shopping district.

4. Tired of procrastinating, Robert finally repaired the tears in the screens on the porch.

5. Of every type of recreation, swimming laps is at the top of my list.

6. My summer job at the theater involves taking tickets.

7. Tricia enjoys reading and relaxing in the den of her new house.

8. Knowing the answer, Jeff waved his hand in the air.

9. The pizza devoured last night was made from scratch.

10. Cooperating with others is important to the success of the group.

11. Praised by all, the victorious team returned about noon.

12. Tad and Hiroshi enjoyed painting the fence in Mrs. Rivera's backyard.

13. Moving the piano from the living room to the family room was difficult for my dad.

14. His enthusiastic applauding was heard by everybody.

15. In the chemistry lab are many vials labeled as dangerous.

16. Baking bread is easy since we bought a bread machine.

17. Using a thesaurus, Hasan wrote an English paper with many descriptive words.

18. The proud parents listened to their son singing a solo at the concert.

19. Singing the solo was the highlight of their son's choir experience.

20. The kite swirling in the air abruptly landed in the big oak tree.

▶ **Exercise 2** **Write in the blank the correct form of the verb in italics. If the verb is correct, write *C* in the blank.**

_____collects_____ My aunts or my uncle *collect* rare stamps.

_____ **1.** The English teachers at my high school *helps* the students with their college essays.

_____ **2.** The Art Club *displays* their work in the school lobby.

_____ **3.** Neither Rhonda nor Ariel *know* how to turn on the computers in the computer lab.

_____ **4.** Emilio, together with us, *plan* to go to the county fair.

_____ **5.** Both he and I *hope* to go to the science museum this weekend.

_____ **6.** Each of the pizzas *have* pepperoni.

_____ **7.** Estaban, accompanied by his two collies, *walk* to the park every day.

_____ **8.** The pots in the sink *was* full of soapy water.

_____ **9.** Neither the grass nor the bushes *grows* well in this soil.

_____ **10.** Either they or he *is driving* to the movie.

_____ **11.** He and she *likes* to browse around the library.

_____ **12.** Above the Arctic Circle in Sweden and Norway *lie* a wilderness called Lapland.

_____ **13.** Sweden, as well as Denmark and Norway, *are* a Scandinavian country.

_____ **14.** The other eight planets and Earth *orbits* around the sun.

_____ **15.** Across the street from the theater *stands* two statues made of marble.

_____ **16.** Many kinds of squirrels, especially a tree squirrel or a chipmunk, *are* easy to tame.

_____ **17.** Everyone in our neighborhood *recycle* old cans and newspapers.

_____ **18.** These are the books that my dad *use* for his doctorate research.

_____ **19.** Here *comes* the panda bears out of their dens.

_____ **20.** *Does* your grandparents plan to attend graduation?

Usage

Name _____ Class _____ Date _____

▶ Exercise 3 **Underline the word or words in parentheses that best complete each sentence.**

(Beside, <u>Besides</u>) going to the Empire State Building, we have tickets for a Broadway show.

1. Could you (loan, lend) me ten dollars until I get my paycheck?

2. The team will go (all together, altogether) in the van to the tennis match.

3. In his oral report Rick made several (illusions, allusions) to Greek mythology.

4. The principal said he would study the case (further, farther).

5. Mickey likes everything about camping (accept, except) the bugs.

6. The genetic structure of DNA makes every living thing (different from, different than) every other living thing.

7. When students begin college, they must (adapt, adopt) to a new environment.

8. You (could of, could have) run into a lot of snow when you reached the Rocky Mountains!

9. The great statesman Sir Winston Churchill had a powerful (affect, effect) on world history.

10. My guidance counselor (adviced, advised) me to take physics this year.

11. The marine biologist never went (anywheres, anywhere) without his equipment.

12. Did you (lie, lay) the notebook down on your desk or on the shelf?

13. The optometrist ensured Luba that (this kind, these kinds) of contact lens is easy and comfortable to wear.

14. Mom said that I (can, may) go to the rock concert if I (can, may) get my homework done first.

15. The crowd was (all ready, already) laughing when the comedian came on stage.

16. Cole played the guitar (awhile, a while) before he left for the game.

17. The University of Michigan and Ohio State have a (continual, continuous) rivalry in football.

18. (Bring, Take) your sweats if you're going to the gym to work out.

19. A large star would more than fill the area (between, among) Earth and the sun.

20. Will the humid air (effect, affect) the results of our experiment?

21. Golda (accepted, excepted) the prize with humility.

22. That economics book is (all together, altogether) too long.

23. I was under the (allusion, illusion) that we were going out this weekend.

24. We live (further, farther) from the school now that we've moved.

25. You really threw the ball (good, well)!

*M*echanics

· ·

Unit 11: Capitalization

Lesson 72
Capitalization of Sentences and the Pronoun *I*

Capitalize the first word of every sentence, including the first word of a direct quotation that is a complete sentence.

She should have thought this over more carefully, don't you agree?
According to the product brochure, "**T**he new software will provide complete anti-virus protection as well as hard disk optimization."

Capitalize the first word of a sentence in parentheses that stands by itself. Do not capitalize a sentence within parentheses that is contained within another sentence.

Crush the garlic and mix it with the vinegar. (**T**he garlic may be put through a garlic press if you prefer.)
Although no one suspected that the gardener committed the burglary (**h**e appeared to have a water-tight alibi), the detective skillfully proved the man's guilt.

Do not capitalize the first word of a quotation that cannot stand as a complete sentence.

The Palladian window is "**a**rched with two lower sidelights, framed with columns."

Do not capitalize the first word of an indirect quotation. An indirect quotation, often introduced by *that*, does not repeat a person's exact words.

My grandfather often said that **i**gnorance of the law was no excuse.

Always capitalize the pronoun *I* no matter where it appears in a sentence.

My sister and **I** decided to buy a futon for her new apartment.

Mechanics

▶ **Exercise 1** Mark each letter that should be capitalized by drawing three lines (≡) under it. Mark each letter that should be lowercase by drawing a slash through it (/). If the sentence is correct as written, write *C* in the blank.

_____ a̲ woman at the bank asked me T̶o fill out a questionnaire.

_____ **1.** The advertisement for the car stated, "the five-speed manual transaxle was designed to provide maximum power and ease of shifting."

_____ **2.** Heather said She and I could take some extra flyers to distribute on Saturday.

_____ **3.** the clipper ship had five tremendous masts that looked as if they reached the clouds.

_____ **4.** To many people, Willie Mays (he was the center fielder for the New York and San Francisco Giants in the 1950s and 1960s) was the greatest baseball player of his time.

_____ 5. The candidate promised to Support any bill that would lower taxes on the middle class.

_____ 6. Asunción is the capital of the South American country of Paraguay. (The country is entirely landlocked.)

_____ 7. Don Quixote, the famous Spanish knight created by Miguel de Cervantes, observed that he never thrust his nose "Into other men's porridge."

_____ 8. Mayonnaise (The name comes from a French battle) is a dressing made of egg yolk, oil, and lemon juice.

_____ 9. Speaking of time, the Greek dramatist Aeschylus wrote that it "Teaches many lessons."

_____ 10. Today, parachutes are made of nylon. (formerly, they were made of silk.)

_____ 11. The writer of Proverbs 19 cautions that where "there is no vision, the people perish."

_____ 12. Moles (They are the small, burrowing creatures that cause such damage to gardens and lawns) can barely see at all.

_____ 13. I started dancing lessons when I was five because my parents felt I had a natural gift for movement.

_____ 14. In describing a character in her novel *Sense and Sensibility*, Jane Austen writes, "she was sensible and clever, but eager in everything."

_____ 15. dodging gracefully out of the bull's way, the matador acknowledged the cheers of the crowd.

_____ 16. They certainly surprised everyone in the room when they admitted They took the box of cookies.

_____ 17. Cathedrals are "luxury liners laden with souls," wrote poet W.H. Auden.

_____ 18. Eleanor Roosevelt was one of the most admired First Ladies. (she was the niece, as well as the wife, of a president.)

_____ 19. G.K. Chesterton once said, "The world will never starve for wonders, but only for want of wonders."

_____ 20. Scotland is part of the United Kingdom. (the other countries are England, Wales, and Northern Ireland.)

_____ 21. What could the old woman have meant by her strange remark?

_____ 22. The ominous tolling of the heavy iron bell (it was almost always silent, but that evening was loud and frightening) is a sound I will never forget.

Mechanics

Lesson 73
Capitalization of Proper Nouns

When a proper noun is composed of several words, capitalize only the important words. Capitalize the names and titles of individuals used before a proper name and in direct address.

Dr. Harriet E. Phillips   Yes, **S**enator   **K**ing Frederick the **G**reat

In general, do not capitalize titles that follow a proper name or are used alone. Most writers, however, capitalize *president* when referring to the current president of the United States.

Alpha Konare, the **p**resident of Mali, visited with the **P**resident at the White House.

In general, capitalize a title that describes a family relationship when it is used with or in place of a proper name.

Good morning, **A**unt **M**artha   My **a**unt lives in Phoenix

Capitalize names of ethnic and national groups, and languages.

Mexican **A**mericans   **T**urkish   **L**atin   **M**alaysian   **Z**ulu

Capitalize names of organizations, institutions, political parties and their members, and firms. Do not capitalize the word *party* when it follows the name of a political party.

United Nations   DePaul University   the Republican party
a Democrat   Microsoft   United Airlines

Do not capitalize words such as *university* when they are not part of a proper noun.

Anne's sister plans to go to a **u**niversity after she gets out of the navy.

Capitalize the names of buildings, monuments, and other structures, ships and planes, trade names, and names of documents, awards, and laws.

a Ford Taurus car   the Lincoln Memorial   Airbus A300
the Ten Commandments   the Brady Bill   an Emmy

Capitalize geographic terms.

North America   Lake Erie   the Middle East
Nashville   Main Street   Peru

Capitalize compass points when they refer to a specific area of the country or the world, but not when they merely indicate direction.

East Africa   the **e**ast coast of Panama   go **e**ast for three miles

Capitalize the names of most historical events, eras, and calendar items. A historical period that refers to a general span of time should not be capitalized.

the Civil War   the Renaissance   Memorial Day   the fifties

Mechanics

Capitalize the days of the week and the months, but not the seasons. Capitalize the names of deities, religions and denominations, their adherents, and religious books and events.

Allah   the **B**ible   **H**induism   **L**utherans   **G**od   **P**assover   the **L**ord

Capitalize the names of planets and other heavenly bodies. Do not capitalize *sun* and *moon*. Never capitalize *earth* when it is preceded by *the*.

Jupiter   **O**rion   the **N**orth **S**tar   the **e**arth   the **s**un

In general, do not capitalize the name of a school subject, unless it is a language.

I am taking **a**lgebra.   **S**he is studying **S**panish.

Capitalize the important words in titles.

the ***W**ashington **P**ost*   *Hamlet*   ***T**he **G**reat **G**atsby*   "**S**pring and **A**ll"   *Time* magazine

---

▶ **Exercise 1** **Mark each letter that should be capitalized by drawing three lines (≡) under it. Mark each letter that should be lowercase by drawing a slash through it (/). If the sentence is correct as written, write *C* in the blank.**

_____   Shelley's Father is a democrat, while her Mother usually votes for the republican

party's candidate.

_____ **1.** Have you heard any news about whether Michigan State university has accepted you

for next Fall?

_____ **2.** The reading in Church last Sunday was from the new testament.

_____ **3.** Next year, my Brother is going to start with Geometry and continue with French.

_____ **4.** Ladies and gentlemen, I am pleased to present governor Lois Montoya of Arizona.

_____ **5.** One of my dreams is to travel East and take a tour through new England to see the

gorgeous leaves in autumn.

_____ **6.** Why did you decide to fly with United Air Lines on an Airbus this time, Uncle Harry?

_____ **7.** Monica's father is one-half irish, one-half cherokee.

_____ **8.** Jimi Hendrix, Richard Thompson, and Eric Clapton all played Fender Stratocaster Guitars.

_____ **9.** The main speaker at the world health organization meeting was the Prime Minister of

Pakistan.

_____ **10.** Melinda gave a presentation on southern California's death valley, the lowest place in

the Country.

_____ **11.** In the novel *War of the Worlds* by H.G. Wells, creatures from Mars invade the earth.

_____ **12.** Tom Hanks won the oscar for best actor two years in a row.

Lesson 74
Capitalization of Proper Adjectives

Capitalize proper adjectives (adjectives formed from proper nouns). Proper adjectives include adjectives formed from names of people.

Elizabethan literature   **N**ewtonian physics   **G**regorian calendar

They also include adjectives formed from place names and the names of national, ethnic, and religious groups.

Roman architecture   **M**iddle **E**astern conflict
Buddhist temples   **A**laskan salmon

When used as adjectives, many proper nouns do not change form.

Strauss waltzes   **W**ashington apples
White **H**ouse assistant   **N**ew **Y**ork police officer

▶ **Exercise 1**   **Place a check (✔) beside each sentence that uses capitalization correctly.**

✔   In New Mexico, we attended a performance of Native-American dances.

_____   **1.** The subject of the lecture was great shakespearean heroines, including Juliet, Portia, and Cleopatra.

_____   **2.** The local museum has just opened a new room devoted to Far Eastern art.

_____   **3.** The famous astronomer strongly supported continuing Martian exploration.

_____   **4.** Among the greatest novelists in victorian literature are George Eliot, Emily and Charlotte Brontë, Charles Dickens, and William Thackeray.

_____   **5.** President Kennedy's central american policy was based on a more equal relationship.

_____   **6.** You should taste my dad's homemade Jewish rye bread with caraway seeds!

_____   **7.** A treaty was signed to try to prevent the spread of Atomic weapons.

_____   **8.** Taino's Finnish cousins are visiting from Helsinki this summer.

_____   **9.** That house's heating system relies on Sun, or Solar, power.

_____   **10.** Among the largest and most important islamic countries of the world are Egypt, Indonesia, Pakistan, and Bangladesh.

_____   **11.** We always look forward to our city's Summer festival downtown by the river.

_____   **12.** For their fiftieth wedding anniversary, Jamaal's grandparents took a Caribbean cruise.

_____   **13.** In Alaska, northern Canada, and Greenland, some Inuit, or Eskimo, people maintain their traditional lifestyle.

Mechanics

_____ 14. The music critic for the newspaper praised the performance's mozartean sense of lightness and grace.

_____ 15. Buddhism springs from Hindu roots, similar to the way Christianity is based on the Jewish tradition.

_____ 16. The restaurant's special salad was made from tomatoes, onions, greek olives, and feta cheese.

_____ 17. Ms. Wang was quite active in researching local asian-american history and culture.

_____ 18. I first sampled Ethiopian cooking at the YMCA's community potluck dinner.

_____ 19. In many parts of India, you can see a christian church on one corner, right across the street from a hindu temple or muslim mosque.

_____ 20. You have to pay a little more to buy genuine Idaho potatoes, but I think they are worth the price because they are so good when baked.

_____ 21. Nikki is reading a book about Einsteinian physics, and she says it makes the ideas very clear.

_____ 22. The Church youth group volunteered to clean up the civil war monument on the town square.

_____ 23. Maggie's aunt is the new pastor of the presbyterian church on Elm Street.

_____ 24. The republican proposal to end the programs was defeated by a sound margin in the Senate.

_____ 25. The main character of this new book has been described as huckleberry finn-ish.

_____ 26. He conducts those Vivaldi concertos with liveliness.

_____ 27. Jolene wrote a story in the Dickensian tradition.

_____ 28. A State department spokesperson refused to answer the reporter's questions.

_____ 29. The franklin county Municipal Court issues summons to serve on juries.

_____ 30. Phil may live in New York, but his Californian outlook is still apparent.

_____ 31. We listened to a band play Italian songs as we strolled through the park.

_____ 32. The choir sang a lovely Anglican hymn in church yesterday.

_____ 33. In dance class Melanie is learning the Scottish reel.

_____ 34. The peruvian rug in the lobby looks quite beautiful.

_____ 35. The heroine's gown was made of patterned Indian muslin.

_____ 36. These pancakes are served with vermont maple syrup.

_____ 37. A Turner landscape was my favorite painting in the exhibit.

_____ 38. Wendy always enjoys a spielberg movie.

Mechanics

✓ Unit 11 Review

▶ **Exercise 1** Mark each letter that should be capitalized by drawing three lines (≡) under it. Mark each letter that should be lowercase by drawing a slash through it (/).

Reggae is an infectious, rhythmic type of jamaican music popularized by $\underset{\equiv}{S}$inger Bob Marley and others.

1. In the movie *Casablanca,* Humphrey Bogart says to Ingrid Bergman, "here's looking at you, kid."

2. I received a letter from senator Glenn thanking me for my opinion on the controversial legislation.

3. Erica's Aunt sent her a postcard from Tanzania.

4. For his birthday, my Brother chose to go out to an indian restaurant.

5. The fourth of july celebrates the signing of the declaration of independence.

6. Crossing the 59th Street Bridge, we had a great view of the manhattan skyline.

7. If you travel due East from Farleyville, you should reach the campsite by evening.

8. "Fools rush in," claimed the English poet Alexander Pope, "Where angels fear to tread."

9. Rick had decided to attend the State University, in part because he was so impressed by Alex Williams, Coach of the track team.

10. Many of the Countries of the mediterranean area use garlic and tomatoes in their cooking.

11. How is your Dad getting around on his crutches?

12. Next year, Naura and i have decided to take Journalism.

13. By the time my little Brother got through rearranging his room (*Cage* would probably be a better word for where he sleeps), his bed was in the closet and the chair was nowhere to be seen.

14. The life of a hollywood star isn't all fun and games, I assure you.

15. How do you say hello in russian?

16. The brightest object in the morning Summer sky is often venus.

17. Simple red brick exteriors and classical columns are hallmarks of georgian architecture, a style popular in the eighteenth century.

18. During world war II, the north Atlantic was the scene of submarine warfare.

19. The Prime Minister of Sweden was the guest of the President in Washington, D.C.

20. My great-grandmother often used to say that You could get farther with honey than with vinegar.

Mechanics

Cumulative Review Units 1–11

▶ **Exercise 1** Write the part of speech above each italicized word. Use these abbreviations: *N* (noun), *V* (verb), *pro.* (pronoun), *adj.* (adjective), *adv.* (adverb), *prep.* (preposition), *conj.* (conjunction), and *int.* (interjection).

        conj.   adj.
Rolanda *and* Denise work at *the* video store every weekend.

1. The roller coaster turned and *plunged* downward *with* alarming rapidity.

2. *Joyous* voices could be heard coming from the *arena.*

3. *Dad* is barbecuing chicken while Mom *gathers* the family together.

4. Rain poured *continuously during* the opening ceremony.

5. *Wow!* That is the *greatest* movie I have ever seen!

6. *Either* Timothy *or* Ryan will give the keynote address.

7. The Monroes brought *us* souvenirs from *Mexico.*

8. Hummingbirds sang as Melissa *strolled through* the gardenia-scented garden.

9. Juan *often* helps his uncle plan *interesting* journeys.

10. *They* began their concert by playing several *old* favorites.

11. Martha lives *on* the north side of town, *and* Gerald lives on the east side.

12. The yearbook staff *seek* contributions of *unusual* photographs.

13. *The* basketball *tournament* starts at noon Thursday.

14. A *friendly* cruise director showed *him* the way to the weight room.

15. *Well,* what exactly are we going to do *now?*

16. *Look* at the technique *of* that professional golfer.

17. *Does anyone know* how to use this computer program?

18. Some *persons* may disagree with the board's decision, *but* the decision is final.

19. *At* the end of the long tunnel *glowed* a single valiant light.

20. Carola *slowly* circled the *crowded* lobby looking for her friend.

▶ **Exercise 2** Write in the blank the verb and tense indicated in parentheses.

Susan ___*hopes*___ to be admitted to Stanford University. (present, *hope*)

1. The assembly _____ as soon as the guest speaker arrives. (future, *begin*)

2. Jerry _____ for Christina at the pizza parlor. (past progressive, *wait*)

Name _____ Class _____ Date _____

3. On second thought, Roger _____ Vinnie in many ways. (present emphatic, *resemble*)

4. Sherry _____ on her term paper six weeks by the time it is finished. (future perfect, *work*)

5. We_____ purchasing a new piano. (present progressive, *consider*)

6. The mercury _____ steadily throughout the afternoon. (present, *rise*)

7. Grandmother _____ us amazing stories about her youth in Hong Kong. (present perfect, *tell*)

8. Singers from around the world _____ in the twelfth annual vocal competition. (past, *compete*)

9. Volunteers _____ more money than expected during the telethon. (past perfect, *raise*)

10. Cousin Lucille _____ us a postcard from Brussels. (past emphatic, *send*)

11. Next Tuesday _____ my sister and brother-in-law's second anniversary. (future, *mark*)

12. This novel _____ everyone who reads it. (present, *fascinate*)

13. After the game, Katrina and her friends _____ to the block party. (past, *walk*)

14. Nadine and Cora _____ to move to Philadelphia for nearly three months. (present perfect progressive, *plan*)

15. Two playful squirrels _____ the large oak tree in our backyard. (past progressive, *climb*)

16. The Art Club_____ the entire exhibit by five o'clock. (future perfect, *see*)

17. A dozen roses _____ without a card. (past perfect, *arrive*)

18. Mrs. DiPietro _____ the best cakes I have ever tasted. (present, *make*)

19. One juror _____ the defendant is innocent. (present emphatic, *believe*)

20. The finance committee _____ Monday night at seven o'clock. (future, *meet*)

21. Monique _____ for Paris on the 10:15 A.M. flight. (future progressive, *leave*)

22. The newspapers _____ across the yard and into a neighbor's driveway. (past, *blow*)

23. Emily _____ we should eat first, but I disagreed. (past emphatic, *think*)

24. Wanita _____ a new system for collecting recyclable items. (present progressive, *propose*)

Name _____ Class _____ Date _____

▶ **Exercise 3** **Place a check (✔) in the blank next to each sentence that uses capitalization correctly.**

___✔___   The new Mexican restaurant has excellent food.

_____ **1.** Giovanni said, "Let's plan the best festival this school has ever had."

_____ **2.** Henri Bergson called laughter "Anesthesia of the heart."

_____ **3.** Three movies, including *A Night To Forget,* were playing at the local theater.

_____ **4.** You fulfilled the promise your Father made years ago.

_____ **5.** Margaret returned the dress to Waverly's department store last week.

_____ **6.** The Native American word *hopi* means "peace."

_____ **7.** Our community theater is mounting a production of *Barefoot in the park.*

_____ **8.** Justine is looking forward to the St. Patrick's Day celebration.

_____ **9.** The Figure Skating finals will be held in Conner auditorium.

_____ **10.** Did you see the antique jukebox in Macy's?

_____ **11.** Fifteen facial muscles work together to produce laughter.

_____ **12.** Derek said that the crowd usually thins out around 6:00 P.M.

_____ **13.** Aunt Clara accidentally knocked over a pile of oranges at the supermarket.

_____ **14.** The ambassador declared, "this marks a new era in friendship between my country and the United States."

_____ **15.** A singing Chef was giving demonstrations in one of the tents.

_____ **16.** Mr. Yee and Dr. Gillespie are signing copies of their new books.

_____ **17.** The Democratic Party is having a fund-raiser in the hotel ballroom.

_____ **18.** The Cartesian idea that this life is only a dream is rather appealing.

_____ **19.** Have you seen the Grecian urns at the Different Plane Gallery?

_____ **20.** James says, "if we search long enough, we are certain to find what we are looking for."

_____ **21.** Orange blossoms decorated the parade float.

_____ **22.** Owls could be heard hooting in the April night.

_____ **23.** The president's press conference will begin at two o'clock.

_____ **24.** doris wonders If she made enough food for the reception.

_____ **25.** René Descartes was a French philosopher who lived in the seventeenth century.

Unit 12: Punctuation, Abbreviations, and Numbers

Lesson 75
End Punctuation: Period, Exclamation Point, and Question Mark

Use a period at the end of a declarative sentence and at the end of a polite command.

Nadine Gordimer won the Nobel Prize for Literature in 1991.
Think of another author from Africa who won the Nobel Prize.

Use an exclamation point to show strong feeling and indicate a forceful command.

What a fabulous book!   Read it!

Use a question mark to indicate a direct question.

Did Wole Soyinka of Nigeria win the Nobel Prize in Literature?

A declarative sentence containing an indirect question does not take a question mark.

Juanita asked if Naguib Mahfouz from Egypt had also won the prize.

▶ **Exercise 1** Add end punctuation as needed.

Sarah asked if she could come with us to the dance recital

1. The America's Cup is the world's most important yachting race

2. The race is held every three years in waters near the country that holds the cup

3. The America's Cup has been held 29 times, and one country has won the competition 28 of them

4. The U.S. domination of this race is without parallel in the history of sports

5. Only once, in 1983, has a non-American boat ever won the America's Cup

6. Can you guess from which country this winner hailed

7. The answer is Australia

8. Have you ever wondered what it would be like to sail on one of the sleek yachts that compete in races like the America's Cup

9. Many sailors wonder whether any thrill can match the feeling of sailing a large, beautiful yacht powered only by a stiff breeze

10. However, sailing a big boat like those that compete for the America's Cup is plenty of hard work

11. More than anything, crew members need strong muscles

12. In the 1995 race, a boat with a unique crew competed in the qualifying trials in San Diego

13. The boat, named *America³*, was owned by Bill Koch, who had won the America's Cup in 1992

14. Bill Koch wanted to find out if a crew composed entirely of women could compete in the America's Cup

15. All but one crew member were female

16. Many people wondered if the women of *America³* could compete with more experienced, all-male crews

17. Doubters quickly found out, as *America³* won its first race in San Diego on January 13, 1995

18. Even though many of the crew members did not have much sailing experience, they melded together their experience as rowers, weightlifters, and sailors

19. The crew of 28 worked together to rig sails, maneuver the boat through the course, and react quickly to changes in wind speed and direction

20. Although *America³* did not win the qualifying trials, fans of yacht racing everywhere gained respect and admiration for this groundbreaking crew

▶ **Exercise 2 Place a check (✔) beside each sentence that is punctuated correctly.**

____✔____   Don't touch that wire!

_____   1. Kevin's uncle called to ask whether he would like to go sailing with him?

_____   2. Kevin didn't hesitate a second before saying yes!

_____   3. To Kevin, sailing was the most relaxing—and the most interesting—way to spend time that he knew.

_____   4. To move with the wind across the water made Kevin feel like a part of nature!

_____   5. The trick was to prepare the sailboat to take advantage of the prevailing wind conditions?

_____   6. On the drive to the lake, Kevin smiled when he noticed the leaves on the trees they passed dancing in the stiff breeze.

_____   7. The sun was warm—but not too warm—on his arm!

_____   8. Looks like a perfect day for sailing, he thought to himself.

_____   9. "Don't you love to see all the different-colored sails on the lake?"

_____   10. Kevin had to agree with Uncle Rob?

_____   11. As their van pulled up to the dock next to the boat, several seagulls flew off with a loud braying laugh!

_____   12. Uncle Rob lifted Kevin's wheelchair onto the pier, and Kevin rolled quickly over to the docked sailboat.

Mechanics

Lesson 76
Colons

Use a **colon** to introduce a list, especially after a statement that uses such words as *these*, *the following*, or *as follows*.

To bake the cookies you will need **these** ingredients: flour, sugar, butter, chocolate chips, baking powder, eggs, vanilla, and pecans.

Do not use a colon if a list immediately follows a verb or a preposition.

Elvis Presley's hit singles **include** "Heartbreak Hotel," "Hound Dog," and "Love Me Tender."

Use a colon to introduce material that illustrates, restates, or explains the preceding material. A complete sentence following a colon is usually not capitalized.

The Cleveland Browns, Phoenix Cardinals, and Seattle Seahawks have one thing in common: they have never played in the Super Bowl.

Use colons to introduce a long or formal quotation.

Eudora Welty's famous short story "Why I Live at the P.O." begins with the following words: "I was getting along fine with Mama, Papa-Daddy, and Uncle Rondo until my sister Stella-Rondo just separated from her husband and came back home again."

Quotations of poetry that are longer than one line and quotations of prose that are longer than five lines are generally written below the introductory statement and indented on the page.

William Wordsworth's poem "Tintern Abbey" contains these prayer-like words:
> While with an eye made quiet by the power
> of harmony, and the deep power of joy,
> We see into the life of things.

Use a colon between the hour and minute of the precise time, between the chapter and verse in biblical references, and the salutation of a business letter.

4:12 A.M.   9:03 P.M.   Job 3:11   Dear Sir or Madam:

Mechanics

▶ **Exercise 1** **Add colons as needed. Cross out colons used incorrectly using the delete (ɣ) symbol. If the sentence is correct as written, write *C* in the blank.**

_____   Grandfather's flight was due to arrive at the airport at 7:23 P.M.

_____   **1.** The positions on a basketball team are as follows a center, two guards, and two forwards.

_____   **2.** Paraguay and Bolivia share at least one important feature they are both without a coastline.

_____ 3. This morning's reading comes from II Samuel 7 16-24.

_____ 4. The members of the Rock and Roll Hall of Fame in Cleveland include Chuck Berry, Buddy Holly, and Sam Cooke.

_____ 5. The petition began with this statement "Because of our concern for the future of the earth, we strongly encourage Dunbar High School to begin a recycling program as soon as possible."

_____ 6. Dear Returns Department

_____ 7. Among the ingredients found on the gourmet pizza were goat cheese, spinach, pineapple, dandelion leaves, and duck sausage.

_____ 8. While coffee is very popular in most countries: in a few, tea is the warm beverage of choice.

_____ 9. Alana has a number of unusual hobbies, such as: playing traditional Hawaiian music, raising show pigeons, and collecting old bottle caps.

_____ 10. My favorite line of poetry, because it sounds so much like bees buzzing, is the following by Tennyson: "the murmuring of innumerable bees."

_____ 11. One question was uppermost in the mind of everyone in the room: how had the murderer been able to escape completely unseen by the maid?

_____ 12. The strings of a guitar are tuned: E, A, D, G, B, and E.

_____ 13. Sitting at the piano to help the students keep time properly was a metronome.

_____ 14. It took a long time before I realized where the strange, fretful noises were coming from the llama was making them!

_____ 15. The test in history will cover the following topics the Civil War, Reconstruction, and industrialism.

_____ 16. The captain's decision left the soldiers with two choices obey the orders or be arrested for insubordination.

_____ 17. Says Mark Twain about his beloved Mississippi River "The Mississippi is well worth reading about. It is not a commonplace river, but on the contrary is in all ways remarkable."

_____ 18. The Bible on the table lay open to Jeremiah 35:1-14.

_____ 19. According to the bus schedule, the crosstown bus is supposed to leave here at 1155.

_____ 20. Martha's cat Tigger lives for one thing alone: to be picked up and petted for hours on end.

Mechanics

Lesson 77
Semicolons

Use a **semicolon** to separate main clauses that are not joined by a coordinating conjunction (*and, but, or, nor, yet* and *for*).

The English word *salary* has an interesting history; based on the Latin word for "salt," it comes from the fact that Roman soldiers were paid money to buy salt.

Use a semicolon to separate main clauses joined by a conjunctive adverb (such as *however, therefore, nevertheless, moreover, furthermore,* and *consequently*) or by an expression such as *for example* or *that is.* In general a conjunctive adverb or expression such as *in fact, for example,* or *that is* is followed by a comma.

Which state has the most interesting and unusual place names would be a lively debate; **however,** Maine, with names such as Passamaquoddy, would certainly be in the running.

Use a semicolon to separate the items in a series when these items contain commas.

Interestingly, three important twentieth-century American poets who held jobs outside of literature are William Carlos Williams, a doctor; Wallace Stevens, an insurance company executive; and T. S. Eliot, a banker.

Use a semicolon to separate two main clauses joined by a coordinating conjunction when such clauses already contain several commas.

India is perhaps best known for its masses of poor people living on the edge of disaster, one meal away from starvation; but it must also be remembered as the world's largest, liveliest democracy, where, in spite of its immense difficulties, it manages to maintain electoral freedom for the most people of any country on Earth.

▶ **Exercise 1** Add semicolons as needed. Cross out semicolons used incorrectly, using the delete (⅌) symbol. If the sentence is correct as written, write *C* in the blank.

_____ Many people enjoy feeding birds at a backyard feeder in the winter; the sight of cardinals, chickadees, and nuthatches is a reminder that spring is just around the corner.

_____ 1. A prehensile tail, one that can grasp or wrap around things, has proven to be a valuable aid to survival for many species the North American opossum and South American spider monkey are two animals that have this type of tail.

_____ 2. George Frederick Handel, the German-born English composer of the eighteenth century, is best known for his oratorios, such as *Messiah* and *Solomon* but he was also a master of instrumental music, as his two series of concerti grossi and his ceremonial suites show.

_____ **3.** Brick is a longtime favorite as a building material because of its good looks and sturdiness; moreover, it can be virtually free of maintenance.

_____ **4.** The sphinx is a fascinating creature from ancient mythology its body was that of a lion, while its head was portrayed as that of a man or woman, ram, or hawk.

_____ **5.** The silver-haired senator was considered the *eminence grise* of his party that is, he was its senior statesman, or "gray eminence."

_____ **6.** The list of performers for tonight's talent show includes Marty Allerdyce, who will play the piano Jason McPherson, who will do a tumbling routine and the Chang twins, who will juggle items the audience donates.

_____ **7.** We will not go along with your plan to disrupt the shareholders' meeting; furthermore, we will oppose it with all our strength.

_____ **8.** Self-portraits are among the most powerful of all paintings the self-portraits of Rembrandt and Van Gogh stand out for their revealing intensity.

_____ **9.** Hollywood's first great director, although other candidates have been mentioned from time to time, was without a doubt D.W. Griffith the father of such techniques as the fade-out, close-up, and moving camera, Griffith is best known for his film *The Birth of a Nation.*

_____ **10.** When Mikhail Gorbachev, a Communist party functionary, became general secretary of the party in 1985, few expected him to be the architect of its dismantling but, by the time he left office in 1991, the Soviet Union was transformed beyond anyone's wildest dreams.

_____ **11.** Sonya watched a video the night before the math exam instead of studying consequently, she received a *D* on the test.

_____ **12.** The 1980s were glorious years for the National Basketball Association as numerous great players captured the public's imagination, including Magic Johnson, the Los Angeles Lakers' great point guard and leader Larry Bird of the Boston Celtics, whose passing flair and shooting accuracy led his team to three championships and Chicago Bulls guard Michael Jordan, whom many consider the greatest player of all time.

_____ **13.** The bald eagle faces a raft of serious challenges to its continued survival nevertheless, in many areas it is beginning to make a comeback.

_____ **14.** The mid-nineteenth century saw the rise of nursing as a modern profession; both Florence Nightingale and Clara Barton are pioneers of the field.

Mechanics

Name _____ Class _____ Date _____

Lesson 78
Commas and Compound Sentences

Use **commas** between the main clauses in a compound sentence. Place a comma before a coordinating conjunction (*and, but, or, nor, yet,* or *for*) that joins two main clauses.

Irish playwright John Millington Synge is known for his dramas about rural Irish life, and his play *The Playboy of the Western World* has become a classic.

You may omit the comma between very short main clauses that are connected by a coordinating conjunction, unless the comma is needed to avoid confusion.

Jose opened the refrigerator and he took out the peanut butter. (clear)
Jose opened the refrigerator and the peanut butter fell on the floor. (confusing)
Jose opened the refrigerator, and the peanut butter fell on the floor. (clear)

▶ Exercise 1 **Add commas as needed. Cross out commas used incorrectly, using the delete (⌐) symbol. If the sentence is correct as written, write *C* in the blank.**

_____ Heracles has been portrayed in several movies and his name has come to stand for someone of immense strength.

_____ **1.** Ancient Greek mythology tells of many great heroes but the greatest of all must surely be Heracles.

_____ **2.** This mighty warrior's father was Zeus, and his mother was a mortal woman named Alcmene.

_____ **3.** Many Greek mythological figures were characterized as the children of gods and mortals and they were known as "demigods."

_____ **4.** Zeus's wife Hera became angry, when she learned of the baby born to a mortal woman.

_____ **5.** Zeus named his son Heracles ("glory of Hera") but the jealous queen of the gods hated her namesake.

_____ **6.** Hera sent two snakes to strangle the baby Heracles in his crib but Heracles awoke and squeezed the life out of the snakes.

_____ **7.** From that moment on, people expected marvelous things from the amazing baby and he grew into the world's most powerful man.

_____ **8.** Alcmene's husband was King Amphitrion and he taught the young Heracles how to box, wrestle, and make war.

_____ **9.** Eurystheus was King of Mycenae but his subject Heracles was much better known and more respected.

_____ **10.** Eurystheus grew jealous of Heracles' fame, and ordered him to perform twelve impossibly difficult tasks.

_____ **11.** The king hoped that Heracles would be killed performing the dangerous tasks but even these duties proved no match for the great hero.

_____ **12.** The tasks Heracles performed have become known as the Twelve Labors of Hercules and any task that seems almost impossibly difficult is today known as "Herculean."

_____ **13.** Heracles submitted to the king's command and the first labor he performed was to slay the dreaded lion of Nemea.

_____ **14.** The lion could not be killed with weapons but Heracles caught it, and strangled it with his bare hands.

_____ **15.** Heracles next killed the fearsome nine-headed Hydra and then he captured alive the golden-horned Hind (deer) of Mount Cerynea.

_____ **16.** Perhaps Heracles' most wonderful labor was, cleaning the Augean stables.

_____ **17.** These stables housed 3000 head of cattle, and had not been cleaned for thirty years but Heracles knocked a hole in the stable wall, and diverted two mighty rivers to rush through, and clean the filthy stables.

_____ **18.** The hero performed numerous other fabulous feats but still Eurystheus thought of more to challenge Heracles.

_____ **19.** Heracles was able to fetch the golden apples of the Daughters of the Night, by tricking the Titan Ajax.

_____ **20.** The final labor was to bring to Eurystheus the three-headed dog who guarded the entrance to the Underworld, yet even the forces of the dead proved no match for the hero.

_____ **21.** When he had completed all twelve labors, Heracles was more famous and admired than ever and the jealous King Eurystheus was forced to leave the hero alone.

Mechanics

Lesson 79
Commas in a Series and Between Coordinate Adjectives

Use **commas** to separate three or more words, phrases, or clauses in a series when they are not connected by conjunctions.

The lights blinked, flickered, and went out.
Shelley bought soft drinks, potato chips, and gingersnaps for the party.
I checked the windows, Denise pulled the curtains, and Dad turned out the lights.

Do not use commas to separate nouns used in pairs (*thunder and lightning, salt and pepper, bread and butter*) that are considered single units. The paired nouns are set off from other nouns or groups of nouns in a series, however.

The weather forecast called for cooler temperatures, thunder and lightning, and showers starting tonight.

Place a comma between coordinate adjectives that precede a noun. **Coordinate adjectives** modify a noun equally. To discover whether adjectives are coordinate, reverse their order or put the word *and* between them. If the sentence still sounds natural, the adjectives are coordinate.

The tall, thin, red-haired player on the other team was really good.

If adjectives preceding a noun sound unnatural with their order reversed or with *and* between them, do not use commas. Generally, adjectives that describe size, shape, age, and material do not need to be separated by commas.

Mindy painted a big round face on the mural.

► **Exercise 1 Add commas as needed. Cross out commas used incorrectly, using the delete (⅄) symbol. If the sentence is correct as written, write *C* in the blank.**

_____ Reading, writing, and 'rithmetic were referred to as the three R's.

_____ **1.** The nimble wily stealthy ferret eyed the rabbit cautiously.

_____ **2.** Peter opened the world almanac checked the index and identified the capital of Rwanda.

_____ **3.** The illustrator had drawn the dogs dressed in shoes, and socks, trousers, and sportcoats.

_____ **4.** The hat cost twenty-six dollars the shirt cost another forty dollars and the shoes were priced at thirty-eight dollars.

_____ **5.** The ballet dancers were graceful athletic and suggestive of the animals they were portraying.

_____ **6.** Interested people can give their applications to Jill Jones Lucy Mason or me.

_____ **7.** The cafeteria is serving grilled cheese sandwiches applesauce, and carrot sticks today.

Mechanics

_____ **8.** The pen scratched across the paper, and then ran out of ink.

_____ **9.** The French flag is blue, and white, and red.

_____ **10.** The king considered the rebels outlaws, scoundrels, and good-for-nothings.

_____ **11.** Break the eggs into a bowl, beat them lightly with a fork and then add the melted butter.

_____ **12.** The wind became calm, and gentle as night fell.

_____ **13.** The sad, angry, contestant walked slowly off the stage.

_____ **14.** Lena and Heather researched, wrote, and presented their analysis of the election of 1994.

_____ **15.** Mr. Denune has a valuable, foreign coin collection.

_____ **16.** Thomas Hardy's *Tess of the d'Urbervilles* is a poignant hard-hitting novel of life in rural England at the end of the nineteenth century.

_____ **17.** Among the different types of lettuce available at our grocery store are iceberg, endive, red leaf, and romaine.

_____ **18.** The little brown dog sitting by the corner can catch balls in its mouth.

_____ **19.** Children are taught to stop look and listen before crossing a street.

_____ **20.** A loud, smelly truck pulled into our driveway and turned around.

_____ **21.** Dad thinks he lost his wallet at either the office the swimming pool, or the drug store.

_____ **22.** Mom and I saw a gigantic, brown insect near the drain in the basement.

_____ **23.** The piece began with a clash of cymbals then the trumpets played a fanfare and the violins introduced the main theme.

_____ **24.** The reviewer described the new movie as, action-packed thrilling and breathtakingly realistic.

_____ **25.** The Cajun menu features crayfish casserole, red beans and rice, and poor boy sandwiches.

_____ **26.** Uncle Dan offered Mom Dad and me the extra tickets to the boat show.

_____ **27.** The material Mom chose for the skirt is soft and smooth and warm.

_____ **28.** Horacio ran into Mark Devin and Khalid at the mall near the music store.

_____ **29.** The smoke from the campfire curled upward, mingled with the leaves on the trees and disappeared.

_____ **30.** The gardener dug the hole placed the tulip bulb at the proper depth and covered it with a mixture of dirt and compost.

Mechanics

Lesson 80
Commas with Nonessential Elements, Interjections, Parenthetical Expressions, and Conjunctive Adverbs

Use **commas** to set off participles, infinitives, appositives, and their phrases if they are not essential to the meaning of the sentence. If they are essential to the meaning, do not set them off with commas.

He smiled broadly, waiting for teammates to congratulate him. (nonessential participial phrase)

To go on every one of the club's hikes is my goal. (As the subject of the sentence, the infinitive phrase is essential to the meaning of the sentence.)

Twain's novel *The Adventures of Huckleberry Finn* also takes place on and along the Mississippi River. (If commas were used to set off the essential appositive, *The Adventures of Huckleberry Finn,* the implication would be that this was Twain's only novel, which is not the case.)

Use commas to set off a nonessential adjective clause, but do not use commas to set off an adjective clause that is essential.

Madison, which is in the south-central part of the state, is the capital of Wisconsin. (*Which is in the south-central part of the state* is extra information.)

Tourists who are not fond of cold weather should think twice about vacationing in Alaska. (*Who are not fond of cold weather* is essential to the meaning.)

Use commas to set off interjections (such as *oh* and *well*), parenthetical expressions (such as *on the contrary, in fact,* and *on the other hand*), and conjunctive adverbs (such as *however, moreover,* and *consequently*).

Well, I guess that's the end.   I hope we play better tomorrow, however.

Mechanics

▶ **Exercise 1** Add commas as needed. Cross out commas used incorrectly, using the delete (⟍) symbol. If the sentence is correct as written, write *C* in the blank.

_____ Anyone͜who would like to join the drama club͜should see Mr. Stayman after school this week.

_____ 1. Mr. Norman, who is a former pro football player, is helping to coach the junior varsity team this year.

_____ 2. Bushido the code of honor of the Japanese samurai warriors was the subject of the professor's lecture.

_____ 3. It's one of Marielle's dreams, to see the Chicago Bulls with Michael Jordan.

_____ 4. Susannah, to tell the truth, is not the world's most diligent student.

_____ 5. To get an *A* in Ms. Montenaro's algebra class, requires doing your homework every night.

_____ 6. I prefer eating in a booth, to sitting at the counter.

_____ 7. Oh, I guess you can join us if you want to.

_____ 8. Maria caught a steelhead which is a kind of trout as well as some rainbow trout.

_____ 9. Hikers, who are not prepared for changes in weather, usually pay the price by getting cold, hot, or wet.

_____ 10. Sir Richard Burton, the English explorer of the nineteenth century, tried unsuccessfully to discover the source of the Nile River.

_____ 11. That orange cat, climbing along the fence, has been yowling all night long!

_____ 12. With around 10 million people the Egyptian capital Cairo is the largest city in Africa.

_____ 13. Her brother will see any movie, that gets a thumbs up from the reviewer on Channel 34.

_____ 14. I don't care for that song to be perfectly frank.

_____ 15. Volleyball players, who can spike as she can, are few and far between.

_____ 16. *Jane Eyre* was written by Charlotte Brontë who is Emily Brontë's older sister.

_____ 17. Any car that starts only half the time is not very useful.

_____ 18. A photo essay however is a good way to use several photographs in one layout.

_____ 19. The credit card company, that sent me the application letter, must not know that I'm only in high school!

_____ 20. The captured soldier waited quietly, hoping for the best but preparing for the worst.

_____ 21. The author Raymond Chandler is best known for his detective stories featuring the sleuth Philip Marlowe.

_____ 22. Would you like, to go to the beach with my family next weekend?

_____ 23. Darcie's brother has blond hair, while her sister on the contrary has flaming red hair.

_____ 24. *Meet the Beatles* the Beatles' first U.S. album was one of the fastest-selling albums of all time.

_____ 25. Pete's mom ordered cappuccino a kind of coffee with steamed milk after the meal.

Mechanics

Lesson 81
Commas and Introductory Phrases

Use a comma after a short introductory prepositional phrase only if the sentence would be misread without the comma.

In the barn, cats hunt for mice. (The comma is needed to prevent misreading.)
In the barn we store hay and farm equipment. (comma not needed)

Use a comma after a long prepositional phrase or after the final phrase in a succession of phrases.

At the bottom of the painting in the first room, I saw the artist's signature.
At the bottom of the painting in the first room was the artist's signature.

Use commas to set off introductory participles and participial phrases.

Singing, the protesters marched down the street.
Scampering quickly across the road, the groundhog avoided the car.

Do not use a comma if the phrase is immediately followed by a verb.

▶ **Exercise 1** **Add commas as needed. Cross out commas used incorrectly, using the delete (⅋) symbol. If the sentence is correct as written, write *C* in the blank.**

_____ Studying old pictures and drawings about the American Revolution, I learned quite a bit about the uniforms worn by the various armies.

_____ **1.** During the American Revolution at the end of the 1700s soldiers from four different countries did most of the fighting.

_____ **2.** Of the four two are most familiar to Americans today.

_____ **3.** Risking his life almost daily for less than seven dollars a month the American infantryman was the heart of George Washington's Continental Army.

_____ **4.** Without standard uniforms or weapons for most of the war, American infantrymen often wore their civilian clothes.

_____ **5.** In 1778, the Continental Army received a shipment of blue and brown coats from France.

_____ **6.** For most it was the first time they had seen anything like an official uniform.

_____ **7.** Sporting their homespun shirts, jackets, and coats the Americans would never be confused with the splendidly dressed redcoats of the British army.

_____ **8.** Contrasting sharply with the shabbily clothed Americans, were the British soldiers .

_____ **9.** In the British army of the Revolutionary period, the uniforms were quite elaborate.

Mechanics

_____ 10. Wearing their distinctive hats British soldiers were often blinded by the sun since they had no visors.

_____ 11. Around their necks the soldiers wore stiff collars and leather neck pieces.

_____ 12. Only with difficulty, was a redcoat able to turn his head.

_____ 13. Carrying their regimental flags into battle, the British redcoats were often a splendid sight.

_____ 14. Toward the end of the war French soldiers became a common sight.

_____ 15. Dazzling in their white uniforms trimmed with light blue, yellow, or pink the French soldiers were also seasoned veterans and good fighters.

_____ 16. Ridiculing the elegance of the French uniforms cartoons appeared in British newspapers and magazines.

_____ 17. Throughout the war Britain hired German soldiers called *mercenaries* to reinforce their own army.

_____ 18. Wearing blue or green uniforms depending on their rank and job the German mercenaries were also feared fighters.

_____ 19. Of all the German mercenaries to fight in the war the largest number came from the state of Hesse-Cassel.

_____ 20. For this reason all German mercenaries came to be known as "Hessians."

▶ Exercise 2 **Place a check beside each sentence that uses commas correctly.**

✔ Using history books, maps, and a calendar, we planned our trip.

_____ 1. With a good guide book and a detailed road map, a history buff can take a very interesting vacation exploring battlefields and other sites from the American Revolution.

_____ 2. From Maine in the North to Georgia in the South the eastern seacoast is filled with fascinating reminders of the War of Independence.

_____ 3. Befitting its location as a colonial crossroads, Pennsylvania is home to many important Revolutionary War sites.

_____ 4. Among the most popular Revolutionary War sites, is Valley Forge.

_____ 5. Lying about 20 miles northwest of Philadelphia Valley Forge was the winter camp of Washington's army.

_____ 6. In this eastern Pennsylvania stronghold, the bedraggled Continental Army spent the unusually harsh winter of 1777–78.

Lesson 82
Commas and Adverb Clauses and Antithetical Phrases

Use **commas** to set off all introductory adverb clauses and to set off internal adverb clauses that interrupt the flow of a sentence. Generally, do not set off an adverb clause at the end of a sentence unless the clause is parenthetical or it would be misread without the comma.

Since the concert had already started, we had to wait in the lobby.
David, after he had been accepted into the program, threw his hat into the air and whooped!
Dad was disappointed because he had to miss my softball game.

Use commas to set off an antithetical phrase. In an **antithetical phrase** a word such as *not* or *unlike* qualifies what precedes it.

Melanie, **unlike** her brothers, enjoys sports.

▶ **Exercise 1** Underline each adverb clause. Circle each antithetical phrase. Add commas as needed.

The guidance counselor said I'd have to take algebra ⟨but not calculus⟩, if I want to attend

college.

1. After Heather watered the amaryllis plant she dropped the watering can.

2. My mom enjoys logging on to her computer whenever she wants.

3. Oak, hickory, and ash unlike softwoods such as pine and spruce make good firewood.

4. Before you decide what to eat let's ask the waiter about the specials.

5. This answer if it is true could be of great importance.

6. Melinda decided to build the rocking chair, although she had never bent wood before.

7. Wherever the cat goes the puppy follows, nipping at the cat's tail.

8. Joel not Joe was the name called.

9. His essay since it was turned in late received a lower grade.

10. The rider promised not to use spurs on the horse unless it was absolutely necessary.

11. Whether it rains or not I expect the weather will remain hot and humid.

12. She didn't tell him the news because it was of no interest to him.

13. Dolphins and porpoises in contrast to sharks are not fish.

14. As the boat sailed off into the setting sun we waved farewell to the tropical paradise.

15. My little sister and her friends stayed out sledding in the snow until they were almost frozen!

Mechanics

16. The contest was structured so that all entrants would have an equal chance of winning.

17. My coffee table when finished will have seven coats of varnish.

18. As long as there are people like Mr. Sanchez involved in the effort no one will be disappointed.

19. Unlike English Latin and Russian are heavily inflected languages, which means they add endings to words to change their meaning.

20. Our committee raised the question in order that the whole class could discuss it.

21. If you take my advice you'll forget the whole thing.

22. Call me as soon as you can!

23. While the house burned the owner sat paralyzed with grief and shock.

24. Unless this city institutes a recycling program it will not be eligible for the grant money from the state.

25. William McKinley although he is usually considered a good president was not a great one.

26. When I ripped my new anorak on a nail I was able to mend it with some nylon thread.

27. Jon's father not his mother came to the performance last evening.

28. Brian tried out for the hockey team because he wanted to.

29. Uncle Tim after he decided to go fishing couldn't remember where he had put his gear.

30. The dancing kite went wherever the wind blew it.

31. The decision whether you agree with it or not will become the official policy of the government.

32. The new Chinese restaurant on Third Street although not expensive was delightful.

33. Although they had difficulty with the weather, the mountain climbers vowed to push on.

34. A goat as opposed to a sheep usually prefers to browse, or eat leaves from bushes and trees.

35. Arrange the bedroom furniture where it looks best.

Mechanics

Lesson 83
Commas with Titles, Addresses, and Numbers

Use **commas** to set off titles when they follow a person's name.

Benazir Bhutto, prime minister of Pakistan, visited the White House yesterday.

Use commas after the various parts of an address, a geographical term, or a date.

The advertisement said that entries should be sent to Sweepstakes, 440 Park Avenue South, New York, NY 10016.
When my aunt was in the Peace Corps, she worked in Ouagadougou, Burkina Faso.
Abraham Lincoln was shot on April 14, 1865, and died the next morning.

A comma is not used when only the month and the day or the month and the year are given.

In July 1776 the Declaration of Independence was signed in Philadelphia.
July 4 has become the American national holiday.

Use commas to set off the parts of a reference that direct the reader to the exact source.

The Drama Club performed Act 5, Scene ii, of Shakespeare's *Macbeth.*
You'll find the answer to that question in Part Three, Chapter 89, page 768.

▶ **Exercise 1** Place a check (✔) beside each sentence that uses commas correctly.

✔ _____ The surprise comes in Act 4, Scene ii, of that melodrama.

_____ **1.** Robin's new address is 4789 Speight Avenue Waco Texas 76711

_____ **2.** Marielle's birthday is August 16, 1977.

_____ **3.** Grover Cleveland, governor of New York was elected president of the U.S. two different times.

_____ **4.** Stockholm, Sweden is a lovely city built on hundreds of islands.

_____ **5.** In July, 1956 a Swedish ship, the *Stockholm,* and an Italian one, the *Andrea Doria,* collided off the coast of Massachusetts.

_____ **6.** In "Ode on a Grecian Urn," lines 49-50, what does poet John Keats say about truth and beauty?

_____ **7.** The association has its headquarters at 198 Cross Street, Ypsilanti, Michigan 48198.

_____ **8.** The parade has been rescheduled for Saturday November 30, 1996.

_____ **9.** Mount Saint Helens, a volcano in the state of Washington, erupted in May 1980.

_____ **10.** Daniel Webster, senator from Massachusetts, was an outspoken opponent of slavery in the years before the Civil War.

Mechanics

_____ 11. Franklin Roosevelt was elected president for an unprecedented third time in November, 1940.

_____ 12. Victoria British Columbia, is known for its magnificent public gardens.

_____ 13. The last game of the season is against Ridgedale High on November 12.

_____ 14. The package Mr. Dawson received had a return address of 2 Main Street, Vandalia, Ohio, 45377

_____ 15. The speech that begins "To be, or not to be" can be found in Act 3 Scene i of Shakespeare's *Hamlet*.

_____ 16. Michael leaves for boot camp on August 2.

_____ 17. The motion was introduced by Lucille Montoya councilwoman from the Fourth Ward.

_____ 18. Madison, Wisconsin is named after the fifth president of the United States, James Madison.

_____ 19. Devastating floods struck Johnstown, Pennsylvania, in 1889, 1936, and 1977.

_____ 20. My grandmother still talks about how hot the weather was during August, 1957.

▶ **Exercise 2** **Add commas as needed. Cross out commas used incorrectly, using the delete (℣) symbol. If the sentence is correct as written, write *C* in the blank.**

_____ Jason hopes to get out of the navy in July, 1998.

_____ 1. Dad's work address is 400 Office Park Drive Birmingham Alabama 35223.

_____ 2. This year Independence Day will be celebrated on July 5.

_____ 3. Is there anyone who hasn't seen the terrifying film of the zeppelin *Hindenburg* as it caught fire on, May 6 1937?

_____ 4. The Law Day address will be given by Ms. Phyllis Anderson judge of the First Circuit Court of Appeals.

_____ 5. One of the world's most famous buildings is the opera house in Sydney Australia.

_____ 6. Book 2 Chapter 17 of George Eliot's *Middlemarch* focuses on Mr. Farebrother, the minister of the local church.

_____ 7. The charter of the United Nations took effect on October 24 1945.

_____ 8. Lyndon Johnson vice president of the United States became president when John F. Kennedy was assassinated.

_____ 9. Ludwig van Beethoven was born in Bonn, Germany.

_____ 10. Send your letter to Frank Thomas, Chicago White Sox 333 West 35th Street Chicago Illinois 60616.

Mechanics

Lesson 84

Commas with Direct Address, Tag Questions, and Letter Writing

Use commas to set off words or names used in direct address.

Mom, would you like to attend my high school graduation dinner with me?
Hey, man, that's an incredibly cool guitar!
Thank you for your help, Mr. Chang.

Use commas to set off a tag question.

I didn't see you at Computer Universe yesterday, did I?
Marshall ate all the cashews, didn't he?

Place a comma after the salutation of an informal letter and after the closing of all letters.

Dear Uncle Alex,   Dear Stacey,   Love,   Sincerely,

Use the following style for the heading of a letter:

1908 Coventry Avenue
Alexandria, Virginia 22314
September 6, 1995

▶ **Exercise 1**   **Add commas as needed. Cross out commas used incorrectly, using the delete (⅄) symbol. If the item is correct as written, write C in the blank.**

_____   Walter how on earth do you expect me to read this messy letter?

_____   **1.** The aliens in the movie will definitely return for more hostages won't they?

_____   **2.** I don't know Christy when was the neutron discovered?

_____   **3.** Dear James

_____   **4.** Your brother doesn't plan to major in music, does he?

_____   **5.** Yes my friend relations between our two countries have never been better.

_____   **6.** Listen pal I wouldn't touch that electric wire if I were you.

_____   **7.** You won't forget to call us as soon as you have any news will you?

_____   **8.** Love Mom

_____   **9.** Hey Grandpa, tell me about when Joe Namath guaranteed that his New York Jets would win the Super Bowl!

_____ **10.** I don't suppose I could have another slice of your delicious rhubarb pie could I, Ms. Wheeler?

Mechanics

_____ 11. Bad dog Spot—just look what you've done to my tennis racquet!

_____ 12. This tape player doesn't need the expensive kind of batteries does it?

_____ 13. Dear, Ben

_____ 14. We'll make it in time to see the start of the game won't we?

_____ 15. No, Ms. Palmer, we won't forget to turn off the flames under the Bunsen burners when

we're finished with the experiment.

_____ 16. Andie won't leave without us for the camp site will she?

_____ 17. Your friend Jordan

_____ 18. You're welcome to join us for dinner on the eighteenth Aunt Julia.

_____ 19. Those broken twigs weren't there when we passed this spot this morning were they?

_____ 20. My dear nephew

_____ 21. Rick should be spending more time on his history essay shouldn't he?

_____ 22. Governor we recommend that you veto this bill because of several unclear passages in

the third section.

_____ 23. You wouldn't be interested in purchasing a magazine subscription would you?

_____ 24. Cordially, Elaine Nakamura

_____ 25. Come here Pete.

_____ 26. Sincerely, Aunt Kathleen,

_____ 27. Marcie's guinea pig can't get out of her cage can she?

_____ 28. I did a few of the problems on page 290 for extra practice Mr. Deksulthorn.

_____ 29. Your, best bud Mark

_____ 30. Your Honor I strongly object to that remark as prejudicial to the jury.

_____ 31. I already cleaned that bunch of spinach didn't I?

_____ 32. Thanks Cara

_____ 33. No, sir I'm certain I didn't hear anything in the shed on the night in question.

_____ 34. Dear Dad

_____ 35. That car in the parking lot runs on natural gas instead of gasoline, doesn't it?

_____ 36. Father Andrew, we'd love to have you sit at our table during the reception.

_____ 37. You could give me a hand with those hay bales couldn't, you?

_____ 38. Yes Officer, I understand how important it is to wear my seat belt at all times.

Mechanics

Lesson 85
Misuse of Commas

A comma should not precede a conjunction that connects the parts of a compound predicate when the predicate has only two parts.

Incorrect: Copenhagen and Stockholm are the largest cities in Scandinavia, but are not nearly as large as London or Paris.

Correct: Copenhagen and Stockholm are the largest cities in Scandinavia but are not nearly as large as London or Paris.

An error called a run-on sentence (or a comma splice or a comma fault) occurs when only a comma is used to join two main clauses that are not part of a series. To avoid run-on sentences, use a coordinating conjunction with the comma, or use a semicolon.

Incorrect: The capitals of Denmark and Sweden are port cities, ships from every country call at their harbors.

Correct: The capitals of Denmark and Sweden are port cities, **and** ships from every country call at their harbors.

Correct: The capitals of Denmark and Sweden are port cities; ships from every country call at their harbors.

A comma should never be used between a subject and its verb or between a verb and its complement.

Incorrect: Which of the two cities is more appealing, is up to the individual traveler to decide.

Correct: Which of the two cities is more appealing is up to the individual traveler to decide.

Incorrect: The Scandinavian countries include, Sweden, Denmark, Norway, and Finland.
Correct: The Scandinavian countries include Sweden, Denmark, Norway, and Finland.

Mechanics

▶ **Exercise 1 Correct each sentence as needed by adding commas, semicolons, or a conjunction. Cross out commas used incorrectly using the delete (⌒) symbol. If the sentence is correct as written, write *C* in the blank.**

_____   A good way to begin learning about the history of the states, is to explore their names.

_____ 1. Learning about the origins of the names of the states, can be fascinating.

_____ 2. States' names can reveal much about their history, and tell interesting stories as well.

_____ 3. For example, Pennsylvania means "Penn's Woodland" it was granted to the proprietor of the colony, William Penn.

_____ 4. How Pennsylvania got its name is a good story.

_____ 5. King Charles I of England owed 16,000 pounds to William Penn's father, and gave the land to the son as partial payment of this debt.

_____ **6.** William Penn wanted to call his colony Sylvania this is the Latin word for *woodland*.

_____ **7.** However, King Charles added the name "Penn" to "Sylvania" to honor William Penn's father, a navy admiral.

_____ **8.** The modest William Penn disliked the idea he was a Quaker.

_____ **9.** Many American states have Native American names, and reflect the settlers' respect for the original inhabitants of their states.

_____ **10.** States with Native American names include, Ohio, Tennessee, Kentucky, Iowa, and Wisconsin.

_____ **11.** Settlers in Ohio, one of the first states to be settled west of the Appalachian Mountains, saw a mighty river, and learned to call it by its Iroquois name.

_____ **12.** When the territory became a state in 1803, the residents decided to call it, "Ohio."

_____ **13.** *Ohio* means "beautiful river" in the Iroquois language, and it proved an appropriate description of the important transportation link.

_____ **14.** Who the important political figures were at the time, can also be deduced from state names.

_____ **15.** North and South Carolina, Virginia, and Georgia, are some good examples of states named after contemporary figures.

_____ **16.** *Carolina* is the Latin form of Charles North Carolina and South Carolina are named for King Charles I of England.

_____ **17.** Elizabeth of England, called the Virgin Queen, provided, the name for the first English colony in the New World.

_____ **18.** Sir Walter Raleigh named the colony after Elizabeth he and his monarch were close friends.

_____ **19.** Georgia is also named for an English monarch, but its namesake is a later one than Elizabeth or Charles.

_____ **20.** James Oglethorpe founded the colony in 1732, and named it after George II.

_____ **21.** Several states have the word *New* in their names these include New Hampshire, New York, New Mexico, and New Jersey.

_____ **22.** New Hampshire, New York, and New Jersey were named after places in England Spanish explorers in the Southwest applied the name "New Mexico" to areas west of the Rio Grande in the 1500s.

Mechanics

Lesson 86
Commas in Review

▶ **Exercise 1** Add commas where necessary. Delete commas used incorrectly, using the delete (⅄) symbol.

The important thing to remember about the story is⅄that men, women, and children can accomplish much more⅄when they work together.

1. The bus, waiting in the parking lot, was chartered to take the cross-country team to the state meet.

2. Shakespeare's play, *The Tempest,* deals with magical events among a group of people shipwrecked on an island.

3. Bill Monroe hailed from the Bluegrass State of Kentucky and he called the music he invented "Bluegrass."

4. Grinning from ear to ear Martin accepted the award on behalf of all his teammates.

5. The race horse was swift powerful, and very high-strung.

6. Beside the wheelbarrow in the flower garden in back of the house I saw a weasel.

7. Dundee Scotland is where these delicious shortbread cookies are made.

8. The meteorologist said, she expects a cool wet summer.

9. Mom and Dad, since they got back from their trip to Ireland have talked of little else.

10. Columbus Day is celebrated, on October 12 in many states and cities.

11. The mighty tree made a ripping sound leaned and slowly crashed to the forest floor.

12. She opened the door, and walked out.

13. For Tuesday class please re-read Act 3 Scenes 2 and 3 of *The Merchant of Venice.*

14. The sheep eat grass hay and almost anything else that grows, including my dad's vegetable garden.

15. At our bird feeder in winter we often see chickadees and nuthatches also feed there on occasion.

16. Michela's goal in attending college is, to earn a degree in physical therapy.

17. His parents were married on June 3, 1975 in Portland Oregon.

18. The world almanac is an extremely useful reference tool, because it contains so much information in one place.

Mechanics

19. To be honest that television show seems boring, and outdated.

20. The members of the planning committee are, Dawn, Raquel, Lek, and Anthony.

21. Adenine which is a kind of chemical is a critical element in DNA.

22. Whomever you want to invite to the graduation party, is fine with me.

23. In the left-hand drawer of the dresser in the guest bedroom, sat the lost kitten.

24. The Ecology Club is meeting after school today, and has scheduled a speaker about newspaper recycling.

25. Thomas P. O'Neill speaker of the House of Representatives during the 1980s, replaced John F. Kennedy in Congress.

26. The butler announced a name the couple entered the room ,and everyone turned and stared at them.

27. At first, she refused.

28. To score one hundred points in a professional basketball game, is almost unbelievable, but Wilt Chamberlain did it in 1962.

29. The different kinds of bagels include, poppy, sesame, onion, rye, and egg.

30. Have you seen *Schindler's List* the film by Stephen Spielberg, about the Holocaust?

31. In order to ensure that everyone is treated fairly please do not write your names only your number on your tests.

32. A distant relative of the raccoon the giant panda is one of the world's favorite animals.

33. Andre Agassi won the Wimbledon tennis tournament in July, 1992 in London, England.

34. The lion sleeping by day and hunting by night is the monarch of the African plain.

35. Dear Brandy

36. During the movie stars made cameo appearances.

37. The new movie was fast-paced, and thrilling and humorous as well.

38. The association had its headquarters at 6749, 56th Street, Kansas City, MO, 64153.

39. Anyone, who would risk her life for another person, is a real hero!

40. I apologize for the inconvenience Mr. Alvarez.

41. For dinner, Dad is preparing spaghetti, and meatballs, green salad, and garlic bread.

42. Laughing I left the theater, and walked home.

Mechanics

Lesson 87
Dashes to Signal Change and to Emphasize

On a typewriter, indicate the **dash** with two hyphens (--). Do not place a comma, semicolon, colon, or period before or after a dash. Use a dash to indicate an abrupt break or change in thought within a sentence.

At the museum in Williamsburg, we saw a pillory—it is a kind of wooden frame that held the arms and head of wrongdoers—that had been built around 1695.

Use a dash to set off and emphasize supplemental information or parenthetical statements.

Mr. Davidson left on his trip to Denmark last Friday—exactly 20 years to the day after he first saw his ancestral home.

▶ **Exercise 1** **Add dashes where necessary. If the sentence is correct as written, write *C* in the blank.**

_____ The soloist performed the piece on a harpsichord—it is an early ancestor of our piano—amazing the audience with her virtuosity.

_____ 1. The German shepherd and the Belgian Malinois share a common background both were developed as guard dogs for sheep flocks and do, in fact, look somewhat similar.

_____ 2. It's a good idea many people seem to neglect this common courtesy to write a thank-you note whenever you receive a gift.

_____ 3. Because Holly helped Jason study for the algebra final, he sent her a dozen roses when he passed.

_____ 4. Crazy quilts those with irregular-shaped pieces of fabric instead of regular shapes such as squares, diamonds, or hexagons can be quite ingenious.

_____ 5. Don't look back someone may be gaining on you!

_____ 6. Slowing the erosion of our country's shoreline all 50,000 miles of it is a high priority.

_____ 7. The magician proceeded to pull three rabbits out of his hat, not one.

_____ 8. Volunteering at the humane society it's on Columbus Road just past the trailer park is an awful lot of fun.

_____ 9. Dad ordered *hummous* a delicious paste made from chick peas and sesame seeds and a salad called *tabouli.*

Mechanics

_____ **10.** Disneyland in Anaheim, California, is more than twenty years older than Disney World in Orlando, Florida.

_____ **11.** The world's population is growing at an alarming rate fast enough to double in only forty-three years!

_____ **12.** You can determine how effective a sun block is by checking the number on the bottle.

_____ **13.** The Aurora Borealis, or Northern Lights the Aurora Australis is the same phenomenon in the southern hemisphere is a breathtaking display of lights often seen in the summer sky.

_____ **14.** New York City has the highest percentage of people who take public transportation to work San Francisco is second among the country's fifteen largest cities.

_____ **15.** Juanita's brother has started his own business as a food caterer.

_____ **16.** Surprisingly, the two states that grow the most cotton they are Texas and California are not in the South at all.

_____ **17.** The Toronto Blue Jays, one of two Canadian teams the Montreal Expos are the other are the first baseball team to win consecutive World Series since the New York Yankees.

_____ **18.** The real name of the comic actor and director Albert Brooks is believe it or not Albert Einstein!

_____ **19.** On our trip west, we toured the Northern Cheyenne reservation in Montana.

_____ **20.** The percentage of women on active duty is highest in the Air Force in 1994, almost 15 percent and lowest in the Marines.

_____ **21.** When swimming at the beach, it's important to be aware of the undertow.

_____ **22.** Among the languages other than English spoken in American homes are Spanish, French, and Tagalog, the language of the Philippines.

_____ **23.** Few people know that the song "America the Beautiful" was inspired by the view from a specific place Pikes Peak in Colorado.

_____ **24.** James Madison he was the fourth president was a good friend and political ally of Thomas Jefferson, the man he succeeded in the nation's highest office.

_____ **25.** The film *Schindler's List*, directed by Steven Spielberg, won the Oscar for best picture in 1993.

_____ **26.** Jerome's eight-year-old brother don't ask me why wondered if he could borrow my electric shaver.

Mechanics

Lesson 88
Parentheses, Brackets, and Ellipsis Points

Use **parentheses** to set off supplemental material that is not meant to be part of the main statement.

Jupiter, the largest planet in the solar system is 88,000 miles (about 140,000 kilometers) in diameter.

Generally, a comma, a semicolon, or a colon appears *after* the closing parenthesis. A period, a question mark, or an exclamation point appears *inside* the parentheses if it is part of the parenthetical expression but *outside* the closing parenthesis if it is part of the sentence.

The author in the photo was Katherine Anne Porter (1890-1980), author of the novel *Ship of Fools*.
Be sure to look for the sign (is it blue or green?) above the door of the hobby shop.
Have you read "The Musgrave Ritual" (the fifth of eleven Sherlock Holmes stories in the book)**?**

Use **brackets** to enclose information that you insert into a quotation from someone else's work in order to clarify the quotation.

"His [Daniel Day-Lewis's] performance as Christy Brown, the Irish writer with cerebral palsy, won an Academy Award in 1989."

Use brackets to enclose a parenthetical phrase that already appears within parentheses.

Robert James Waller's first novel (*The Bridges of Madison County* [the action takes place in the author's home state of Iowa]) is one of the highest-selling hardcover novels of all time.

Use a series of equally spaced points, called **ellipsis points**, to indicate the omission of material from a quotation. If the omission occurs at the beginning of a sentence, use three spaced points. Use the correct punctuation (if any) plus three spaced points if the omission occurs in the middle or at the end of the sentence. In using a period plus three spaced points, do not leave any space between the last word before the omission and the first point, the period.

. . . It was clear to me . . . that Saddam Hussein was quite prepared to suffer a great deal. . . . Meanwhile Kuwait was being destroyed.

—Gen. Colin Powell

▶ **Exercise 1** **Place a check beside each sentence that uses parentheses, brackets, and ellipsis points correctly.**

___✔___ "Martin [Luther King Jr.] knew that character and ability are formed in the home . . . ," Colin Powell has written, "and in the school."

Mechanics

_____ 1. Colin Powell (the future chairman of the U.S. Joint Chiefs of Staff) was born in New York to Jamaican immigrant parents on April 5, 1937.

_____ 2. His father worked long hours (as a clerk in a shipping company;) his mother also worked, as a seamstress.

_____ 3. Colin Powell recalls his childhood as a happy one, although his neighborhood of Hunt's Point (in New York's South Bronx) has since become impoverished.

_____ 4. Hunt's Point was a relatively prosperous working-class neighborhood of blacks (many, like the Powells, of West Indian descent), Latinos, Jews, and other ethnic groups.

_____ 5. On several occasions he has said, "[Hunt's Point] was a neat place to grow up."

_____ 6. "Growing up in New York," Powell wrote in 1988, "everybody was a minority...I did not know what a majority was."

_____ 7. The young Colin Powell worked part-time in a store owned by a Jewish family, and there he learned to speak some Yiddish (the language of eastern European Jews [from the old German word for *Jewish*]).

_____ 8. The Powells attended St. Margaret's Episcopal Church (The Episcopal Church is the national church of England and was the church of most Jamaicans.).

_____ 9. Colin Powell was able to avoid the many dangers that were beginning to infect the South Bronx (drug use, crime, and poverty,) thanks to his strong, supportive family.

_____ 10. Among his cousins are several state and federal judges, an ambassador to Sierra Leone (a country in west Africa), a psychologist, two Oxford graduates, a leading aerospace engineer, and one of the nation's richest African-American businessmen.

_____ 11. His sister Barbara was U.S. ambassador to Malaysia (she also became an assistant secretary of state.)

_____ 12. Powell's parents (Luther and Maud (who was born McKoy)) take most of the credit for the family's success, according to their famous son.

_____ 13. "Children watch the way their parents live their lives..," Colin Powell said. "If the parents' values seem correct and relevant, the children will follow those values."

_____ 14. He told the *New Republic* magazine that there was an "expectation" in his family: "(You) were supposed to do better."

_____ 15. At Morris High School and later at City College of New York, Powell was only an average student (Did you know that he began college as an engineering major, later switching to geology)?

_____ 16. In college, Powell joined the Reserve Officers' Training Corps (ROTC), and he became a second lieutenant when he graduated in 1958.

_____ 17. Powell said later about his school career, ".... it gave me an insight into the fundamentals of government [and] a deep respect for our democratic system."

_____ 18. Powell found that he enjoyed the disciplined life of the army (Perhaps it was this discipline, as much as any other element, that led him to decide to become a career officer.)

Lesson 89
Quotation Marks for Direct Quotations

Use **quotation marks** to enclose a direct quotation. In general, separate introductory or explanatory remarks from the quotation with a comma.

"Once you've seen Niagara Falls, you'll never forget its awesome power," my grandfather said solemnly.

Grandmother added with a laugh, "I agree with you, dear, but when we were there, you complained the whole time about the roar!"

When a quotation is interrupted by explanatory words such as *he said* or *she wrote*, use two sets of quotation marks. Begin the second part of the quotation with a capital letter if it is a complete sentence.

"Notre Dame, Michigan, and Alabama are the teams," said the coach, "with the best records in college football."

"Alabama coach Bear Bryant has won the most games," she continued. "He won 323 games in his career."

Never use quotation marks in an indirect quotation (a quotation that does not repeat a person's exact words).

Original quotation: "I don't care about your horrid little frog," Valerie screeched.
Indirect quotation: Valerie screeched that she didn't care about the horrid little frog.

Use single quotation marks around a quotation within a quotation.

During the discussion, he said, "Remember that she ends the novel by stating, 'The land went slowly back to pasture and then to forest. In a hundred years, no one knew it had ever existed.'"

In writing dialogue, begin a new paragraph and use a new set of quotation marks every time the speaker changes.

"What do you feel like doing?" Mark asked when we had all gathered at the corner.
"How about we go shoot some hoops at the playground," suggested Khalid.
"We could do that—if we had a basketball," answered Mark.

▶ **Exercise 1** **Add quotation marks where necessary. If the sentence is correct as written, write *C* in the blank.**

_____   "No man ever became extremely wicked all at once," wrote the Roman dramatist

Juvenal.

_____ **1.** While it is not surprising that Texas has the most farms of any state, the state in second

place may surprise you,the speaker said.It's Missouri.

_____ **2.** The only reason for her lateness, sniffed Marian, is that she doesn't respect us enough to try to be on time.

_____ **3.** Did Jason explain to you what he wanted?

_____ **4.** The Persian cat is considered the height of elegance, the book stated, with its long, luxurious fur and haughty, regal manner.

_____ **5.** I remember very clearly, said Grandfather, when President Franklin Roosevelt said, The only thing we have to fear is fear itself.

_____ **6.** Let me tell you about our special, said the waiter with a smile. Today we're featuring roast leg of lamb with mint jelly, roast potatoes, and green beans.

_____ **7.** The police officer said that Mom was going 42 miles an hour in a 35-mile-an-hour zone.

_____ **8.** What do you think you're doing with that can of shaving cream? Dad asked sharply.

_____ **9.** I'm afraid you've forgotten, said William, that the coach said, The first three finishers in each event will advance to the finals.

_____ **10.** Pointing to the slide, the lecturer said, The platypus is without question one of the oddest mammals on Earth.

_____ **11.** Abraham Lincoln said that there is no grievance that is a fit object of redress by mob law.

_____ **12.** Put the pie plate on the counter when you're finished, Dad said.

_____ **13.** Danielle said with a laugh, I really screamed when that person jumped out and said Boo!

_____ **14.** Don't shoot! cried the commander. They're carrying a white flag!

_____ **15.** Jeff screamed at the top of his lungs, Come on, Panthers!

_____ **16.** The French essayist Michel de Montaigne believed that saying is one thing and doing another.

_____ **17.** Some circumstantial evidence is very strong, says Thoreau in *Walden,* such as when you find a trout in the milk.

_____ **18.** If you will read page 6 of your manual, said the computer technician, shaking his head, you'll find it says, Never place food or drinks on top of your monitor.

Mechanics

Lesson 90
Quotation Marks: Other Uses

Use **quotation marks** to enclose the titles of short works, such as short stories, short poems, essays, newspaper and magazine articles, book chapters, songs, and single episodes of a television series.

"Peasants" (short story)   "The Green Jaguar" (chapter)
"Tintern Abbey" (poem)   "Poor Wandering One" (song title)
"Stay Fit with Exercise" (article)   "Fall Into Life" (essay)
"A Holiday Celebration" (episode of a television series)

Use quotation marks to enclose unfamiliar slang and other unusual or original expressions.

When she was little, my sister wouldn't go anywhere without her "bunkie," a dreadfully ratty old blanket that she loved dearly.

Use quotation marks to enclose a definition that is stated directly.

Smorgasbord is the Swedish word meaning "sandwich table."

Always place a comma or a period *inside* closing quotation marks.

"Can't Explain," "I Can See for Miles," and "Happy Jack" were three of the Who's early hit songs.

Always place a colon or a semicolon *outside* closing quotation marks.

Mom pointed out why I should read the article "Organizing Your Life": my room is a total mess.

Place the question mark or exclamation point *inside* the closing quotation marks when it is part of the quotation.

My favorite song from the musical *Oliver* is "Where Is Love?"

Place the question mark or exclamation point *outside* the closing quotation marks when it is part of the entire sentence.

Have you ever read the short story "To Build a Fire"?

If both the sentence and the quotation at the end of the sentence need a question mark (or an exclamation point), use only one punctuation mark and place it *inside* the closing quotation marks.

Who called and asked "Would you like to go to the soccer game?"

Mechanics

▶ **Exercise 1** Add quotation marks and other punctuation as needed.

"There's no question that Colonel Sidebottom committed the crime," the detective said. "What puzzles me is how he got out of the locked room."

1. When the old fisherman asked me if I was using spinners or bobbers I had to admit I was just putting pieces of bread on my hook.

2. "The angelfish in Maria's aquarium I cried, "are the most beautiful things I've ever seen

3. Music tempo notation includes some of the following terms: *largo,* meaning slow *allegro,* meaning fast and *presto,* meaning very fast

4. For Tuesday, please read the chapter entitled Energy and Metabolism

5. I've never seen Mom laugh so hard in her life as when the jar of mayonnaise fell on the floor and Dad just looked up from his book and said, "No, thank you

6. A gherkin, a kind of small pickle, comes from the Dutch word *gurken,* the plural of cucumber

7. The airplane flight attendant introduced himself as Sean and asked, "Would anyone like a magazine

8. Do you know who wrote the short story The Lady or the Tiger

9. "Excuse me, where is the social security office the woman asked at the desk.

10. My mom's favorite song is Angie by the Rolling Stones.

11. "That girl will be a success at anything she tries Ms. Porter said, "because she has confidence in herself

12. Here's the reason I don't like Matthew Arnold's poem Dover Beach it's entirely too melancholy.

13. "It's possible that you could have seen a copperhead the ranger said, "although that snake is rare in this part of the country

14. Who asked, "Which way to the cafeteria

15. "I wonder if I could reach that window the cat thought as she eyed the slightly opened first-floor window.

16. To learn more about solar power, I read the article entitled Harnessing the Sun's Awesome Energy

Mechanics

Lesson 91
Italics (Underlining)

Italic type is a special slanted type. (*This is printed in italics.*) Italics is indicated on a typewriter or with handwriting by underlining. (This is underlined.) Most computer word processing programs can print italic type.

Italicize (underline) titles of books, lengthy poems, plays, films and television series, paintings and sculptures, long musical compositions, and court cases. Also italicize the names of newspapers and magazines, ships, trains, airplanes, and spacecraft.

Bleak House (novel)	*Song of Myself* (long poem)
Twelfth Night (play)	*American Gothic* (painting)
Gaslight (film)	*Mad About You* (television series)
The Thinker (sculpture)	*Rigoletto* (musical work)
Detroit Free Press (newspaper)	H.M.S. *Bounty* (ship)
Marbury v. *Madison* (court case)	*Challenger* (spacecraft)

Italicize (underline) and capitalize articles (*a, an, the*) written at the beginning of a title only when they are part of the title itself. It is common practice not to italicize (underline) the article preceding the title of a newspaper or magazine. Do not italicize the word *magazine* unless it is a part of the title of the periodical.

A Winter's Tale   a *Time* magazine cover

In forming the possessive of italicized titles, do not italicize the apostrophe and *-s*.

Sports Illustrated's article   *Macbeth*'s plot

Italicize (underline) foreign words and expressions that are not used frequently in English. If foreign words and phrases are commonly used in English, do not italicize them.

In the Italian restaurant the waiter asked if I wanted my ham *cotto* or *crudo*.

Italicize (underline) words, letters, and numerals used to represent themselves.

Dina's handwriting is hard to read because her *g* looks just like her *s*.

▶ **Exercise 1** **Underline words and phrases that should be italicized. If the sentence is correct as written, write *C* in the blank.**

_____ Thomas Hardy's last novel was Jude the Obscure.

_____ 1. The spacecraft Viking I was launched on August 20, 1975, and landed on Mars exactly

11 months later.

_____ 2. In art class we saw a slide of Brancusi's fascinating abstract sculpture The Kiss.

_____ 3. Megan got most of the information for her report from a long Washington Post

newspaper article.

_____ 4. Did you know that Charles Lindbergh's plane, in which he flew from New York to Paris in 1927, was called the Spirit of St. Louis?

_____ 5. We have been receiving sketchy reports on TV about the *coup d'etat* in Nigeria.

_____ 6. If you're looking for an exciting train ride, I suggest you take the Bergen Express from Oslo, Norway to Bergen on the North Sea.

_____ 7. The reporters took down the witness's statement verbatim.

_____ 8. A submarine called the U.S.S. Nautilus was the first to be powered by atomic energy.

_____ 9. I agree that Martin Chuzzlewit's plot is complicated, unbelievable, and manipulative, but I loved the book anyway!

_____ 10. With my pasta the waitress brought me what the menu called ensalada verde, which turned out to be a tossed green salad.

_____ 11. My brother checks the baseball statistics every week in The Sporting News.

_____ 12. The name they gave to their summer cottage was Tiocfaidh An Samhradh, Irish for "summer will come."

_____ 13. The story about the breakdown of the peace talks was originally published in the Los Angeles Times.

_____ 14. After the game, we all went over to Melissa's house to play with her mom's karaoke machine.

_____ 15. What did you think of the New York Times's coverage of the presidential inauguration?

_____ 16. In 1954, the Supreme Court decided unanimously in Brown v. Board of Education that segregated schools were unconstitutional.

_____ 17. It bothers my uncle that this magazine spells out the word percent instead of using the % symbol.

_____ 18. Michela's favorite opera by Mozart is The Marriage of Figaro.

_____ 19. Our panel discussion is going to be about Mikhail Gorbachev's revolutionary policy of perestroika in the Soviet Union of the 1980s.

_____ 20. My grandfather sent me a postcard of Rembrandt's Man in the Golden Helmet.

_____ 21. The name of the interesting Swedish casserole with potatoes, onions, and anchovies was Janssons Frestelse, or "Johnson's Temptation."

_____ 22. I want to finish my homework early so I can watch the Pearl Jam concert on MTV Unplugged.

Mechanics

Lesson 92
The Apostrophe

Use an **apostrophe** and -*s* for the possessive of a singular indefinite pronoun. Do not use an apostrophe with any other possessive pronouns.

everyone**'s** duty   one**'s** own recipe   whose car   its paw

Use an apostrophe and -*s* to form the possessive of a singular noun, even one that ends in -*s*.

the boy**'s** mountain bike   the fox**'s** tail   the glass**'s** rim

Use an apostrophe alone to form the possessive of a plural noun that ends in -*s*. Use an apostrophe and -*s* if the plural does not end in -*s*. Do not use an apostrophe to form the plural of a date.

the Lions**'** meeting   children**'s** literature   the 1950s

Put only the last word of a compound noun in the possessive form.

the secretary of state**'s** speech   her mother-in-law**'s** house

If two or more persons (or partners in a company) possess something jointly, use the possessive for the last person named. If two or more persons (or companies) possess an item (or items) individually, put each one's name in the possessive form.

Procter and Gamble**'s** products   Gibson**'s** and Fender**'s** guitars

Use a possessive form to express amounts of money or time that modify a noun. The modifier can also be expressed as a hyphenated adjective, in which case the possessive form is not used.

three hours**'** time   a three-hour trip

Use an apostrophe in place of letters omitted in contractions and in place of the omitted numerals of a particular year.

you**'**re = you + are   the class of **'**96

Use an apostrophe and -*s* to form the plural of letters, numerals, symbols, and words used to represent themselves. Italicize (underline) only the letter, numeral, symbol, or word.

His *n***'s** look exactly like his *u***'s**.   This page is full of *@***'s**, not letters.

▶ **Exercise 1 Underline the answer in parentheses that correctly completes the sentence.**

After my (<u>great-grandfather,</u> great's-grandfather) retired, he moved to Las Cruces.

1. New Mexico is a state (whose, who's) history, cultural traditions, and natural beauty deserve to be better known.

2. The first Europeans to explore the area that became the state of New Mexico were the Spanish in the late (1530's, 1530s).

3. Franciscan father Marcos de Niza and an enslaved person named Estevan entered the area in 1539, and their (explorations', exploration's) goal was finding precious metals.

4. (De Niza's and Estevan's, De Niza and Estevan's) journey did not, however, yield any discoveries of gold or silver.

5. It did result, though, in the (European's, Europeans') settlements in San Juan Pueblo in 1598.

6. In a few (year's, years') time, a second settlement was founded in Santa Fe.

7. This city, founded in 1610, would become more than three hundred years later (New Mexicos, New Mexico's) state capital.

8. The (Spaniards', Spaniard's) influence grew and today represents one of the state's three main cultural traditions.

9. A second cultural heritage is the Native American tradition, the gift of the many different (groups, group's) who had lived in the Southwest long before the arrival of the Spanish.

10. One of the earliest was the Pueblo, who usually built (they're, their) cities in the form of connected apartmentlike dwellings.

11. Visitors can study one of these unusual dwellings at Chaco Canyon, where Pueblo ruins believed to be over 1900 (year's, years) old still remain.

12. In (today's, todays') New Mexico there are nineteen Pueblo, two Apache, and four Navajo reservations.

13. Tourists interested in learning more about (men's and women's, mens' and womens') lives in these Native American societies can visit many of the reservations.

14. One of the most interesting and beautiful of the (states, state's) Pueblo villages is near the city of Taos.

15. (Taos', Taos's) reputation as an important art center and home of painter Georgia O'Keeffe also helps attract visitors.

16. The Navajo reservation shared by New Mexico and neighboring Arizona is the (United States', United State's) largest.

17. (Native Americans', Native American's) influence on the culture of New Mexico continues to be strong, and they form the second strand in this multicultural state.

18. Beginning in the early (1800s, 1800's), settlers from the East began to arrive in what was then the Spanish territory of New Mexico.

19. If there is one major cause of the movement of American settlers into New Mexico, (its, it's) the opening of the fabled Santa Fe Trail in 1821.

20. Leading from Missouri to the town square in Santa Fe, the trail was many (people's, peoples') road west.

Mechanics

Lesson 93
The Hyphen

Ordinarily a hyphen is not used to join a prefix to a word. Exceptions are as follows:

Use a hyphen after any prefix joined to a proper noun or a proper adjective. Also use a hyphen after the prefixes *all-, ex-* (meaning "former"), and *self-* joined to any noun or adjective.

pro-Canadian   ex-governor   all-knowing   self-awareness

Generally, hyphens are used to avoid confusion, such as between words beginning with *re-* that could be mistaken for another word different in meaning and pronunciation. Also use a hyphen to separate the prefix *anti-* when it joins a word beginning with *i-*. Always hyphenate the prefix *vice-* and any succeeding word, except in *vice president.*

re-creation of a historical scene   outdoor recreation
anti-industrialism   vice-mayor

Use a hyphen in a compound adjective that precedes a noun. When compound adjectives beginning with *well, ill,* or *little* are modified by an adverb, they are usually not hyphenated. An expression made up of an adverb ending in *-ly* and an adjective is not hyphenated.

a dark-colored hat   The hat was dark colored.
a well-known musician   a very well known musician
a poorly written play   a tightly packed container

Hyphenate any spelled-out cardinal or ordinal number up to ninety-nine or ninety-ninth. Hyphenate a fraction used as an adjective (but not one used as a noun).

a two-thirds vote   two thirds of the voters

Hyphenate two numerals to indicate a span. When you use the word *from* before a span, use *to* rather than a hyphen. When you use *between,* use *and.*

pages 568-643   1914-1918   **from** 1914 **to** 1918   **between** 12:00 **and** 1:45

In general divide words at the ends of lines between syllables or pronounceable parts. Consult a dictionary if necessary.

light-ning   clip-per   sell-ing   tast-ier   scorn-ful   short-est

Mechanics

▶ **Exercise 1 Draw a slash through each word where it should be divided at the end of a line.**

cor|rect

1. access

2. stopping

3. shorter

4. smoothest

5. boastful

6. whisper

7. blossom

8. immense

9. expand

10. morning	**14.** coffee	**18.** instant
11. quarter	**15.** structure	**19.** shopping
12. fulfill	**16.** member	**20.** vibrate
13. conduct	**17.** madder	

▶ **Exercise 2** **Add hyphens where necessary. Cross out hyphens used incorrectly using the delete symbol (ꙮ). If the sentence is correct as written, write *C* in the blank.**

_____ The display on this computer is easily-read and adjusted.

_____ **1.** The history quiz on Monday will cover pages 221 244.

_____ **2.** The speaker called herself the author of a little read novel that everyone had heard about.

_____ **3.** Nine-tenths of the students voted to donate the leftover money to SADD.

_____ **4.** I got to supervise the youngest campers' re-creation period at the crafts cabin.

_____ **5.** Most of our lambs this year were born between midnight and 3:30 A.M.

_____ **6.** Stacie's grandmother complimented Michael for being so well-read.

_____ **7.** Nicole was happy to finish twenty first in the gymnastics meet.

_____ **8.** The witness just repeated that he did not re-collect anything unusual happening on the morning in question.

_____ **9.** The material I purchased for the blouse was a loosely-woven linen/cotton blend.

_____ **10.** Harry Truman was elected vice-president in 1944 and assumed the presidency on the death of Franklin Roosevelt in 1945.

_____ **11.** The news report stated that antigovernment forces had moved to within three miles of the presidential palace.

_____ **12.** John F. Kennedy was president of the U.S. from 1961 to 1963.

_____ **13.** Matthew was the best we had ever seen at the valuable skill of self promotion.

_____ **14.** The surprise guest was the very well-known star of such films as *Hercules Slays the Monster, Don't Answer That!,* and *Calling All Cornballs.*

_____ **15.** My brother was quite stunned when he learned that the Jets had hired the ex-coach of the Philadelphia Eagles.

_____ **16.** Forty four entries to the essay contest were received by the deadline of midnight last night.

Mechanics

Lesson 94
Abbreviations

Use only one period if an **abbreviation** occurs at the end of a sentence that would normally take a period of its own. If an abbreviation occurs at the end of a sentence that ends with a question mark or an exclamation point, use the period and the second punctuation mark.

Danitra left at 9:00 P.M.   Did you read the article by Felicia Martinez, **M.D.**?

Use all capital letters and no periods for abbreviations that are pronounced letter by letter or as words. Exceptions are U.S. and Washington, D.C., which do use periods.

NBA   EPA   AIDS   ACT   OSHA

Use the abbreviations A.M. (*ante meridiem,* "before noon") and P.M. (*post meridiem,* "after noon") for exact times. For dates use B.C. (before Christ) and, sometimes, A.D. (*anno Domini,* "in the year of the Lord," after Christ.)

Use abbreviations for personal titles appearing before names and for those titles indicating professional and academic degrees. When abbreviating a person's first and middle names, leave a space after each initial. When using three initials, use no periods and leave no spaces between initals.

L. L. Bean   **Maj.** Susan Jones   **Rev.** Robert Davis **Jr.**   Anna Wang, **Ph.D.**   **JFK**

Abbreviate units of measure used with numerals in technical or scientific writing. Do not abbreviate units of measure in ordinary prose, however. These abbreviations stand for plural as well as singular units. Metric abbreviations do not require periods.

mm millimeter	**oz.** ounce	**kg** kilogram	**m** meter
tsp. teaspoon	**lb.** pound	**km** kilometer	**in.** inch
1 liter	**yd.** yard	**qt.** quart	**g** gram

▶ **Exercise 1 In the blank write the correct abbreviation for the word in italics.**

_____Mr._____   The faculty sponsor for the Computer Club is *Mister* Peña.

_____   **1.** Deena's dream is to see a *National Football League* game.

_____   **2.** *Major* Ruben Sanchez gave the opening welcome to the new recruits.

_____   **3.** Historians usually date the fall of Rome as *anno Domini* 476.

_____   **4.** Please welcome, from the Olivet Baptist Church, *Reverend* Marshall C. Thomas.

_____   **5.** The concert is scheduled to start at 8:00 *post meridiem.*

Mechanics

_____ **6.** I wrote to the *Federal Bureau of Investigation* for information.

_____ **7.** Haqim Lamar, *Doctor of Philosophy,* is the center's new director.

_____ **8.** No, *Doctor* Andrews, I haven't had any pain in my finger.

_____ **9.** Our industrial economics class toured the local *General Motors* auto plant.

_____ **10.** Sophocles' most famous play was written around 442 *before Christ.*

_____ **11.** Jason will take the *American College Test* in May.

_____ **12.** Julie Ruhl, *Doctor of Dental Science,* is our family dentist.

_____ **13.** My brother plays racquetball at the *Young Men's Christian Association.*

_____ **14.** Ken Griffey *Junior* was the leading vote getter on the 1996 All-Star team.

_____ **15.** Why in the world would anyone schedule a meeting for 5:30 *ante meridiem?*

▶ **Exercise 2** **Write the correct abbreviation for each of the following.**

1. Doctor of Social Work _____

2. National Organization for Women _____

3. liter _____

4. Drug Enforcement Administration _____

5. National Aeronautics and Space Administration _____

6. kilometer _____

7. ounce _____

8. General _____

9. teaspoon _____

10. National Collegiate Athletic Association _____

11. kilometer _____

12. John Fitzgerald Kennedy _____

13. pound _____

14. millimeter _____

15. American Medical Association _____

16. American College Test _____

17. Strategic Arms Limitation Talks _____

18. Bachelor of Arts _____

19. Occupational Safety and Health Administration _____

Lesson 95
Numbers and Numerals

Spell out any **number** that occurs at the beginning of a sentence. Also spell out cardinal and ordinal numbers that can be written in one or two words. Numbers written in more than two words are usually expressed in **numerals** (numbers expressed in figures). A very large number can be written as a numeral followed by a noun of amount, such as *million* or *billion*.

Three hundred and sixty-four people signed up for the home energy audit.
Mars has **two** moons, Deimos and Phobos.
The earth's population is now thought to be about **5.8 billion** people.

If related numbers appear in the same sentence and some can be written out while others should appear as numerals, use all numerals.

More than **350** entries were received, but only **12** were selected for the final round of judging.

Use numerals to express decimals, percentages, and amounts of money involving both dollars and cents. Write out amounts of money that can be written in one or two words.

Multiply that sum by **$2.78** to get the right answer.
Dad paid **thirty-nine** cents a pound for these slightly bruised peaches.

Use numerals to express the year and the day, to express the precise time, and with the abbreviations A.M. and P.M. Spell out expressions of time that are approximate or that do not use the abbreviations A.M. or P.M.

Author Maxine Hong Kingston was born on October **27, 1940,** in Stockton, California.
Volunteers should meet at the shelter house at around **nine** o'clock in the morning.

To express a century when the word *century* is used, spell out the number. To express a decade when the century is clear from the context, spell out the number. When a century and a decade are expressed as a single unit, use numerals followed by an *-s*.

These coins were used in the **fourth** century!
Buddy Holly was one of the superstars of rock and roll in the **fifties**.
According to the author, the modern world was born during the decade of the **1820s**.

Use numerals for streets and avenues numbered above ten and for all house, apartment, and room numbers. Spell out numbered streets and avenues with a number of ten or under.

I think this dog belongs to the woman in Apartment **12G** on **Third** Avenue.

Mechanics

▶ **Exercise 1** **Underline the answer in parentheses that correctly completes the sentence.**

I believe this subway stops at (Eighty-Second, <u>82nd</u>) Street.

1. The (1850s, eighteen-fifties) were a decade of rising tension in the United States because of the coming battle over slavery and states' rights.

2. Of the 136 people who applied to the program, only (nine, 9) failed to pass the entrance test.

3. The nature walk is to begin at around (one o'clock, 1:00).

4. The national debt of the U.S. has surpassed (4 trillion dollars, $4,000,000,000,000).

5. Nina bought a used Toyota for ($2,000.00, two thousand dollars).

6. Astronomers now believe that there may be more than (9, nine) planets in our solar system.

7. Stephanie's art class starts at (9:45, nine forty-five) A.M. and usually runs until lunchtime.

8. My brother and his wife celebrated their (3rd, third) wedding anniversary by going out to dinner at the fanciest restaurant in town.

9. The profits of the cleaning business were up (39, thirty-nine) percent over this time last year.

10. The Great Depression and the economic hardship it brought colored the entire decade of the (thirties, 30s).

11. (Nine hundred fifty-three, 953) people paid to see all four performances of the class play, a

    new attendance record!

12. To find the amount of tax you owe, multiply the amount on line 42 by (point nine hundred thirty-five, .935).

13. Monique rolled a strike in the (8th, eighth) frame, allowing our bowling team to take the lead in the game.

14. I have my eye on a computer at Computer Wonderland, but it costs (twelve hundred fifty-nine dollars, $1259), so I probably can't afford it.

15. Jason's favorite uncle joined the navy on December (third, 3), 1971.

16. Alexis scored in the (ninety-ninth, 99th) percentile nationwide on the math test, meaning she

    did better than almost every student in the country!

17. (5, Five) of the 126 teams in the district had undefeated records going into the last game of the

    season.

18. Many historians believe that the (sixteenth, 16th) century produced the greatest literature in European history.

19. There are more than (12, twelve) million Methodists in the United States, making it one of the largest denominations.

20. A pack of gum costs (27 cents, twenty-seven cents) with tax.

21. ($1250, One thousand, two hundred-fifty dollars) was raised in the scrap paper drive last year.

22. Melanie had (three, 3) hits, including a home run and a double, in the softball game against Ryder High.

23. The Latin Club banquet is scheduled to start at (six o'clock, 6:00) P.M.

24. The recent earthquake in Mexico measured (6.4, six point four) on the Richter scale.

☑ Unit 12 **Review**

▶ **Exercise 1** **Place a check beside each sentence that uses punctuation, abbreviations, and numbers correctly.**

___✔___   I had my silhouette cut at the state fair (Did you know it was named after a French government official of the eighteenth century?).

_____   **1.** The man, singing the tenor part, won an award for his last role.

_____   **2.** The distance from Cleveland to Cincinnati is 249 miles (four hundred kilometers).

_____   **3.** The tightrope walker had herself blindfolded—people were absolutely amazed—and then proceeded to cross the wire without a net!

_____   **4.** Can you remember who said, "Don't fire until you see the whites of their eyes?"

_____   **5.** The morning dawned cool, breezy, and cloudless.

_____   **6.** 105 different books were nominated by the senior class as their favorite.

_____   **7.** The art critic felt that the new portrait of the mayor was poorly-drawn.

_____   **8.** I'm happy to introduce our speaker for this evening, Rev. Jeremy H. King of St. George's Episcopal Church.

_____   **9.** A woodchuck burrow consists of an entrance, a nest, and a spy hole which is a little opening near the entrance.

_____ **10.** In my opinion, *The Scarlet Letter* is Nathaniel Hawthorne's best novel, and "Young Goodman Brown" is his best story.

_____ **11.** The chestnut horse with the light-colored saddle is the one I'd like to ride.

_____ **12.** James Monroe, the fifth president of the United States, was reelected in 1820 with all but one electoral vote; his election ushered in the "Era of Good Feeling."

_____ **13.** At the top lefthand corner of the house painters were working feverishly to finish the job before it rained.

_____ **14.** For the party I'm going to make my specialty, chili.

_____ **15.** That pen you're using is leaking ink, you might want to try another one.

_____ **16.** UCLA won the NCAA men's basketball championship in 1995.

_____ **17.** I felt sorry for the raccoon that had injured it's paw.

_____ **18.** Which of your friends left you the note asking "What are you doing next Saturday?"

_____ **19.** Heather's three first choices are: Indiana University, the University of Michigan, and Stanford University.

_____ **20.** Brian's sister Jan has decided to attend Cornell University in New York.

Mechanics

Cumulative Review: Units 1–12

▶ **Exercise 1** Underline the word in parentheses that best completes each sentence.

The speaker started out (bad, <u>badly</u>).

1. I finished my homework (already, all ready).

2. This dessert tastes (all together, altogether) too sweet for my teeth!

3. I (can't hardly, can hardly) stand it when people scratch a blackboard with their fingernails.

4. When was this warning (hanged, hung) on the wall?

5. Don't (loose, lose) your hall pass or the guard will stop you.

6. We won't be there for (a while, awhile), so go ahead and eat without us.

7. Alice (doesn't, don't) live here anymore.

8. Well, the refrigerator is practically empty, so I guess someone (must of, must have) been really hungry!

9. Meet me for basketball practice (in, into) the gym.

10. Standing up here so high, it's hard to believe that a major river (lays, lies) far below.

11. (Besides, Beside) your cello lessons, what else do you do after school?

12. I don't know if I (can, may) make it up that cliff.

13. Well, this is certainly (a, an) inconvenience, Stanley!

14. The sporting event will take place (irregardless, regardless) of the weather.

15. Your twin sister, Anastasia, acts very (different than, different from) you, Alice.

16. Even from the air, we could see that the damage from the earthquake looked (bad, badly).

17. I don't like (these kinds, this kind) of pencils because they smear.

18. The grand jury will look into the matter (farther, further).

19. (Take, Bring) this video back when you go to the store.

20. I don't know what else to do (accept, except) to admit I was wrong.

▶ **Exercise 2** Underline the verb form in parentheses that best completes each sentence.

Billy and Sheila always (mislays, <u>mislay</u>) their toys.

1. The mayor, together with his staff, (has, have) left for the day.

2. The highest wave during the storm (was, were) ten feet!

3. The long-term effects of pollution (remains, remain) yet to develop their full ramifications.

4. In a case at the back of the antique store (sits, sit) several priceless vases.

5. Ashford (has, have) the mumps!

6. The students painted the mural that (covers, cover) those three walls of the cafeteria.

7. I think she (gives, give) too much money for her clothes.

8. Every article, advertisement, and graphic (was, were) checked for accuracy.

9. Each of the violinists (plays, play) at least one other instrument in the youth orchestra.

10. My hat, in addition to my gloves and pants, (is, are) caked with mud from the horseback ride

    in the rain.

11. A group of several hundred protesters (gathers, gather) in front of the courthouse.

12. Neither the driver nor the passenger (seems, seem) hurt from the crash.

13. None of the boys on the team (likes, like) their defeat at the hand of their archrivals.

14. Can you believe that some of these clothes (has, have) already faded?

15. Several members of our carpool (wants, want) to start biking.

16. Either an opossum or some raccoons (strews, strew) the garbage all over the porch.

17. Where (does, do) these shoes go?

18. Either the radio or the newspapers (covers, cover) all our championship games.

19. Neither of those talk shows that you insist on listening to all the time (interests, interest) me at all!

20. (Is, Are) either of the office telephones in the conference room free now?

▶ **Exercise 3 Add all necessary punctuation marks, including end punctuation. Draw a line under words or phrases that should be in italics.**

If you want to read a weird novel, and I know you do, try Thomas Pynchon's <u>V.</u>

1. The blues a specifically American form of music was popularized by three giants Bessie

   Smith Ma Rainey and Louis Armstrong

2. Scott Joplin composer of the song Maple Leaf Rag 1899 is the best known composer of the music

   known as ragtime surely you remember his music from the movie The Sting

3. Onomatopoeia is the forming of words that imitate sounds buzz hiss and twitter are good

   examples

4. J M Barrie wrote Peter Pan or the Boy Who Wouldnt Grow Up yes it s a long title which is why

   everyone just calls it Peter Pan

5. Mary Renault the pen name of Mary Challans 1905 1983 wrote wonderful historical novels about Athens and Sparta including The King Must Die

6. William Kennedy wrote the novel Ironweed that became a film and also wrote the script for Francis Ford Coppola s film The Cotton Club 1984

7. Big jazz festivals are held in Newport Rhode Island and Monterey California

8. Jack Kerouac wrote the novel On the Roadwhich has become synonymous with the period of American writing known as the beat movement

9. Can there be a movie called Alien 4 if the heroine you know Sigourney Weavers Ripley died in Alien 3

10. Aren t you confusing Francis Scott Key 1779 1843, who wroteThe Star-Spangled Banner with Francis Parkinson Keyes 1885 1970 who wrote the novel Dinner at Antoine s (1948)

11. When the writer Thoreau was arrested for refusing to pay taxes to support the Mexican War his friend Emerson visited and said Henry what are you doing in here

12. Supposedly they are making Star Wars movies that predate the current ones for example I guess well get to know the ancestors of Luke Skywalker and Han Solo

13. American humorist James Thurber who was a cartoonist for the New Yorker is often identified with his short story The Secret Life of Walter Mitty

14. Bill Haley and His Comets were the first famous rock band and their recording of Rock Around the Clock from the film Blackboard Jungle 1955 was a major hit

15. A A Milnes characters Pooh Tigger Roo and Piglet are some of the most beloved in all of children s literature

16. Georgia O'Keeffe 1887 1986 painted haunting pictures of the Southwest andhey youre not listening to a thing I say are you

17. Do you know if its Jim or Tim the one with the beard who published a story in The Antioch Review

18. Nina a member of the seraph society is the headstrong heroine in a Teresa Vitale book.

Mechanics

Vocabulary and Spelling

Unit 13: Vocabulary and Spelling

Lesson 96
Building Vocabulary: Learning Words from Context

Clues to the meaning of an unfamiliar word may be found in its context, or the words and sentences surrounding it. These clues may be in the form of specific clues or general context.

INTERPRETING CLUE WORDS

Definition—The unfamiliar word is actually defined after a clue word. Clue words include *which is, which means,* and *that is.*

Ms. Meyers was *ambiguous* in her instructions, **which means** that her directions were not clear.

Example—The unfamiliar word is illustrated by an example or an analogy. Clue words include *like, for example, for instance, these, including,* and *especially.*

Remnants of ancient cultures, **like** mounds, tell us much of their way of life.

Comparison—The unfamiliar word is likened to a familiar one. Clue words include *like, also, likewise, similarly, in the same way, similar to, resembling,* and *as.*

Jason *gorged* on snacks; **similarly,** Yoshika overate until she felt uncomfortable.

Contrast—The unfamiliar word is shown as the opposite of a familiar word. Clue words include *whereas, but, although, on the contrary, however, on the other hand,* and *in contrast to.*

Although her husband was careless with his checkbook, Mrs. Nguyen *assiduously* recorded every transaction in hers.

Cause and effect—An unfamiliar cause is explained by a familiar effect. Clue words include *because, as a result, therefore, when,* and *consequently.*

The man was *indigent* and **therefore** could not afford even necessities.

Restatement—An unfamiliar word is explained by a more familiar expression. Clue words include *or, in other words, also known as,* and *also called.*

The alarm system was very *sophisticated;* **in other words,** it was complicated.

▶ **Exercise 1** **Draw a line under specific clue words. From the context, write a definition for the italicized word.**

Most of the sailors were eager volunteers, <u>but</u> some of the crew were *conscripts.*

<u>sailors that were forced into service</u>

Vocabulary and Spelling

1. For many years that government has been *autocratic,* which means it is controlled by a single

   power. _____

2. Geraldo lost many friends because of his *prevarications,* that is, he told lies.

   _____

3. The losers were very *despondent,* in contrast to the winners, who were cheering and laughing.

   _____

4. Many senators left the session during the *filibuster* because the long pointless speeches were

   boring. _____

5. Mr. Chin *coddled* his granddaughters, just as most grandparents spoil their grandchildren.

   _____

6. A good plumber carries a complete set of *paraphernalia* including wrenches, a torch, and a

   pipe threader. _____

7. George Sand was the *nom de plume* or pen name of Amandine Aurore Lucie Dupin, Baroness

   Dudevant. _____

8. The stranger committed one *faux pas* after another; for example, he insisted on talking in a

   very loud voice. _____

9. Carly made *elaborate* plans for her vacation, whereas Allison preferred a simpler getaway.

   _____

10. Margarita *relinquished* her chairmanship since she no longer had the time to devote to the

    committee. _____

11. Juan experienced a *paucity* of ideas for the membership drive. Likewise, we couldn't think of

    any either. _____

12. Because of the heavy traffic fine, Harley was *impecunious;* consequently he had to wait until

    payday to purchase the new CD. _____

13. The eight-bit computer has become *obsolete;* in other words, it is generally no longer used.

    _____

14. Eduardo *reneges* under criticism in the same way that Teresa fails to keep her promises.

    _____

15. The extra review session was *superfluous* since everyone had already passed the test.

    _____

Vocabulary and Spelling

Lesson 97
Building Vocabulary: Word Roots

The main part of a word is called its **root**. When the root is a complete word, it is called a **base word**. The root can suggest the basic meaning of a word. Roots are often combined with a **prefix** (a part preceding the root), a **suffix** (a part following the root), or another root. These parts can change the direction of a word's meaning. Here is a list of some common roots.

ROOTS	MEANINGS	ROOTS	MEANINGS
aqua, aqui	water	junct	join
astr, astro	star	jur, jus	law
biblio	book	logy, log	word, thought, speech
bio	life	metr	meter, measure
chron	time	nym	name
clin	bend, lean	op, oper	work
cogn	know	patho	path, suffering
crypt	hidden, secret	ped	foot, child
culp	fault, blame	psych	soul, mind
fin	end, limit	reg, rig	rule, straight
fix	fasten	scop	examine, instrument
gen	birth, kind	spect	sight
graph, gram	write, writing	terra	earth
jac, ject	throw, cast, hurl	verb	word
jud	judge	vid, vis	see

▶ **Exercise 1** Draw a line under the root of each word. Define each word, using a dictionary if necessary. If there is more than one meaning, use the one that emphasizes the root.

aqua̲phobe   one who has a fear of water _____

1. jury _____

2. advise _____

3. biosphere _____

4. trajectory _____

5. monogram _____

6. degenerate _____

7. terra-cotta _____

8. verbose _____

9. introspection _____

10. telescopic _____

11. fixation   _____

12. regimented   _____

13. definitive   _____

14. parapsychology _____

15. culpable   _____

16. pedestal   _____

17. pediatrics   _____

18. pathogenic   _____

19. incognito   _____

20. inclination   _____

21. operative   _____

22. chronological   _____

23. pseudonym   _____

24. biomass   _____

25. metricate   _____

26. analog   _____

27. astral   _____

28. justification   _____

29. aquaculture   _____

30. adjunct   _____

31. hydraulic   _____

32. distract   _____

33. manacles   _____

34. epigram   _____

35. nurture   _____

36. intercede   _____

37. psychosis   _____

38. congenital   _____

39. equinox   _____

40. pastorate   _____

Lesson 98
Building Vocabulary: Prefixes and Suffixes

Prefixes are attached to the beginnings of roots or words to change their meaning. They may show quantity, size, negation, time, direction, or position.

PREFIX	MEANING	PREFIX	MEANING
post-	after	pre-, pro-	before
re-	again	syn-	together
a-, an-	not, without	ant-, anti-	against
de-, dis-	do the opposite	non-, un-	not
semi-, hemi-	half	bi-, di-	two
uni-, mono-	one	cent-	hundred
circum-	around	in-, im-	into or not
sub-	below, outside of	trans-	across, over

Suffixes are added to the end of a root or a word to make a new word with a new meaning. A suffix may change the part of speech of a word.

SUFFIX	MEANING	SUFFIX	MEANING	
-ee	receiver of action	-ance, -ence	state, quality	
-ant, -eer	agent, doer	-ist	one who	} noun-forming
-ness	action, state	-tion, -ion	the act of	
-ate	become, form	-en	make, cause to be	} verb-forming
-ify	cause, make	-ize	make, cause to be	
-ic	characteristic of	-ous, -ful	full of, having	} adjective-forming
-ial	relating to	-al	characterized by	
-ly	akin to	-less	lacking	

▶ **Exercise 1** Draw a line under at least one prefix or suffix in each word. Write the meaning of the prefix or suffix in the first blank and the meaning of the word in the second. Use a dictionary if necessary.

circumnavigate   _around_   _to sail or fly completely around_

1. prejudge   _____   _____

2. improper   _____   _____

3. subliminal   _____   _____

4. hypersensitive   _____   _____

5. transmit   _____   _____

6. uniform   _____   _____

7. monotheist   _____   _____

8. embed   _____   _____

9. antithesis _____ _____

10. ingrate _____ _____

11. payee _____ _____

12. recipient _____ _____

13. accordance _____ _____

14. imitation _____ _____

15. unction _____ _____

16. fallacious _____ _____

17. cranial _____ _____

18. fallible _____ _____

19. solemnize _____ _____

20. flautist _____ _____

21. expatriate _____ _____

22. misperceive _____ _____

23. predate _____ _____

24. capable _____ _____

25. ornate _____ _____

26. bucolic _____ _____

27. hyperextend _____ _____

28. deify _____ _____

29. auctioneer _____ _____

30. marginal _____ _____

31. odious _____ _____

32. agitator _____ _____

33. severance _____ _____

34. perambulate _____ _____

35. vengeful _____ _____

36. secrecy _____ _____

37. amoral _____ _____

38. commute _____ _____

Vocabulary and Spelling

Lesson 99
Basic Spelling Rules: I

Adding a prefix does not change the spelling of the original word. Use a hyphen when the original word is capitalized or with the prefixes *ex-* (meaning *previous* or *former)*, *self-*, and *all-*.

anti- + social = **anti**social   *un-* + stable = **un**stable   *self-* + serve = **self**-serve
non- + British = **non**-British   *ex-* + director = **ex**-director   *all-* + around = **all**-around

SUFFIXES

Most words do not change spelling when a suffix is added. When adding *-ly* to a word that ends in a single *l*, keep the *l*. If the word ends in a double *l*, drop one *l*. If the word ends in a consonant + *le*, drop the *le*.

partial + *-ly* = partia**lly**   dull + *-ly* = dul**ly**   dangle + *-ly* = dang**ly**

Drop a final silent *e* before a suffix that begins with a vowel. Keep the silent *e* before adding a suffix beginning with a consonant.

line + *-er* = lin**er**   value + *-able* = valu**able**   infinite + *-ly* = infinite**ly**

Exceptions: judge + *-ment* = judg**ment**   argue + *-ment* = argu**ment**   due + *-ly* = du**ly**

Keep the final *e* when the word ends in *-ee* or *-oe*, before the suffix *-ing*, and with words ending in *-ce* or *-ge* that have suffixes beginning with *a* or *o*.

see + *-ing* = see**ing**   woe + *-ful* = woe**ful**   trace + *-able* = trace**able**

Double the final consonant if the original word is a one-syllable word, if the accent remains on the last syllable of the original word after the suffix is added, or if the original word is a prefixed one-syllable word.

stop, stopped   regret, regretting   reset, resetting

Do not double the final consonant if the accent is not on the last syllable, if the accent shifts when the suffix is added, if the final consonant is *x* or *w*, or when the original word ends in a consonant and the suffix begins with a consonant.

confer, conference   row, rowing   ship, shipment

▶ **Exercise 1** Write the word that results when the given prefix or suffix is added to the supplied word. Check your dictionary for variations in spelling.

sight + *-ing*   _____sighting_____

1. *dis-* + like   _____   3. *ex-* + wife   _____

2. *counter-* + productive _____   4. *un-* + American _____

5. mortal + -ly _____

6. smell + -ly _____

7. tingle + -ly _____

8. whine + -er _____

9. true + -ism _____

10. polite + -ness _____

11. pollute + -ing _____

12. grace + -ful _____

13. pine + -ing _____

14. advance + -ment _____

15. supreme + -acy _____

16. flee + -ing _____

17. stop + -er _____

18. repel + -ent _____

19. defer + -ence _____

20. allow + -ance _____

21. full + -ly _____

22. excel + -ent _____

23. change + -able _____

24. mix + -ing _____

25. serve + -ile _____

26. confer + -ing _____

27. place + -ment _____

28. propel + -er _____

29. remit + -ance _____

30. infer + -ence _____

31. obscure + -ly _____

32. hoe + -ing _____

33. flow + -ing _____

34. due + -ly _____

35. member + -ship _____

36. style + -ize _____

37. complete + -tion _____

38. replace + -able _____

39. argue + -ment _____

40. austere + -ity _____

▶ Writing Link Choose ten verbs not found in this exercise, make them into nouns, and use them to write a coherent paragraph.

_____

_____

_____

_____

_____

_____

_____

_____

_____

Lesson 100
Basic Spelling Rules: II

PLURALS

Add -*s* to most nouns (including proper nouns) to form the plural. Add -*es* to nouns ending in -*ch*, -*s*, -*sh*, -*x*, or -*z*. When a noun ends in a consonant + *y*, change the *y* to *i* and add -*es*. Some nouns ending in -*f* (especially -*lf*) become plural by changing the *f* to *v* and adding -*es*.

girl + -*s* = girls   fox + -*es* = foxes   bush + -*es* = bushes   country + -*es* = countries
wharf + -*es* = wharves   puff + -*s* = puffs   thief + -*es* = thieves   calf + -*es* = calves

Some nouns have irregular formations for the plural, and some are the same for both singular and plural.

ox + -*en* = oxen   goose, geese   moose, moose   deer, deer

WORDS WITH *IE* AND *EI*

The *i* comes before the *e* except when both follow a *c* or when they are sounded together as an $\bar{a}$ sound, as in *weigh*. However, there are many exceptions.

shriek (**i** before **e**)   receive (**e** before **i**)   deign ($\bar{a}$ sound)   leisure (exception)

WORDS WITH -*CEDE* AND -*CEED*

Three words end with -*ceed*: *exceed*, *proceed*, and *succeed*. Most words that end with a $s\bar{e}d$ sound use the root -*cede*. *Supersede* is the exception.

se**cede**   ac**cede**   con**cede**

UNSTRESSED VOWELS

An unstressed vowel is a vowel that is not emphasized in pronunciation. To determine correct spelling, think of a related word where the vowel or syllable is stressed.

lam**e**ntation, lam**e**nt   desp**e**rate, desp**e**ration

COMPOUND WORDS

Compound words usually do not change spelling when formed. Some compound words form one word, however, some use a hyphen, and some remain two words. The dictionary is a great help with these.

fast + ball = fastball   strong + arm = strong-arm   chain + mail = chain mail

CHALLENGING WORDS

Many spelling challenges exist with words that are homonyms or near homonyms. Other words contain unusual combinations of letters. When in doubt, use a dictionary. Be aware that computer spell-checkers do not find wrong word choices or errors that result in a correct word that is wrong for the context. Proofreading is still necessary.

Vocabulary and Spelling

▶ **Exercise 1** Write the new word in the blank. Use a dictionary to check your answers.

plural of *cake* ___cakes___   shoe + tree ___shoetree___

1. plural of *half* _____   17. plural of *mouse* _____
2. plural of *rhapsody* _____   18. plural of *clef* _____
3. rain + maker _____   19. green + back _____
4. plural of *pitch* _____   20. plural of *porch* _____
5. plural of *tendril* _____   21. flat + worm _____
6. plural of *matrix* _____   22. plural of *press* _____
7. milk + shake _____   23. plural of *leaf* _____
8. plural of *sheep* _____   24. plural of *fox* _____
9. cake + walk _____   25. green + card _____
10. plural of *chief* _____   26. plural of *deer* _____
11. plural of *doe* _____   27. plural of *mass* _____
12. president + elect _____   28. plural of *buzz* _____
13. flea + bitten _____   29. great + grand + father _____
14. plural of *ditch* _____   30. plural of *dish* _____
15. plural of *mathematics* _____   31. after + math _____
16. book + keeper _____   32. plural of *spine* _____

▶ **Exercise 2** Write the missing letter or letters in each word.

rec ___ei___ ve   com ___a___ tose   re ___cede___

1. interce _____   11. bel _____ f   21. ach _____ ve
2. rec _____ pt   12. gr _____ f   22. retr _____ ve
3. h _____ ght   13. pun _____ tive   23. pr _____ st
4. proce _____   14. h _____ r   24. ch _____ f
5. dec _____ t   15. f _____ gn   25. fr _____ ght
6. w _____ gh   16. rece _____   26. s _____ ve
7. prece _____   17. fall _____ cy   27. dec _____ ver
8. ex _____   18. antece _____   28. magn _____ tize
9. bell _____ cose   19. dram _____ tize   29. conce _____
10. com _____ dy   20. effic _____ nt   30. perc _____ ve

Unit 13 Review: Building Vocabulary

▶ **Exercise 1** Write the definition of the word in italics. Use a dictionary if necessary. Draw a line under any clue words.

The audience rose in *unison;* <u>that is,</u> they stood up at the same time. __all together; as one__

1. Calvin didn't fear the *interrogation* because he had nothing to hide. _____

_____

2. When this project comes to *fruition*, it will provide many benefits to all of us. _____

_____

3. Like a gentleman from olden days, Mario was known for his *gallantry;* for example, he held doors

for others and always rose when someone entered the room. _____

4. Annie never let the *gibes* or heckles of the fans break her concentration at the free-throw line.

_____

5. The assembly was organized to pay *homage* to Gillian because she had won a full scholarship.

_____

6. The lack of sleep *impeded* Juan's judgment. As a result, he had difficulty making a decision.

_____

7. Kwaku consistently showed *ingenuity* in contrast to Lilla's single-minded approach.

_____

8. Karen's *jejune* or childish behavior shocked everyone that knew her. _____

9. The truck driver provided a *bill of lading;* consequently, we were able to check the accuracy of

the cargo. _____

10. Carmen chose the theme for the dance *unilaterally;* therefore, she received all the criticism

when conflicts arose. _____

11. Steel is not very *malleable,* but iron and brass are much easier to shape. _____

_____

12. Tai's entry for the art show was a *montage,* while all the other entries focused on single subjects.

_____

13. This story is very good, but count on Abu to *nitpick.* _____

14. The senator gave *oblique* answers to my questions rather than addressing them directly.

_____

15. The new lounge was merely an *opiate* for the employees with the hope that they would forget

their real grievances. _____

16. In contrast to his generous brothers, Alberto always took a *parsimonious* approach to his money.

_____

17. Her lack of enthusiasm for the project *perturbed*, or upset, Mr. Hayashi greatly.

_____

18. The odor in the building made us so *queasy* that we could not eat lunch.

_____

19. Amy slept so soundly that even a blast from Kevin's tuba didn't *rouse* her.

_____

20. This tournament is *sanctioned* by the golf association, which means that the winners will

accumulate points for player of the year. _____

21. Estella's dancing was very *sinuous* in contrast to Marla's stiff and rigid movements.

_____

22. Ms. Ito's *benevolence* to the family included new clothing and several appliances.

_____

23. The fire marshall pronounced the blaze *spontaneous* because the wet hay in the mow built

heat and ignited on its own. _____

24. After hearing the two witnesses' conflicting stories, the jury was *confounded*. _____

_____

25. Audiences are very *fickle* when it comes to loyalty; that is, they will switch favorites often.

_____

26. Merry spent the entire evening trying to impress the mayor while Joan was less *gushy*.

_____

27. Dwain made an *eloquent* defense of his opinion; as a result, several persons switched to his side.

_____

28. The Royal Dalton dinnerware was stored in a mahogany *hutch* that was my grandmother's

favorite piece of furniture. _____

Vocabulary and Spelling

Unit 13 Review: Basic Spelling Rules

▶ **Exercise 1** Underline the correct spelling of the word in parentheses. Use a dictionary if necessary.

How many (<u>receivers</u>, recievers) went deep on that play?

1. How many members (normaly, normally) attend?

2. At the lost child's return, his parents greeted him with many hugs and (kiss's, kisses).

3. Harley conducted himself with impeccable (demeenor, demeanor).

4. The pasta at The Florentine is (dalicious, delicious).

5. Does Kim participate in many (extracurricular, extra-curricular) activities?

6. The rain started while I was (hoing, hoeing) the garden.

7. Billie and Marie had fun playing among the (sheafs, sheaves) of wheat.

8. Tell me exactly what happened, but keep it (brief, breif).

9. One of Ms. Markle's strengths in cooking is her creative use of (condaments, condiments).

10. In only a few years the Internet has effectively (spaned, spanned) the world.

11. After the boring speech, we appreciated Kang's (humerous, humorous) remarks more than usual.

12. The popularity of this proposal depends on how it will be (percieved, perceived).

13. The museum has a large collection of antique swords and (knives, knifes).

14. Carlita's ebony (tresses, treses) were shiny and silky.

15. Dad's vote for the Republican (nullafied, nullified) Mom's Democratic vote.

16. The House Committee on (UnAmerican, Un-American) Activities met this week.

17. Pablo's (deceit, deciet) eventually caught up with him.

18. Piano music is written using both bass and treble (cleffs, clefs).

19. The surroundings were rather (homly, homely), but loving warmth was obvious.

20. (Single-handedly, Single handedly), Mr. Espinosa rescued the girl from the river.

21. Their clandestine approach was given away by the (niegh, neigh) of one of their horses.

22. What type of (conveyance, conveiance) will be used for the shipment?

23. Mark's hilarious (paridies, parodies) made it difficult for Elmo to contain his laughter.

24. Saturday afternoon we will take our (motorboat, motor-boat) to the river.

25. The city has a twelve-foot (easment, easement) on the south side of our property.

26. Who has the (knowhow, know-how) to place a splint on a victim's leg?

27. Children and (match's, matches) make a deadly combination.

28. Emilio's unemployment (weighed, wieghed) heavily on his mind.

29. Does the doctor have the correct (antivenom, antivenin)?

30. My father attended a (conferrence, conference) on world hunger.

31. One must be on guard against the many (streses, stresses) of the competitive world.

32. I will stir the stock while you are (diceing, dicing) the carrots.

33. Andrea (preceded, preceeded) Roxie by fifteen minutes.

34. I have a huge urge to go (skiing, sking) this weekend.

35. Ms. Adamson is the most competent (advisor, adviseor) I have ever had.

36. Have you ever met my (mother in law, mother-in-law)?

37. All the deputies have been (duely, duly) sworn to uphold the law.

38. My sister purchased three tops and two new (dress's, dresses).

39. At what time did the president (conceed, concede) defeat?

40. This is the exhibit of the African (wildebeest, wildubeast).

41. There is nothing (foreseable, foreseeable) that will prevent me from attending.

42. Shall we take a (candlestick, candle stick) and some candles in case our batteries die?

43. Are you in the mood for (weiners, wieners) and sauerkraut?

44. During this special sale, you may have your payments (defered, deferred) for six months.

45. The dictator (dissolved, disolved) the parliament.

46. The fort looks to be (inapproachible, inapproachable) from here.

47. Thank you for your timely (referal, referral).

48. My penpal makes her own (stationary, stationery).

49. I hate to see anything (suffering, sufferring).

50. Wow, look at that herd of (elks, elk)!

51. My dog is very (long-lived, long lived).

52. You can find temporary (logement, lodgment) in the old inn.

53. That movie was pretty (wierd, weird).

54. Dedra and Shawna are full of (merriment, merryment).

55. I can't believe you made that (statment, statement)!

Composition

Unit 14: Composition

Lesson 101
The Writing Process: Prewriting

Before you can begin to write, you need to arm yourself with information and ideas. This stage of writing is called prewriting. In the prewriting stage you decide *what* you want to say (topic), *why* you want to say it (purpose), and *to whom* you want to say it (audience).

First, decide on your topic or subject by using the following methods:

Freewrite: Write down anything that comes into your mind. Write in a random fashion letting your ideas flow freely. This method is like thinking on paper.

Collect Information: Gather information from several different sources about topics that interest you. A newspaper headline, magazine article, or a photograph in a book can give you interesting ideas for topics.

Make Lists: Make lists of events, experiences, people, ideas, or even words that interest you. Use these lists to generate ideas for topics.

Ask Questions: Write down questions that you would like to find the answers to. Answers to questions such as *What if...? How...?* or *Who...?* might provide an interesting topic for your writing.

After choosing your topic, it is time to determine your purpose, or reason for writing. Your purpose might be to inform, to persuade, to entertain, to describe, or to analyze. Deciding on a purpose can help you narrow your topic.

Finally, determine what audience you are trying to reach with your writing. Knowing your audience will help you to decide on what writing style and what level of vocabulary to use. For example, writing a lab report for a group of environmental scientists would be very different from writing a report on pollution to present to a group of second-graders.

▶ **Exercise 1** **Spend 10 minutes prewriting, using any of the methods described above.**

_____

_____

_____

_____

_____

_____

_____

_____

Composition

Name _____ Class _____ Date _____

▶ Exercise 2 **Select five possible writing topics from your prewriting in Exercise 1. Write the topic, a possible purpose, and a possible audience for each topic.**

_____

_____

_____

_____

_____

_____

_____

_____

_____

_____

▶ Exercise 3 **Determine a purpose and an audience for each topic listed below.**

1. instructions on how to change an oil filter on an American car _____

_____

2. a humorous poem describing children _____

_____

3. tips on Japanese business etiquette _____

_____

4. how to determine the volume of a cylinder _____

_____

5. recipes for making quick and easy meals _____

_____

6. criticism of a new law _____

_____

7. warning that a lake is polluted _____

_____

8. announcement of a seminar on raising dairy cattle _____

_____

Composition

9. opinion of a new movie _____

_____

10. forecast of what fashion will be like in twenty years _____

_____

▶ **Exercise 4** **Find five different photographs or illustrations that interest you. Briefly describe each photo or illustration, then write a list of four questions that you have about each. Use these questions to come up with a possible writing topic.**

1. Description: _____

_____

Questions: _____

_____

_____

_____

Possible topic: _____

_____

2. Description: _____

_____

Questions: _____

_____

_____

_____

Possible topic: _____

_____

3. Description: _____

_____

Questions: _____

_____

_____

_____

Possible topic: _____

_____

Composition

4. Description: _____

_____

Questions: _____

_____

_____

_____

Possible topic: _____

_____

5. Description: _____

_____

Questions: _____

_____

_____

_____

Possible topic: _____

_____

▶ Exercise 5 **Tell what style and vocabulary is appropriate for each audience. Then choose one audience, and write a short paragraph about your immediate plans after graduation.**

1. Audience: you—in your personal journal _____

2. Audience: a specific family member _____

_____

3. Audience: a future employer _____

4. Audience: a college admissions office _____

5. Audience: a friend in another city _____

_____

_____

_____

_____

_____

_____

Composition

Lesson 102
The Writing Process: Drafting

Once you've gathered ideas and information in the prewriting stage, it's time to start putting them on paper. This stage of the writing process is called drafting, and it will be the first time that you write your ideas in paragraph form. The first paragraph of your draft should state the theme or the main point of your writing. This is called a thesis statement. Often your purpose and audience can help you formulate your thesis statement. Paragraphs that follow your first paragraph should have a topic sentence that supports the thesis statement and details to support the topic sentence. The theme, audience, and purpose of your writing will also help you to determine the way, or style, in which you write. The writing style that you adopt will give the piece its tone or "feel."

▶ **Exercise 1 Use each theme to write a complete thesis statement.**

1. Theme: 17-year-olds should be allowed to vote _____

_____

2. Theme: exposure to paint containing lead is harmful _____

_____

3. Theme: music today is better than it used to be _____

_____

4. Theme: the role of robots in the future _____

_____

5. Theme: earning money for college _____

_____

6. Theme: the most difficult stage of growing up _____

_____

7. Theme: playing only to win _____

_____

8. Theme: significance of the destruction of rain forests _____

_____

_____

Composition

9. Theme: my favorite painting _____

_____

10 Theme: reasons for the Persian Gulf War _____

_____

▶ **Exercise 2** **Write an appropriate topic sentence for each of the following paragraphs.**

Only about 20 percent of the people in China live in cities. However, the cities are growing rapidly as people from rural areas move to the cities in search of jobs. In some areas there is a lack of housing and people must live in crowded apartments or homes with relatives until they can find a place of their own.

_____

_____

As soon as you hear the warning, turn on the television or radio to get more information. If a tornado has been sighted nearby, go to a basement. If you do not have a basement, take cover under a heavy piece of furniture away from windows.

_____

_____

Today, movies are produced all over the country. Many southern states, such as North Carolina and Florida, have large movie studios. Because labor is often cheaper in these states, movies can be produced for less money than in Hollywood.

_____

_____

First and foremost make sure you get to your job on time. Cooperate with your coworkers, follow the company's policies, and carry out your manager's instructions carefully when performing your duties. Try to learn more about the company you are working for and, if you think you can handle it, ask to be given more responsibility.

_____

_____

_____

Composition

▶ **Exercise 3** Write a brief paragraph on each theme. Use a style that is appropriate for the given audience. Each paragraph should contain a topic sentence and details to support it.

1. **Theme:** complaint that compact discs are overpackaged and produce too much waste; **Audience:** compact disc manufacturers _____

_____

_____

_____

2. **Theme:** a set of instructions for a young person who has to stay home alone for a few hours after school; **Audience:** a thirteen-year-old relative or neighbor _____

_____

_____

_____

3. **Theme:** reasons why your city or area should be the next site of the summer or winter Olympics; **Audience:** Olympic officials _____

_____

_____

_____

4. **Theme:** tried and true methods for asking someone out on a date; **Audience:** friend

_____

_____

_____

5. **Theme:** invitation to speak at your graduation ceremony; **Audience:** mayor or city council member _____

_____

_____

_____

6. **Theme:** a request for information on how to apply for a college scholarship; **Audience:** college admissions office _____

_____

_____

_____

Composition

7. Theme: an apology for not following through on a promise; **Audience:** friend or relative

_____

_____

_____

8. Theme: a description of your favorite song or type of music; **Audience:** someone who has never

heard this song or type of music _____

_____

_____

_____

▶ **Exercise 4** **Write two questions that you would need to answer in order to create a good paragraph from each topic sentence below.**

1. Most of the world's civilizations began near a source of water. _____

_____

2. If you can swim, hold your breath for a full minute, and lift at least sixty pounds, then you may

be the person for this job. _____

_____

3. The Sherpas' knowledge of the Himalayas makes them valuable guides for mountain climbers.

_____

_____

4. When you go white-water rafting you may leave with a boatload of strangers, but you return

with a boatload of friends. _____

_____

5. This artist uses willow branches to craft her delicate furniture. _____

_____

6. Many immigrants from southwestern Asia travel to Europe in search of jobs.

_____

7. The value of ivory is destroying Africa's elephant population. _____

_____

8. Broccoli provides the body with many health benefits and can even help to prevent some

diseases. _____

Composition

Lesson 103
The Writing Process: Revising

After you have completed your draft, the next step is to revise, or improve, your writing. First, reread your draft carefully. Have you stated your purpose clearly in your thesis statement? Have you included all the details necessary to support your thesis? Next, check for unity. Is the organization logical? Are the details presented in a way that the reader will understand how they relate to your thesis statement? Finally, check for coherence. Is each sentence clear? Does the writing flow smoothly from sentence to sentence and paragraph to paragraph? Have you provided clear transitions from one idea to the next? Rework your writing to make it clear. Add or replace words to convey meaning as precisely as possible. While putting your ideas on paper, you may have left out adjectives or adverbs that can make your writing more interesting. Now is the time to add color and action to your writing by adding more descriptive words.

▶ **Exercise 1** Revise and rewrite the paragraphs below for clarity, unity, and coherence.

1. Sitting in his small office in Southsea, England, in the 1880s, Dr. Arthur Conan Doyle passed the time by writing stories. The author introduced his new detective in a story called "A Study in Scarlet." In 1886, However, Conan Doyle had the idea of basing a character on a clever and observant teacher at his Edinburgh medical school, Joseph Bell. He tried his hand at adventure yarns, science fiction, and history, but enjoyed only a moderate success. The character's name, which was soon to become known throughout the world, was Sherlock Holmes. The most famous of all literary detectives sprang from the mind of a bored and relatively unsuccessful doctor.

_____

_____

_____

_____

_____

_____

_____

_____

_____

Composition

2. Natural rubber has been replaced by many new synthetic materials. Natural rubber, though, is still used in tires, electrical insulation, and for waterproofing. Natural rubber is made from latex, which comes from rubber trees. Latex is a milky liquid. To gather latex, workers must be hired and then they make shallow cuts in the trunks of rubber trees to gather the latex. They attach a spout to the tree and a small cup. The cup is used to collect the latex. Removing the latex does not hurt the tree. Latex is not the sap of the tree. One worker can tap as many as 350 trees each day.

_____

_____

_____

_____

_____

_____

_____

_____

▶ **Exercise 2** **The sentences in each paragraph below are not organized in a logical order. Number the sentences in the order they should appear. Delete sentences that do not support the main idea.**

1. _____ As perfume use became more popular, the custom spread to Europe. _____ The use of perfumes can be traced back to ancient Egypt. _____ Some people are allergic to perfumes. _____ Remains of vials containing perfumed oils and ointments have been discovered in early Egyptian tombs. _____ Farms in southern France grow fragrant flowers and plants for use in the profitable perfume industry. _____ Today, France manufactures much of the world's perfumes.

2. _____ If you want to get a job at a hospital, previous experience as a hospital volunteer will give you an edge over other applicants. _____ If you like working with young children, spending time at a daycare facility will give you valuable job experience. _____ When you start looking for your first job you will likely run into a problem that every first time job hunter faces—a lack of experience. _____ Recreation centers, childcare facilities, homeless shelters, hospitals, and fund-raising organizations are always in need of dedicated people to help them a few hours a week. _____ My brother is a volunteer at a local nursing home. _____ One way to get some on-the-job experience before you start looking for a job is to do volunteer work

in your community. _____ Finally, when you volunteer, you'll not only be learning skills

but providing a valuable service to your community.

▶ **Exercise 3** **Rewrite each sentence adding details to make it more interesting and descriptive.**

1. After the tornado, only two buildings were left standing.

_____

_____

2. Whenever we eat at our favorite restaurant, we order our favorite food.

_____

_____

3. My cousin Germaine lives in the house on the corner.

_____

_____

4. A hero is someone whom you respect.

_____

_____

5. Visiting the beach was the best part of my vacation.

_____

_____

6. He was lost in the forest for three days before they found him.

_____

_____

7. Chris decided to wear red to the game.

_____

_____

8. Our boat was able to make it through the storm.

_____

_____

Composition

9. There were ten people and only one car.

_____

_____

10. I was confused when all the reporters began asking me questions about what had happened.

_____

_____

11. It bothers me when people are impolite.

_____

_____

12. We walked through the woods after it snowed.

_____

_____

13. I've seen my favorite movie at least eight times.

_____

_____

14. My car was making a funny sound, so I took it in for repairs.

_____

_____

15. My best friend is different from everyone else.

_____

_____

16. I filled out an application, but I'm not sure if I'll get the job.

_____

_____

17. By the time I'm twenty-one, I hope to have reached my goals.

_____

_____

18. I was quite embarrassed when I realized I was the only person in costume.

_____

_____

Composition

Lesson 104
The Writing Process: Editing

After you have revised your work, the next step is to edit what you have written. As you edit, look for correct word usage, subject-verb agreement, correct verb tenses, clear pronoun references, run-on sentences, and sentence fragments. When editing, cross out words and write new words in margins and spaces between the lines. Next, proofread your writing to correct spelling, punctuation, and capitalization errors. Use the following proofreading marks:

insert ∧   coördinate

delete ⅃   printingg

insert space #   onehundred

close up space ⌒   over head

capitalize ≡   Canary islands

make lowercase /   Mayor

check spelling (sp)   Phillipines sp

switch order   people twelve

new paragraph ¶   ¶The last person . . .

▶ **Exercise 1 Edit and proofread each sentence.**

I have just enuogh money to by a tankof gas.

1. The instructions for asembling the model was confuseing.

2. Arti facts from Tutankhamen's tomb help us understand more about life in Anceint egypt.

3. Twentytwo people, signed up for the senior class trip to Boston massachusettes.

4. Does you have any batterys I could borrow for my calculater.

5. The movies special affects were reallistic.

6. After falling at least fourty times, Ive finallly learnt to skate backwards?

7. Sparse plant life exists in the interior of Antartica.

8. The writeing contest deadline was extended to june 15.

Composition

9. Many of japans Buildings have been built to withstand the stress of earthqaukes.

10. Lets be sure to pack some Sunscreen if were going to daytona beach.

11. Stastistics show that red cars are stopped for sppeeding more often then any other type.

12. The louvre in Paris France and the uffizi in Florence italy house some of the worlds most famous art work.

13. Fruits and vegetables and peas contain large amounts of vitamin a and c.

14. The photgraphers gathered at the white house.

15. The whether forcaster said that two tornadoes had been sighted south of the city.

16. The food is usualy good at Mortons café but some times the steak is over done.

17. I was surprised to see the Spring fashions in Mason's department store when there was still snow on the ground.

18. The tropic of cancer is located just a few miles southern of the Florida keys.

▶ Exercise 2 **Proofread the paragraph to correct spelling, punctuation, and capitalization.**

Have you ever wondred how the speed of an airborn baseball is measured? Its done the same way that the highway patrol measures the sped of a auto mobile—with a radra gun. A person holding a radar gun stands behind home plate. The radar gun emits a microwave beams. When the basebeall moves into this beam, it reflects the beam backto the gun. When the diference inthe reflected bean and the orignial beam is measured, the miles per hour can be calculateed. Some of baseballs best pitchers can fire a fast ball across the plate at speeds close to one hundred miles an per hour.

Lesson 105
The Writing Process: Presenting

After completing a piece of writing, you may want to share your work with others. You can begin thinking about your presentation as early as the prewriting stage when you define your audience. The nature of your writing will affect how and where you might present your writing.

An outlet for presenting your writing to a specific audience is called a market. As a twelfth-grade student several markets are available to you. Some of these markets may be related to school, such as school newspapers and classroom presentations. Others might be in your community, such as local organizations and community newspapers. Other markets include contests sponsored by magazines or special-interest publications and newsletters. The *Market Guide for Young Writers,* available in many libraries, will provide many ideas for marketing your work.

To decide how to present your writing, first analyze the piece and pinpoint the audience. Then search for an outlet that serves that audience. Some outlets, such as classroom presentations, radio programs, community productions, or speech contests offer a chance to give oral presentations. In these cases, visual aids may enhance your presentation.

▶ Exercise 1 **Suggest an outlet or market for each piece of writing described below.**

a story for children about endangered animals   a children's magazine or a community environmental fair
_____

1. an essay discussing violence on television _____

_____

2. lyrics for a song about surfing _____

_____

3. a description of your vacation on a western cattle ranch _____

_____

4. an explanation of how to prevent a virus from entering your computer _____

_____

5. a recipe for holiday cookies _____

_____

6. a speech on the increase of crime in your community _____

_____

7. a how-to article on grooming a dog for a national dog show _____

_____

Composition

8. a complaint about an unsafe feature on your car _____

_____

9. an editorial praising the actions of your local fire department _____

_____

10. a comedy routine based on the experiences of your first date _____

_____

▶ Exercise 2 **Suggest a visual aid that would increase the effectiveness of each presentation below.**

a play about the history of the wild west   *costumes from the time period*

1. a presentation about how to perform first aid _____

_____

2. a class report on how whales and other animals communicate _____

_____

3. a speech outlining the dangers of using drugs _____

_____

4. a magazine article describing a new restaurant in your area _____

_____

5. a scientific report on the effectiveness of ten different cancer drugs _____

_____

6. an essay on how the government is wasting money _____

_____

7. a report on a famous television personality _____

_____

8. explanation telling first graders the difference between a circle, square, rectangle, and triangle

_____

9. a presentation describing the different spices used in Indian cooking _____

_____

10. a science class report on how heredity determines what traits are passed from one family

member to another _____

_____

Composition

Lesson 106
Outlining

Outlining is a way to organize your information before you begin writing. In the prewriting stage you gather information and generate ideas. Outlining gives you a way to structure those ideas. One way to make an outline is to transfer information from your prewriting material to index cards. You can then arrange the cards by main topic and supporting details. In an outline, use roman numerals to indicate main topics and use capital letters for subtopics. Under each subtopic, list details using regular numbers and lowercase letters. If you divide a topic into subtopics, always use at least two subtopics. Part of an outline for a report on Renaissance figures might look like this:

I. Renaissance artists
   A. Leonardo da Vinci
      1. Born 1452 in Vinci, Italy
      2. Artist, scientist, and inventor
      3. Major artistic achievements
         a. *Mona Lisa*
         b. *Last Supper*
         c. *Adoration of the Magi*
   B. Michelangelo
      1. Born 1475 in Arezzo, Italy
      2. Painter, sculptor, and architect
      3. Major artistic achievements
         a. *Sistine Chapel*
         b. *The Pietà*
II. Renaissance philosophers

▶ **Exercise 1** **Use the information presented in the following outline to write a one- or two-paragraph report about vitamins.**

   I. Water-soluble vitamins
      A. Characteristics
         1. Dissolve in water so they pass easily into the bloodstream
         2. Not stored in body tissue, but excreted in urine
         3. Must be replenished every day
      B. Examples
         1. B-complex vitamins
         2. Vitamin C
  II. Fat-soluble vitamins
      A. Characteristics
         1. Absorbed and transported by fat cells
         2. Stored in body's fatty tissue
         3. Excess build-up can have a toxic effect
      B. Examples
         1. Vitamin A
         2. Vitamin D
         3. Vitamin E

Composition

_____

_____

_____

_____

_____

_____

▶ **Exercise 2** **Organize the following topics and details into an outline for a report on air pollution. Create three main topics in your outline.**

Photochemical smog	Exhaust from vehicles
Eyes water and sting	Heart and brain receive less oxygen
Acid rain	Types of air pollution
Industry	Trash burning
Major causes of air pollution	Smog
Effects of air pollution on our health	Irritates nose, throat, and lungs
Sulfurous smog	

_____

_____

_____

_____

_____

_____

_____

_____

_____

_____

_____

_____

Composition

Lesson 107
Writing Effective Sentences

Effective sentences are one of the most powerful tools a writer has. You can alter the tone and style of your writing simply by changing the patterns of your sentences. Consider these strategies when writing sentences. Vary the length of your sentences. Don't use all long sentences or all short sentences. Also vary the structure of your sentences. Following a rigid sentence pattern can become repetitive and boring. In some cases, parallelism (the deliberate repetition of certain words, phrases, or sentence structures) can be used to achieve a desired effect. Another strategy is to use interruption for emphasis. A sudden break in thought calls attention to itself. Use this device to emphasize an important point or detail. Another way to add emphasis is to use an unusual sentence pattern that stands out from the rest.

Pay special attention to topic sentences. When writing a topic sentence for a paragraph make it specific enough to arouse or "hook" your readers so that they will want to read on.

Use the active voice as often as possible in your sentences. In a sentence in the **active voice**, the subject performs the action. *(He grabbed the last sandwich.)* In a **passive-voice** sentence, the subject is acted upon. *(The last sandwich was grabbed by him.)* Active-voice sentences are stronger than passive-voice sentences. As a general rule, use passive voice only when the subject performing the action is not known, when the subject is unimportant, or when you want to emphasize something other than the subject.

▶ **Exercise 1** **Rewrite each sentence below to create one or two sentences that are more interesting and effective.**

We smelled smoke as we entered the house. We saw flames climbing up the kitchen curtains.

As we entered the house, we smelled smoke and saw flames climbing up the kitchen curtains.
_____

1. A space station has more room than a spaceship. Skylab was a space station built by the United

States. It had separate living quarters, separate work areas, and separate exercise areas.

_____

_____

2. My diploma was given to me at graduation. The principal congratulated me and shook my hand.

_____

_____

3. In Bangkok, Thailand, there is a system of waterways that are used as roads by the people.

People use boats instead of cars to carry goods. Some boats transport people to and from work.

_____

_____

Composition

4. We went to the first baseball game of the season. A foul ball was hit into our section. I was competing with hundreds of other people to snag a foul ball and I actually got one.

_____

_____

5. His landlord doubled the rent. His boss doubled his workload. His paycheck was half of what it usually was. _____

_____

6. Africa's Sahara grows larger every year. Overgrazing and poor farming methods are eroding the once fertile soil. _____

_____

7. The city streets were filled with people. Then the dark clouds moved in. At that point everyone disappeared. _____

_____

8. The hike into the canyon was relatively easy. We forgot that hiking out of the canyon would be all uphill. We were tired, sore, and thirsty by the time we got back. _____

_____

9. The quarterback fumbled the ball in the first quarter. He stumbled and fell in the second quarter. He bungled the play in the third quarter. By the fourth quarter all hope for winning the game had crumbled. _____

_____

10. Rachel Carson was a scientist and nature-lover. She wrote the book *Silent Spring*. The book revealed the dangerous effects of some pesticides on wildlife. _____

_____

▶ Exercise 2 **Use the subject, verb, and object provided to write one active-voice sentence and one passive-voice sentence.**

grandfather, gave, watch

Active: My grandfather gave me a watch for graduation.

Passive: For graduation I was given a watch by my grandfather.

Composition

1. he, completed, final exam

   Active: _____

   Passive: _____

2. twenty fans, blocked, entrance

   Active: _____

   Passive: _____

3. Paulo, resolved, conflict

   Active: _____

   Passive: _____

4. Painter, applied, color

   Active: _____

   Passive: _____

5. Hannah, purchased, red vest

   Active: _____

   Passive: _____

6. Scouts, packed, first-aid kit

   Active: _____

   Passive: _____

7. Franklin, borrowed, money

   Active: _____

   Passive: _____

8. Sara and Mallory, saw, movie

   Active: _____

   Passive: _____

9. Shakespeare, wrote, plays

   Active: _____

   Passive: _____

10. Collision, shattered, windshield

    Active: _____

    Passive: _____

Composition

▶ Exercise 3 **Rewrite the following paragraph using more effective sentences.**

   "Ring-Around-the-Rosie" is a popular children's rhyme. Most people don't know about its history. It was really written during the Middle Ages. It's actually about what happened during the Great Plague or Black Death. The Great Plague was an epidemic that killed lots of people. It had killed about a third of the people who lived in Europe by the late 1300s. "Rosie" was the rash that was caused by the disease. "A pocketful of posies" were the herbs that people carried. They believed these herbs might keep them from getting the disease. "We all fall down" means that people were dying from the disease.

_____

_____

_____

_____

_____

_____

_____

_____

_____

_____

_____

_____

_____

_____

_____

_____

_____

_____

_____

_____

Composition

Lesson 108
Building Paragraphs

Supporting details in a paragraph can be arranged in several ways. Chronological order places events in the order in which they happened. Spatial order describes how objects might appear to an observer. Compare/contrast order shows similarities and differences among the items you are writing about.

The first of the following paragraphs illustrates the use of chronological order; the second, spatial order; and the third, compare/contrast order.

We arrived in New York at 5:05, just in time for rush hour. It was 6:15 by the time our cab driver inched his way to our hotel. We had just enough time to scramble out of the taxi and run to our rooms to get ready. We wanted to be there when the curtain opened at 7:00.

When we flew into New York I was surprised to see the layers and layers of tall buildings on what seemed like such a tiny island. As I hailed a cab, I became instantly aware of the crush of people and cars in this bustling city. Traffic was bumper-to-bumper, and horns blared as cars and buses jockeyed for position. I was anxious to get to my hotel room where I might find a few minutes of solace behind a closed door.

Some people describe New York as a city with the best and worst of everything. It has some of the world's top artists, most successful businesses, and most impressive museums, but it's also overcrowded, expensive, and has a high rate of crime. Most people say they either love or hate the city of New York. Few visitors leave the city without forming any opinion at all.

▶ **Exercise 1** **Read each sentence. Write *C* if you think the sentence would most likely appear in a paragraph using chronological order, *S* if it would appear in a paragraph using spatial order, and *CC* if it would appear in a paragraph using compare/contrast order.**

__CC__ The British game of cricket and the American game of baseball have many similarities.

_____ 1. As you walk into the building, you'll see a mirrored wall to the left and a marble staircase to the right.

_____ 2. I'm still trying to decide whether to take the Chinese cooking class or the oil painting class.

_____ 3. The gift from my aunt was wrapped in bright green paper with a bright yellow ribbon.

_____ 4. Before you plant your garden, turn over the soil and add fertilizer.

_____ 5. The doctor told me to take the pills she gave me and then call her in two weeks.

_____ 6. Her bright red dress and flowered hat made her stand out in the crowd.

_____ 7. The animal and plant life in the Himalayas changes dramatically as you move to higher elevations.

Composition

_____ 8. There are many differences between the way a television reporter covers an event and the way a newspaper reporter covers an event.

_____ 9. As we approached the cabin we heard a low growl and saw a bear peering in the window.

_____ 10. After you enter your data, the next step is to save it before you turn off the computer.

_____ 11. Although both artists paint seascapes, one uses watercolors and the other uses oil paints.

_____ 12. The actors rehearsed at four o'clock to make sure they were prepared for the eight o'clock performance.

_____ 13. We looked toward the horizon and saw a storm approaching from the southwest.

_____ 14. When I was younger I enjoyed reading mysteries, but now I prefer historical novels.

_____ 15. If we take the main highway it may be faster, but the back roads are much more scenic.

▶ Exercise 2 **Number the following sentences in chronological order.**

_____ The officer will ask you to fill out an application.

_____ The register is important because it helps you keep track of how much money you have in your account.

_____ First, ask a parent or another adult to recommend a local bank.

_____ Then visit the bank and talk to a bank officer.

_____ After you have had your checking account for about a month, you will receive a statement from the bank that lists all of your transactions for that month.

_____ Call the bank and ask what its procedures are for opening an account.

_____ After you fill out the application, you will receive your checkbook filled with blank checks.

_____ Here is what you need to do if you want to open a checking account.

_____ Inside the checkbook is a check register where you can record the checks you write and their amount.

Composition

▶ **Exercise 3** **Use the details below and your own knowledge to write a paragraph about the sport of lacrosse. Your paragraph can be written in either chronological, spatial, or compare/contrast order. Indicate which order you are going to use.**

Lacrosse originated with the Native Americans.

Native American teams had as many as 200 people to a side.

The Native American game was called "baggataway."

The game was later named "lacrosse" by French Canadians, because the netted stick used to throw the ball resembled a cross.

The first modern game was played by two Native American teams in 1834 using formal rules on an enclosed field.

Lacrosse is a team sport.

Players use a netted stick to throw or hit a ball into a goal net.

A lacrosse ball is a little smaller than a baseball and is made of rubber.

A lacrosse field is 110 yards long.

A men's team is made up of 10 players and a women's team has 12 players.

Players pass the ball back and forth by flipping the crosse with their wrists.

Only goalies can use their hands to deflect the ball.

Games are divided into four 25-minute periods.

_____

_____

_____

_____

_____

_____

_____

_____

_____

_____

_____

_____

_____

_____

_____

_____

Composition

▶ **Exercise 4** **Choose one topic from the list below. Use the same topic to write one paragraph using chronological order, one using spatial order, and one using compare/contrast order.**

your favorite or least favorite movie

an embarrassing moment

a trait or habit someone has that bothers you

your dream vacation

what you would do if you were the last person left in the world

a description of someone you admire

Chronological order:

_____

_____

_____

_____

_____

_____

_____

_____

Spatial order:

_____

_____

_____

_____

_____

_____

_____

Compare/contrast order:

_____

_____

_____

_____

_____

_____

Composition

Lesson 109
Paragraph Ordering

When you revise a first draft, check the unity and coherence of paragraphs. Each paragraph should include a topic sentence, which states the main idea of the paragraph, as well as supporting details related to the topic sentence. Be sure the comparisons are understandable. Check chronological details for proper order and make sure that spatial details are clear. Finally, link the ideas together properly by using effective transitions.

▶ **Exercise 1** **Revise the following paragraphs for unity and coherence. Rewrite the paragraphs based on your revisions.**

There are about a half a million Cajuns in the state of Louisiana. Did you know that they are originally from Canada? In the 1700s thousands of French settlers called "Acadians" lived in eastern Canada. The Cajuns are ancestors of this group of French settlers in Canada. Canada was controlled by Britain then. The Acadians were deported from Canada when France and Britain went to war. The British deported them because they would not support Britain in the war.

British soldiers put the Acadians on ships. Some made it back to France, but many died. Some—about 4,000—made it to Louisiana. Some settled on the eastern coast of the United States. The Acadians are the ancestors of the Cajuns who live in Louisiana today.

Today in Louisiana some of the Cajuns are farmers. Some fish for a living. Some Cajuns have ranches. There are some interesting things about the Cajun culture. They speak a dialect of the French language. They are known for their spicy foods. Their music is also very popular and is played on fiddles and accordion-like instruments called "squeeze boxes."

Some Acadians were able to return to Canada. Many live there today. Most are living in New Brunswick, Nova Scotia, and Prince Edward Island. The Acadians, like the Cajuns, have their own unique culture. Many of the Acadians still have Cajun relatives. These Cajun relatives live in the state of Louisiana.

_____

_____

_____

_____

_____

Composition

Lesson 110
Personal Letters

A **personal letter** is usually a letter to a friend or a relative written in an informal tone. Personal letters are written to inform others of recent events in your life and to ask the recipient questions about his or her life. Personal letters often contain your opinions, thoughts, and feelings about various topics. They can help maintain friendships and deepen understanding between two people. A personal letter can also be an invitation or a thank-you note.

Personal letters are usually written in indented form. Each paragraph is indented, as well as each line in the heading, the complimentary close, and the signature.

▶ **Exercise 1** **Read the following personal letter. Answer each question.**

>   2320 Sawmill Drive
>   Montgomery, TX 75081
>   July 24, 1996

Dear Nora,

   You probably are wondering why I haven't written. We promised each other when you moved that we would write each other every week. I'm sorry, and I vow to do better!

   It's been a crazy summer for me. I took the job I told you about at the hospital, and I'm working four days a week. I work in the children's ward with a woman who plans activities for the children. We put on puppet shows, do art projects, and most of the time just play with the kids. Some of the kids don't have many visitors, so it makes me feel really good to spend time with them.

   I had lunch with Gina and Coretta yesterday. We all miss you and are anxious to see you when you come in August. We're planning a party so we can spend some time together. Is that OK with you? I hope everything is going well for you. Let me know how your interview for the new job went. Miss you!

>   Your friend,
>   *Anna*

1. What is the relationship between Anna and Nora? _____

_____

2. Why do you think Anna wrote this letter to Nora? _____

_____

3. How is this a good example of a personal letter? _____

_____

_____

Composition

4. What might Nora include in a response to Anna's letter? _____

_____

_____

▶ **Exercise 2 Write a personal letter to a friend.**

_____

_____

_____

_____

_____

_____

_____

_____

_____

_____

_____

_____

_____

_____

_____

_____

_____

_____

_____

_____

_____

_____

_____

Composition

Different situations call for different kinds of personal letters. You would probably use a different tone and style in writing to an adult than you would use in writing to your best friend. Your letter to your relative would probably be more formal, while you might make use of slang or secret code words in writing to your best friend. You would also use a different tone and style when writing to a favorite author, performer, or sports figure.

▶ **Exercise 3** Write a letter to an adult relative telling him or her about your plans after graduation. Your letter will also give you an opportunity to invite the relative to your graduation ceremony.

_____

_____

_____

_____

_____

_____

_____

_____

_____

_____

_____

_____

_____

_____

_____

_____

_____

_____

_____

_____

_____

_____

Composition

▶ **Exercise 4** **Write a letter to an author, performer, or sports star whom you admire.**

_____

_____

_____

_____

_____

_____

_____

_____

_____

_____

_____

_____

_____

_____

_____

_____

_____

_____

_____

_____

_____

_____

_____

_____

_____

_____

_____

_____

_____

_____

_____

_____

Composition

Lesson 111
Business Letters: Letters of Request and Complaint

A letter of request is a letter that asks for information or service. When you write a letter of request, always be clear and courteous. Explain what information you need and why you need it. Include any information the receiver may need to answer your request.

Business letters are usually written in block form or semiblock form. In block form, everything is lined up with the left margin. In semiblock form, the heading, complimentary close, and signature are placed on the right side of the page.

▶ **Exercise 1** **Examine the following letter. Is it a good example of a letter of request? Why or why not? Write your critique below.**

Dear College Admissions Department:
    I need some information. I want to attend your school next year and will need some sort of financial aid. Can you send me something on this? I don't have much time so you'll need to get it to me as quickly as you can, OK?

Sincerely,
Brad Franklin

_____

_____

_____

_____

▶ **Exercise 2** **Write a short letter requesting information on one of the following topics. Use proper business-letter format.**

a letter to one of your senators requesting information on her or his voting record on a particular issue
a letter to an art school requesting more information on a class you are interested in taking
a letter to a recreation center asking if they need anyone to volunteer as a referee for the summer

_____

_____

_____

_____

_____

Composition

A letter of complaint describes a problem or concern and sometimes is a request for action. It should be clear, concise, and reasonable. Never let your anger show when writing a letter of complaint. Avoid insults and threats. Begin by stating the problem and telling briefly how it happened. Then use supporting details as evidence of your problem. End your letter by explaining what you would like done about the matter.

▶ **Exercise 3** **Read the following letter of complaint. Describe any problems and suggest how to correct them.**

8614 14th Street
New York, New York 10036
September 20, 1996

Dear Cinema One Manager:

    I can't believe what you did to my friend and me the other night. We paid good money to get into your seven o'clock show, but when we walked into the theater it was completely packed. We asked for our money back and they said "Forget it!" They said there were two seats in the first row and to take them or else. You must be crazy to think anyone would want to sit in the front row. I haven't done that since I was five years old! Hey mister, we want our money back or free tickets to another show. Do I have to call a lawyer?

Not sincerely,
Shannon Crawford

_____

_____

▶ **Exercise 4** **Revise and rewrite the above letter of complaint.**

_____

_____

_____

_____

_____

_____

_____

_____

_____

_____

Composition

Name _____ Class _____ Date _____

Lesson 112
Business Letters: Résumés and Cover Letters

A résumé is a summary of your work experience, school experience, talents, and interests. You use it to apply for a job or for admittance into a school or academic program. A résumé should be clear, concise, expressive, and informative. Because a résumé is a summary, it is not necessary to use complete sentences. However, the format you use should be consistent, as in the following example.

Lionel Jefferson
1804 Becker Street
Atlanta, GA 30303
(404) 964-3209

Objective:	Full-time summer employment as a park ranger assistant
Work Experience:	Volunteer nature tour leader, Metropolitan Park
Education:	King High School, September 1995–present, 3.0 grade point average
	Atlanta Middle School, August 1992–1994, 3.3 grade point average
Accomplishments:	Community service award for participation in river cleanup program; president of student chapter of Sierra Club
References:	Martin Pavlich, teacher, King High School (404) 555-6340
	Julia Harmon, Park Ranger, Metropolitan Park (404) 555-8787

▶ **Exercise 1 Write a résumé to apply for one of the following:**

summer job as a lifeguard
part-time job at a recreation center or daycare center
scholarship to pay for a summer computer camp
membership in an honors science class

_____
_____
_____
_____
_____
_____
_____
_____
_____

Composition

Unit 14, Composition **341**

A cover letter is a brief letter of introduction that usually accompanies a résumé. It states what you are applying for and where you can be contacted. It also refers the reader to your résumé for additional information. By using your cover letter to call attention to certain abilities, interests, and experiences, you can create a "customized" presentation, tailored to a specific job or program.

The following is an example of a well-formatted, concise cover letter. Note that the letter follows business letter style rules and that it is directed to a specific person.

Lionel Jefferson
1804 Becker Street
Atlanta, GA 30303
(404) 964-3209

Mr. Howard Ramirez
Director, Georgia State Parks
678 River Valley Road
Atlanta, GA 30306
April 16, 1996

Dear Mr. Ramirez:

I am responding to the notice that you posted on the King High School job search board. I am a senior at King High School in Atlanta and am interested in obtaining full-time summer employment as a park ranger assistant. I am very interested in nature studies and plan to major in natural resources management when I attend Community College in the fall.

I have worked at Atlanta's Metropolitan Park as a tour guide and am familiar with some of the responsibilities of park management. I am a hard worker and am anxious to gain more experience in this field. I hope you find that my qualifications meet some of your needs at this time. I have enclosed a copy of my résumé for your review.

Sincerely,

Lionel Jefferson

▶ **Exercise 2** **Write a cover letter to send with the résumé that you wrote in Exercise 1.**

_____

_____

_____

_____

_____

_____

_____

Composition

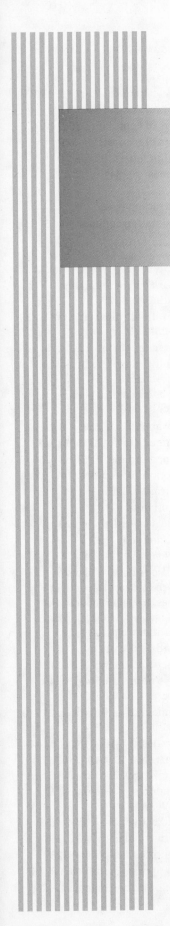

*I*ndex

Index

Positive degree (form), modifiers, 9–10, 61, 195, 197

Possessive apostrophes, 16, 40–41, 277

Possessive pronouns, 2, 9, 41, 51, 61, 175, 277

Possessive nouns, 2, 16, 41, 47, 61, 277

Precede, proceed, 13, 224

Predicate adjective, 6, 82

Predicate nominative, defined, 6, 8, 82

Predicates
  complete, 6, 74
  compound, 6, 75
  simple, 6, 73

Prefixes, 16–17, 295, 297
  and hyphens, 16, 279, 297

Prepositional phrases, defined, 6, 65, 85
  as adjectives, 85
  as adverbs, 85
  commas with, 255
  object of the preposition, 6, 65, 85
  recognizing, practice in, 65–66, 85–86
  subject-verb agreement, 26, 155

Prepositions, defined, 5, 65
  compound, 5, 65
  list, 5, 65
  objects of, 6, 65, 85
  recognizing, practice in, 65–66

Present perfect tense, 3, 137, 139

Present tense, 3, 135, 139

Presentation, of writing, 18, 321
  market, 321

Prewriting, 18, 307
  audience, 18, 307
  freewriting, 18, 307
  practice, 307–310
  purpose, 18, 307
  topic, 18, 307

Principal parts of verbs, 3–4, 131, 133

Proceed, precede, 13, 224

Progressive verbs, defined, 4, 141

Pronouns, defined, 2, 51, 175
  after *than* and *as,* 9, 177
  agreement with, 8, 29–34, 183, 185, 187, 189
  antecedents of, 3, 9, 30–34, 51, 183, 185, 187, 189
  as appositives, 6, 90, 177
  cases of, 2, 8–9, 51, 175
  demonstrative, 2, 54

gender of, 9, 183, 185

incorrect shifts, 34, 185

indefinite, 2, 29, 54, 167, 187

intensive, 2, 52, 179

interrogative, 2, 9, 53, 181

personal, 2, 51, 175

possessive, 2, 9, 41, 51, 61, 175, 277

reflexive, 2, 9, 52, 179

relative, 2, 53, 103

who, whom, 9, 13, 181, 225

Proofreading, 319

Proper adjectives, 5, 61
  capitalization of, 14, 237

Proper nouns, 2, 49, 235

Punctuation rules. *See specific types.*

Purpose, prewriting, 18, 307

Q

Question marks, 14, 243
  and quotation marks, 16, 273

Quotation marks, 15–16, 271, 273
  with colons or semicolons, 16, 245, 273
  with commas or periods, 16, 271, 273
  with definitions, 273
  in direct quotations, 15, 271
  in indirect quotations, 235, 271
  with question marks or exclamation points, 273
  within a quotation, 15, 271
  with titles of short works, 15, 273
  with unusual expressions, 15, 273

Quotations, capitalizing, 13, 233

R

Raise, rise, 13, 224

Reason is because, avoiding, 13, 224

Reflexive pronouns, 2, 9, 52, 179

Regardless, not *irregardless,* 12, 222

Regular verbs, principal parts, 3–4, 131

Relative pronouns, 2, 53, 103
  list, 53, 103

Respectfully, respectively, 13, 225

Résumés, 20, 341–342

Revising, 18, 315, 333
  coherence, 315, 333
  meaning, 315
  unity, 315, 333

Rise, raise, 13, 224

Roots of words, 17, 293

Run-on sentences, defined, 24–25, 113, 263

S

Said, says, 13, 225

Scarcely, in double negatives, 11, 220

Semiblock form of letters, 19, 339

Semicolons, 14–15, 16, 99, 247
  to correct run-on sentences, 24–25, 113, 247, 263

Sentence fragments, 22–23, 111

Sentence outlines, 19

Sentence structure
  complex, 7, 101
  compound, 7, 99
  compound-complex, 7, 101
  simple, 7, 99

Sentences, effective, 145, 325
  active voice, 145, 325
  interruption, 325
  parallelism, 325
  passive voice, 145, 325
  unusual patterns, 325
  varied length, 18, 325
  varied structure, 18, 325

Sentences, kinds of
  declarative, 8, 109
  exclamatory, 8, 109
  imperative, 8, 109
  interrogative, 8, 109

Sentences, inverted, 6, 8, 26–27, 77, 159

Sentences, run-on, 24–25, 113, 263

Series
  commas in, 15, 44, 251
  colon before, 14, 245

Set, sit, 13, 225

Should of, avoiding, 12, 220

Simple predicates, defined, 6, 73

Simple sentences, defined, 7, 99

Simple subjects, defined, 5, 73

Singular nouns, 2, 47, 183

Sit, set, 13, 225

Spatial order, 18, 327

Spelling
  adding -*ly* and -*ness,* 18, 297
  doubling the final consonant, 18, 297
  forming compound words, 18, 299
  of -*cede,* -*ceed,* and -*sede,* 17, 299
  of *ie* and *ei,* 17, 299

of plural nouns, 16–18, 277, 299
  with prefixes, 16, 297
  with suffixes, 17–18, 297
  of unstressed vowels, 17, 299
Style or voice, 311
Subject complements, 6, 82
  predicate nominatives, 6, 82
  predicate adjectives, 6, 82
Subject-verb agreement, 8, 26–29,
  153, 155, 157, 159, 161, 163, 165,
  167, 169
  and adjective clauses, 8, 169
  and collective nouns, 27, 161
  and compound subjects, 8,
    28–29, 163
  and indefinite pronouns, 8, 29,
    167
  and intervening expressions, 8,
    29, 165
  and prepositional phrases, 8, 26,
    155
  in inverted sentences, 8, 26–27,
    77, 159
  and linking verbs, 8, 26, 157
  and predicate nominatives, 8, 26,
    157
  and special subjects, 8, 161
  with titles, 8
Subjects
  agreement of verb with, 8, 26–29,
    153, 155, 157, 159, 161, 163,
    165, 167, 169
  complete, 6, 74
  compound, 5, 75, 163
  gerunds and infinitives as, 89, 91
  noun clauses as, 107
  simple, 5, 73
Subjunctive mood, verbs, 4, 147
Subordinate (dependent) clauses, 7,
  42, 97, 101, 103, 105, 107, 181,
  257
Subordinating conjunctions, 5, 67, 97
  list, 67, 97
Suffixes, 17–18, 295, 297
Superlative degree (form), 9–10, 61,
  195, 197

T

Take, bring, 11, 220
Teach, learn, 12, 223
Tenses, defined, 3, 35–37, 135, 137,
  139
  compatibility, 35, 143
  distinguishing, 36–37, 139
  future, 3, 135, 139
  future perfect, 3, 137, 139
  past, 3, 135, 139
  past perfect, 3, 137, 139
  present, 3, 135, 139
  present perfect, 3, 137, 139
  shifts in, avoiding, 35, 143
Than, then, 13, 225
That there, this here, avoiding, 13,
  225
Theme, writing, 18, 311
Then, than, 13, 225
Thesis statement, writing, 18, 311
This here, that there, avoiding, 13,
  225
This kind, these kinds, 12, 223
Topic outlines, 19, 323
Topic, prewriting, 18, 307
Topic sentences, 311, 333
Transitive verbs, defined, 3, 55

U

Underlining, 16, 275
Understood subject, 77, 109
Unity, in writing, 315, 333

V

Verb phrases, defined, 3, 6, 59
Verbal phrases, 7, 87, 89, 91, 93
Verbals, defined, 7, 93
  See also Gerunds, Infinitives,
  Participles
Verbs, defined, 3, 55
  action verbs, 3, 55
    intransitive, 3, 55
    transitive, 3, 55
  agreement with subjects, rules, 8,
    26–29, 153, 155, 157, 159,
    161, 163, 165, 167, 169

auxiliary (helping), 3, 59
  emphatic, 4, 142
  intransitive, 3, 55
  irregular, regular, 3–4, 131, 133
  linking, 3, 57, 157
  list, 3–4, 133
  moods of, 4, 147
    imperative, 4, 147
    indicative, 4, 147
    subjunction, 4, 147
  principal parts of irregular, 3–4,
    133
  principal parts of regular, 3, 131
  progressive, 4, 141
  tenses of, 3, 35–37, 135, 137, 139
    See also Tenses
  transitive, 3, 55
  voice of, active and passive, 4,
    145, 325
Vocabulary building, 17–18, 291,
  293, 295
  from context, 17, 291
  prefixes and suffixes, 17–18, 295,
    297
  word roots, base words, 17, 293
Voice of verbs, defined, 4, 145, 325
  active, 4, 145, 325
  effective use of, 145, 325
  passive, 4, 145, 325
Voice or style, 311, 323

W

Well, good, 12, 201, 222
Who, whom, 9, 13, 53, 181, 225
Would of, avoiding, 12, 220
Writing letters, 19–20, 335, 337,
  339–342
Writing paragraphs, 18–19, 329, 333
Writing process. *See specific steps.*
Writing sentences, 325

Y

You, as understood subject, 77, 109